IMAGES
of America

ALONG THE SANDUSKY RIVER

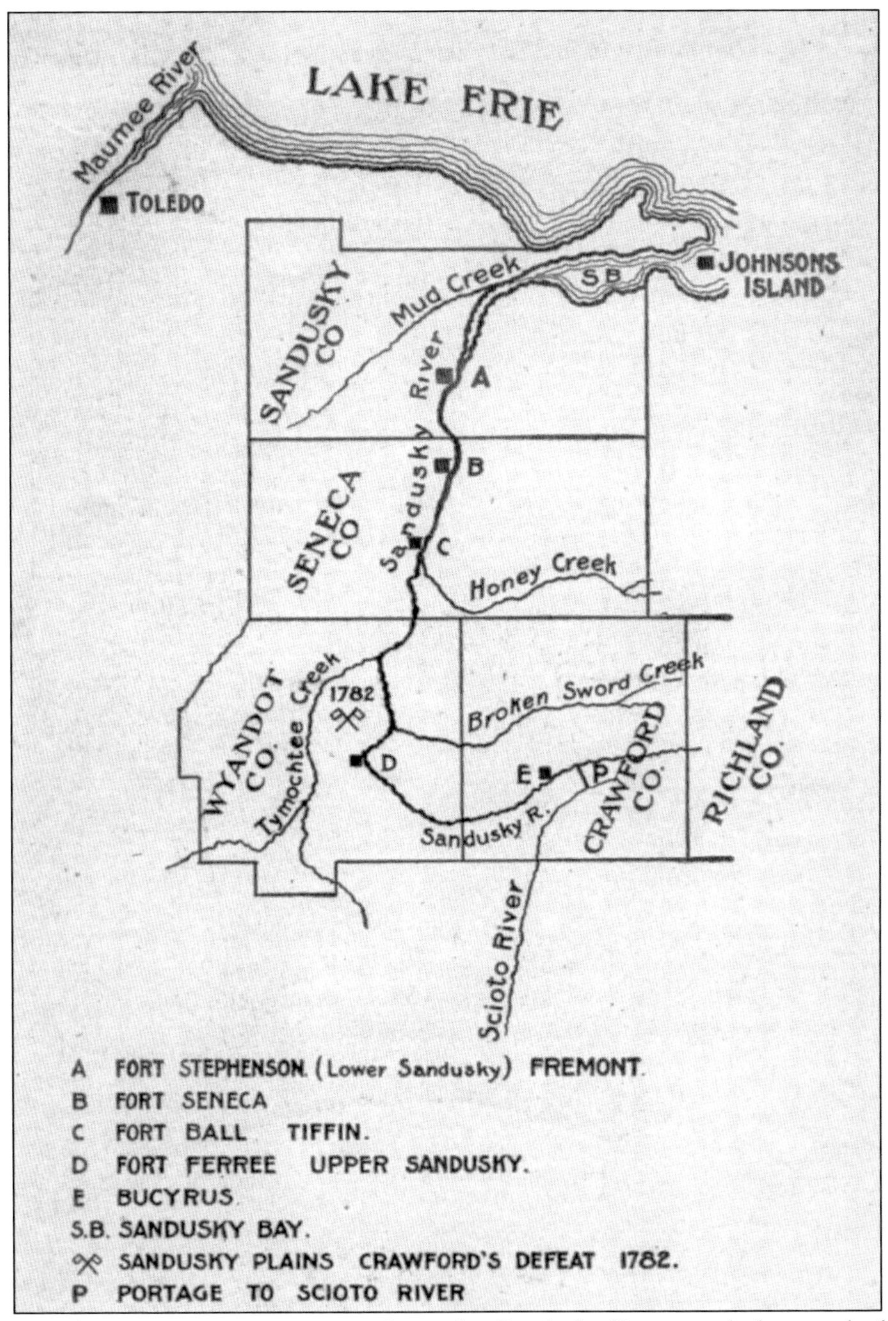

This map designates important sites along the Sandusky River, including early forts and battlefields, as well as tributaries and the narrow portage to the upper Scioto River used by Native American tribes. (Authors' collection.)

ON THE COVER: The Sandusky River winds its way north toward Fremont in this mid-20th-century aerial view. The open areas in the foreground south of town have since been developed into parks along the river, and the nearest railroad bridge is now part of the North Coast Inland Trail. (Authors' collection.)

IMAGES
of America

ALONG THE SANDUSKY RIVER

Brandon Hord and Larry Michaels

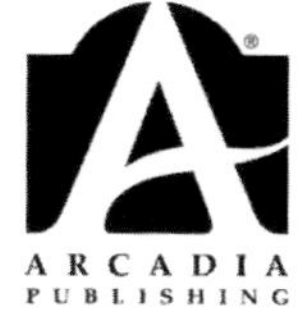

Copyright © 2016 by Brandon Hord and Larry Michaels
ISBN 978-1-4671-1588-9

Published by Arcadia Publishing
Charleston, South Carolina

Printed in the United States of America

Library of Congress Control Number: 2015950084

For all general information, please contact Arcadia Publishing:
Telephone 843-853-2070
Fax 843-853-0044
E-mail sales@arcadiapublishing.com
For customer service and orders:
Toll-Free 1-888-313-2665

Visit us on the Internet at www.arcadiapublishing.com

To Ray Grob, a champion of natural habitat, preservation, and the Sandusky River, who was instrumental in achieving its 1970 designation as an Ohio Scenic River

Contents

Acknowledgments

This book would not have been possible without the kind help and resources of Tonia Hoffert and the Seneca County Museum, the Hayes Presidential Center, and the Johnson's Island Preservation Society along with the Friends and Descendants of Johnson's Island. Thanks also go to Bill Stein, Ken Dumminger, Krista Michaels, and all who have helped preserve local historical photographs. Additional thanks go to Suzi Michaels for helping conduct research for this book. And in particular, the authors would like to thank Ray Grob, a longtime area resident whose passion for the river is unsurpassed.

The authors would also like to thank their title manager at Arcadia Publishing, Jesse Darland, for his patience and encouragement in working through tight deadlines and his help in the production of this book. Unless otherwise stated, the images that appear in this volume have been collected by the authors.

INTRODUCTION

At the confluence of Allen Run and Paramour Creek east of Bucyrus in Richland County lies the humble beginning of one of the major river systems in Ohio—the Sandusky River. The name of the river is derived from three Wyandot words that roughly mean "cool water gathered in pools of water." It meanders its way west through Bucyrus and Crawford County as little more than a stream. In Wyandot County, the river turns north, flowing through Upper Sandusky, Tiffin, and Fremont in Seneca and Sandusky Counties. It gains strength from tributaries such as Tymochtee, Wolf, and Green Creeks before it finally empties into Sandusky Bay, terminating in Lake Erie after a journey of 133 miles.

The watersheds of the river and Sandusky Bay drain a total of 1,828 square miles and flow through all or part of 12 counties. Designated one of Ohio's scenic rivers in 1970, the Sandusky River is the lifeblood of the people who have lived along its banks the last 300 years, from early native tribes such as the Seneca and Wyandot to the more than 50,000 residents who live in the communities along its shores today. This book seeks to celebrate this significant river by presenting snapshots of history across time with the hopes of reminding people what a treasure it is and the importance of preserving it for future generations.

In the first chapter, we will travel back several hundred years to look at the early days of life along the Sandusky. The chapter begins with James and Elizabeth Foulkes Whitaker, the first permanent white settlers in Ohio, and their home, the 1,280-acre Whitaker Reserve. The remaining part of it is known today as Peninsular Farms, set aside in an easement preserved for generations to come. We then fast-forward to a more tumultuous time when the Sandusky River played an important role in the fight between the British and Americans for control of northwest Ohio in the War of 1812. The British, after being rebuffed at Fort Meigs on the Maumee River in April 1813, turned their attention to the Sandusky River and launched an invasion up the river to capture the fort at Lower Sandusky where modern Fremont now stands. In what some have called the Gettysburg of the Old Northwest, an army of over 500 British veterans of the Napoleonic Wars, under Gen. William Proctor and along with several hundred Native Americans, was decisively defeated at Fort Stephenson by about 160 soldiers led by Maj. George Croghan and just one piece of artillery, known as Old Betsy. The chapter ends with a close look at the Confederate prison on Johnson's Island in Sandusky Bay, situated where the river empties into Lake Erie.

We will then look at the scenic aspects of the river. In 1970, the Ohio Department of Natural Resources designated the Sandusky River as the second Ohio Scenic River, after the Little Miami. The river features a wide variety of habitats. It is home to Ohio's largest inland population of bald eagles, as well as many species of fish and amphibians. Walleye and white bass spawning runs draw avid fishermen from around the state to Fremont to partake in the bounties of the river. As one of the major spawning locations for walleye, the Sandusky River plays a vital role in maintaining the Lake Erie ecosystem and the sportfishing industry in the lake. Walleye run late March to the end of April, and white bass peak in May. Early summer is prime time for smallmouth bass that spawn on the shallow flats in June. Channel catfish appear in summer and perch in September and October. The river is also frequently used for recreation, particularly canoeing and kayaking, and it is a perfect destination for campers who enjoy those activities.

The third chapter considers the man-made influences upon the river, including the bridges, dams, and mills that have been constructed along the shore for transportation and power sources. The first road through the Black Swamp and Sandusky County was the Maumee & Western Reserve Turnpike (now US Route 20) laid out in the 1820s. As early as 1828, a bridge was built across the river in Fremont (then known as Lower Sandusky), because it was on the lower rapids of the river. In addition to all the river crossings, including some early covered bridges, many small dams and mills were built to harness river power. The largest—the Ballville Dam, built in 1912—is now no longer needed for electric power or flood control and is likely to soon be removed, opening up an additional 22 miles of river for walleye, white bass, and greater redhorse spawning and providing a boon to the lake and river ecosystem.

As with most rivers, the Sandusky is not a tranquil and meandering river year-round. During late winter and early spring, with the advent of melted ice and heavy rains, the normally peaceful Sandusky can turn into a thundering force of destruction. The fourth chapter graphically shows the devastation caused by the terrible flood of 1913—the highest level of water ever recorded on the river—that caused the death of 22 people.

The book ends with a general look at some early homes, buildings, and other landmarks that reflect the historical significance of the communities along the shores of the Sandusky River.

One

Forts, Battlefields, and Early History

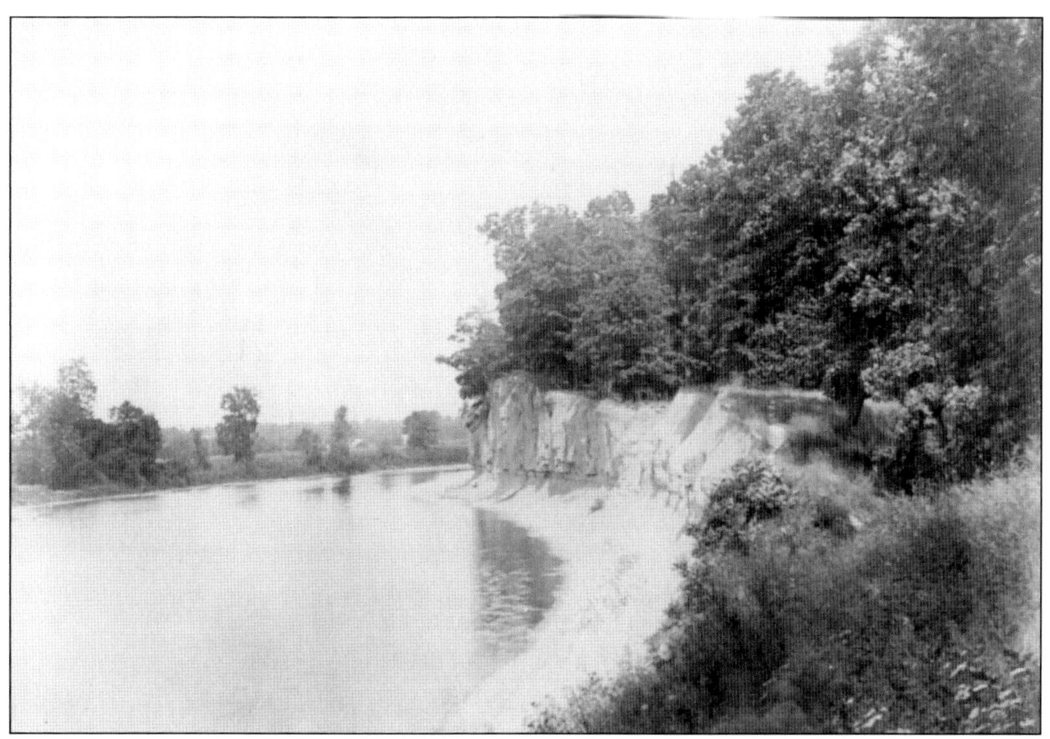

Called the Blue Banks for their deposits of blue clay, these high cliffs on the east bank of the Sandusky River south of Fremont were a gathering place for Native American tribes for centuries. Burial sites have been uncovered along the top of the cliff, and despite more recent erosion, the Blue Banks remain a prominent reminder of the river's long, significant past.

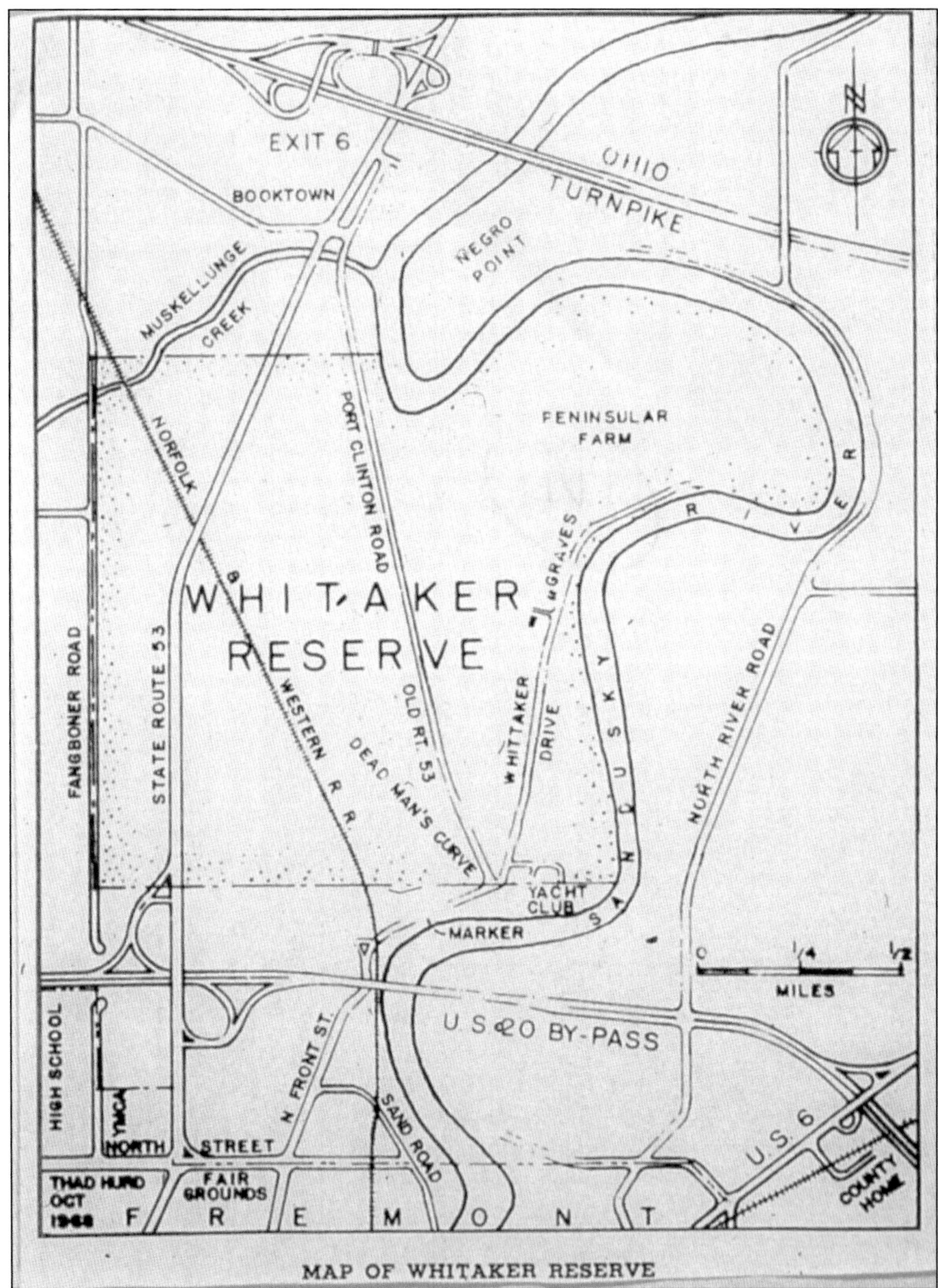

MAP OF WHITAKER RESERVE

About 1778, a young boy named James Whitaker was taken captive by the Wyandot Confederacy and brought to Lower Sandusky, a renowned native prisoner transfer post. As a reward for running the gauntlet, Whitaker was adopted as a Wyandot and given 1,280 acres of pristine land just north of present-day Fremont, as shown on this map. In the early 1780s, he married another former captive, Elizabeth Foulkes; together, they lived on the land called the Whitaker Reserve, becoming probably the first permanent white settlers in Ohio.

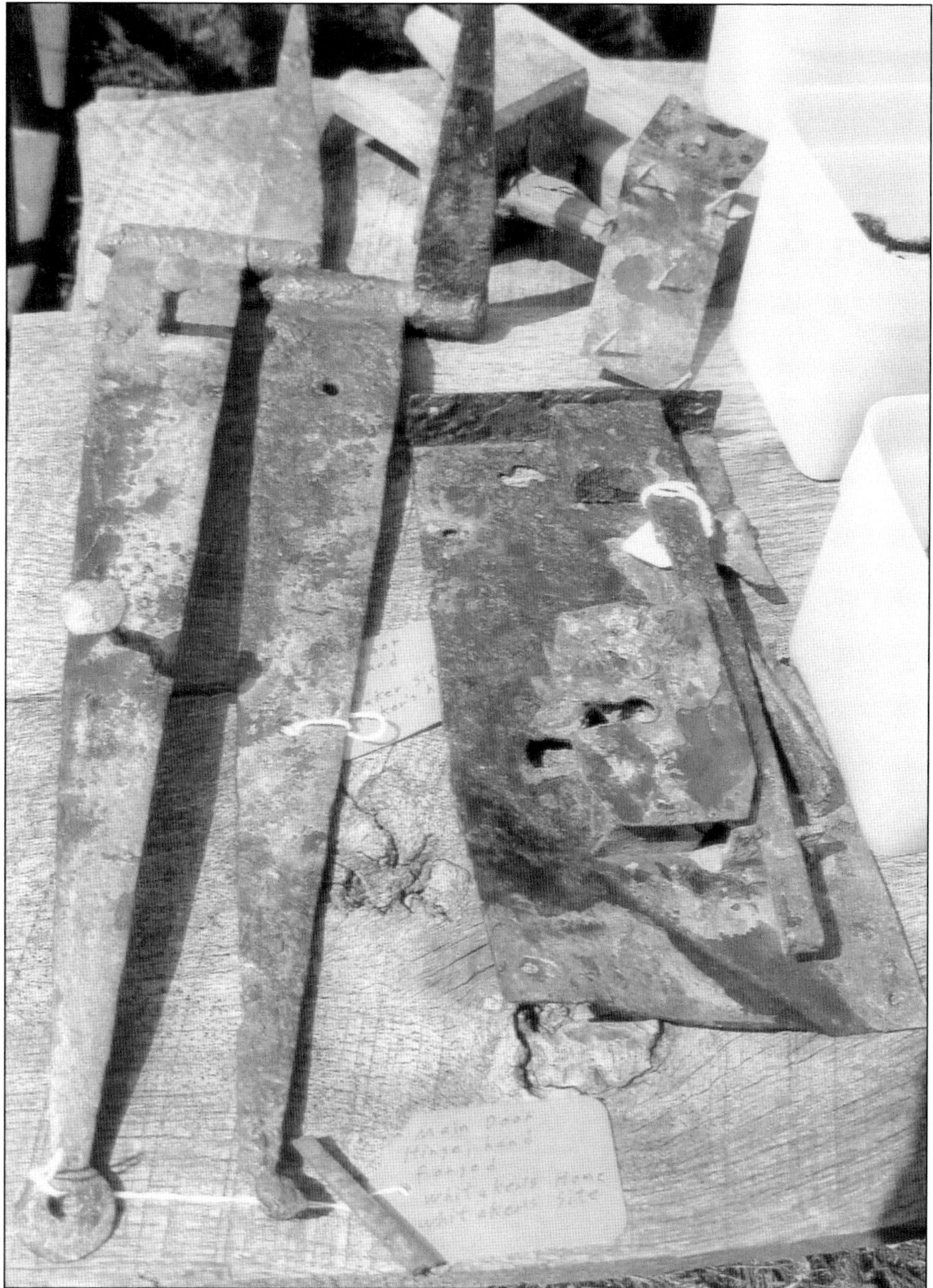

James Whitaker established a trading post on his land and had extensive dealings with the Native American communities in the area and, later, all the way to Fort Wayne. From the original Whitaker Reserve, 474 acres have been preserved via easement by Don Miller, the current owner of the area now known as Peninsular Farms. Many years ago, an archaeological dig was conducted on the property, and the original location of the trading post was uncovered. This photograph shows some of the hinges, locks, and other artifacts found on this more than 200-year-old site.

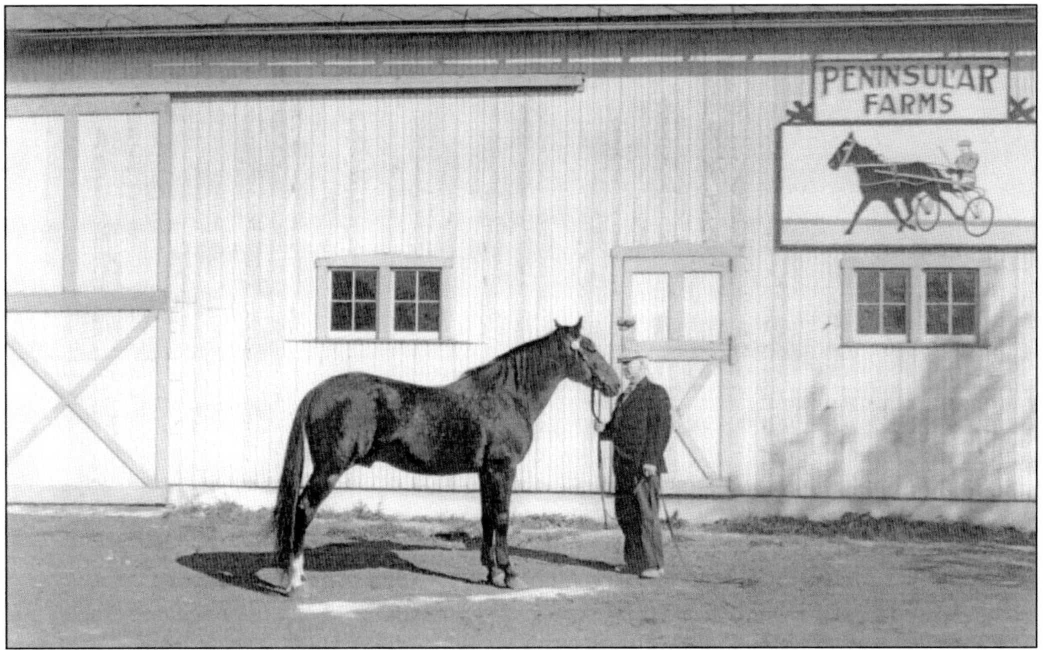

Before Don Miller restored Peninsular Farms in the 1970s, it was owned by the Mooney family. This photograph features John Mooney Sr., who consolidated several small farms on Whitaker land into Peninsular Farms during the 1920s. He raised racehorses on the farm, such as the one pictured here in front of a barn on the property.

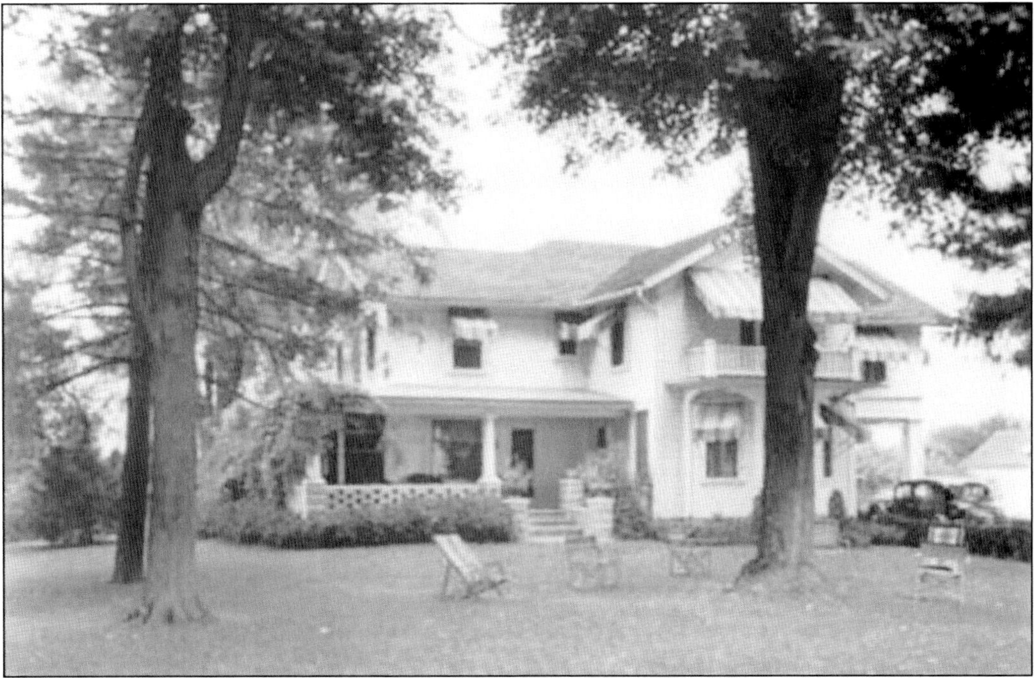

The main farmhouse at Peninsular Farms is pictured about 1940. To get to the farmhouse, visitors can travel down a scenic drive along the river. The early farmhouse has been restored, and the Miller family has graciously hosted many community events.

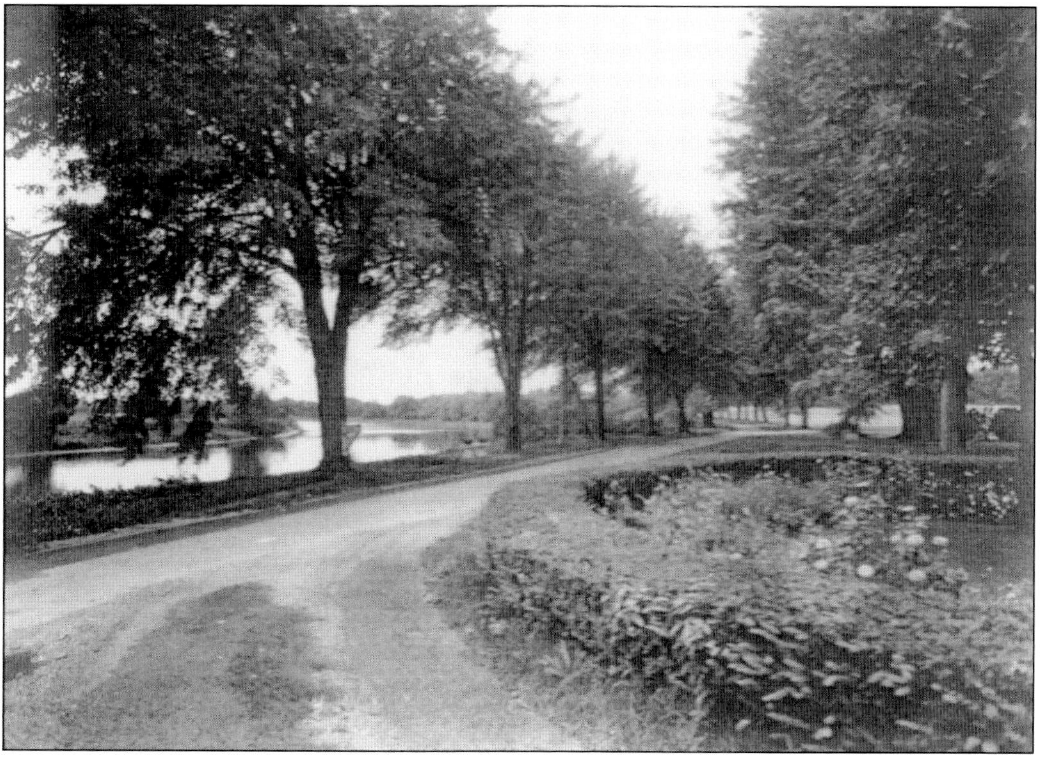

This view looks south from the farmhouse towards Port Clinton Road and the Fremont Yacht Club, showing the lovely tree-lined road on the farm that runs along the shore of the river. All sorts of wildlife can be spotted on the farm, including a large population of deer.

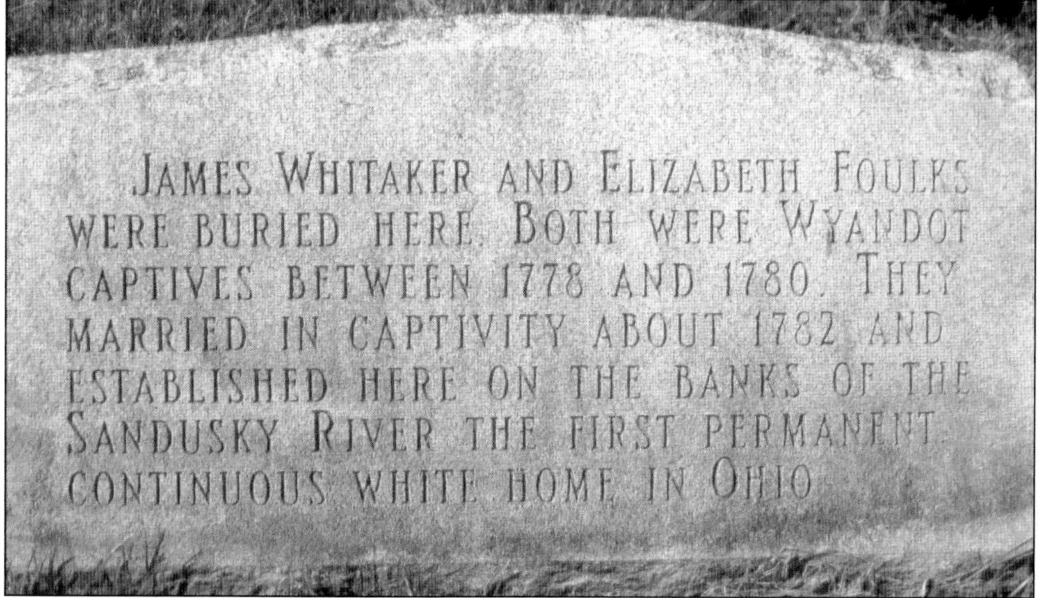

The actual site where James and Elizabeth Whitaker are buried is marked by this stone. It stands humbly along the private access road to the farmhouse from Port Clinton Road and affirms that the first permanent home of a white settler in Ohio was on the banks of the Sandusky River.

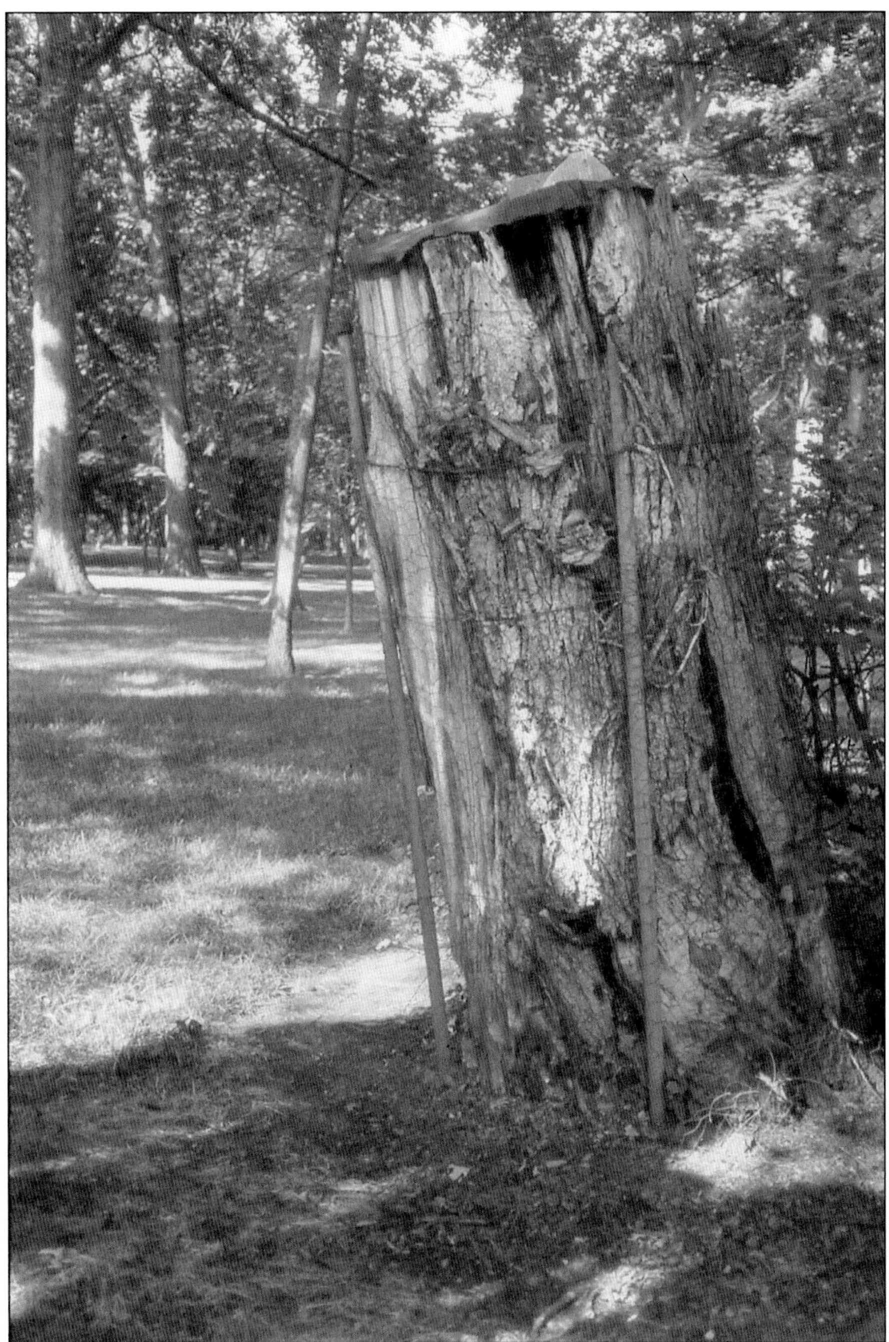

A young lady from Pennsylvania named Peggy Fleming was captured by hostile Indians in 1790 and sentenced to burn to death while tied to this tree. Through the heroic efforts of James Whitaker and Wyandot chief Tarhe the Crane, Fleming was rescued at the last moment before she was to be set on fire. As Fremont grew, the tree was saved because it was within the grounds of Spiegel Grove, the estate of Pres. Rutherford B. Hayes. Only the stump of the historic tree remained when this photograph was taken, and it was recently moved into the Hayes Presidential Museum and a plaque placed on this site.

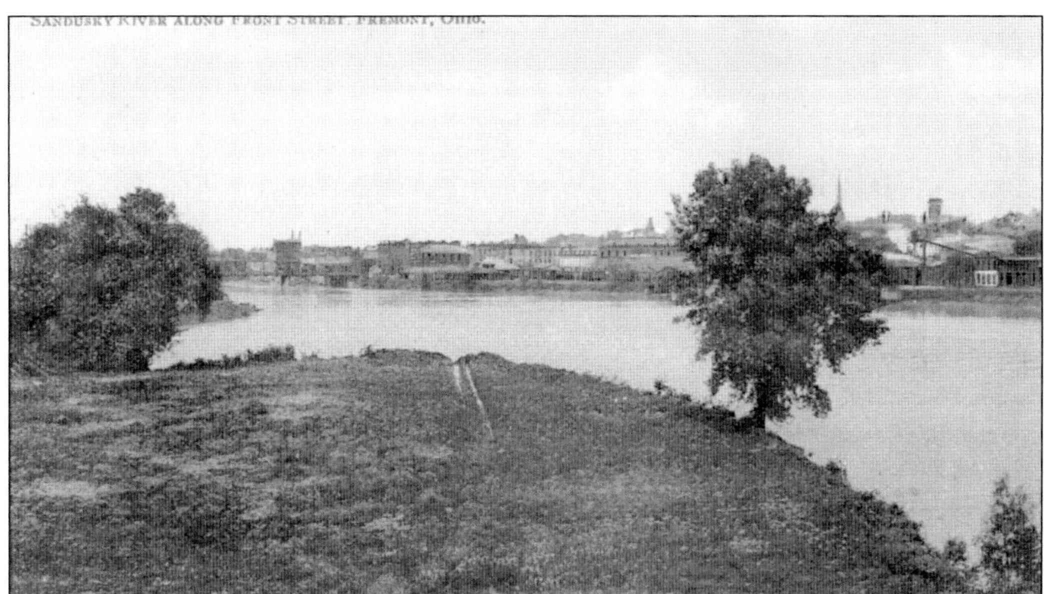

During the Revolutionary War, in 1780, Gen. George Washington sent Capt. George Brady to Northwest Ohio to spy on the Native Americans and ensure they were not planning a campaign against the fledgling country. His first mission was a success, but Brady was captured during a second mission and narrowly escaped death. This view looks south from Brady's Island in the Sandusky River north of Fremont, where he spent several days spying on the natives during his first mission.

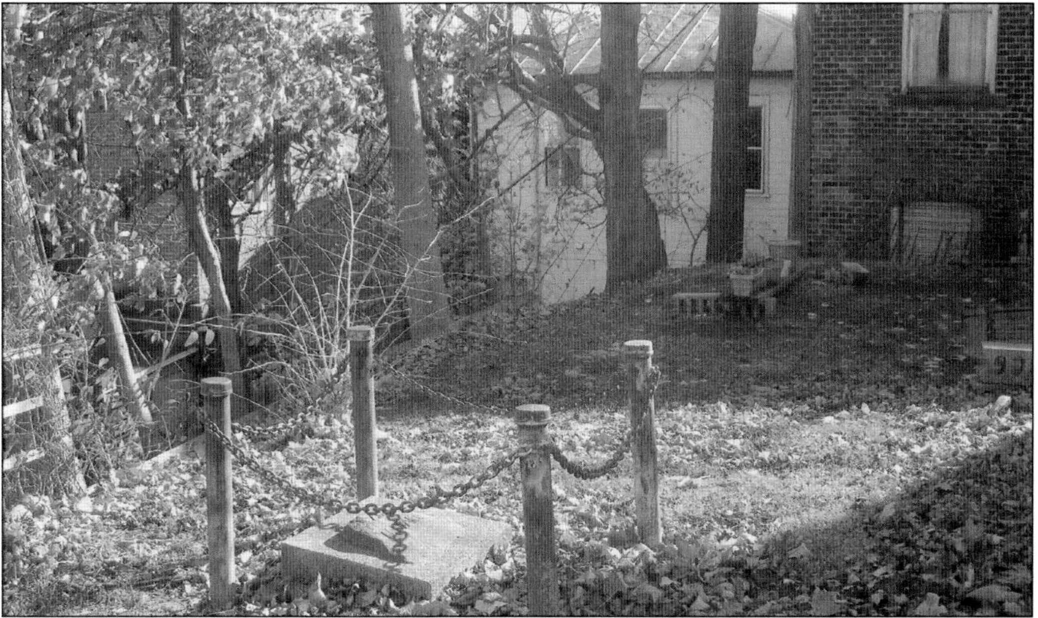

In 1811, postman Uriah Drake was carrying mail through the wilderness when he was murdered while crossing the river, possibly in a robbery attempt. He was buried in this single grave on a hill in Fremont overlooking the river, resting peacefully near the site where British soldiers would attack Fort Stephenson only two years later. The little isolated marker behind these 19th-century storefronts on Croghan Street simply records "U. Drake, 1811."

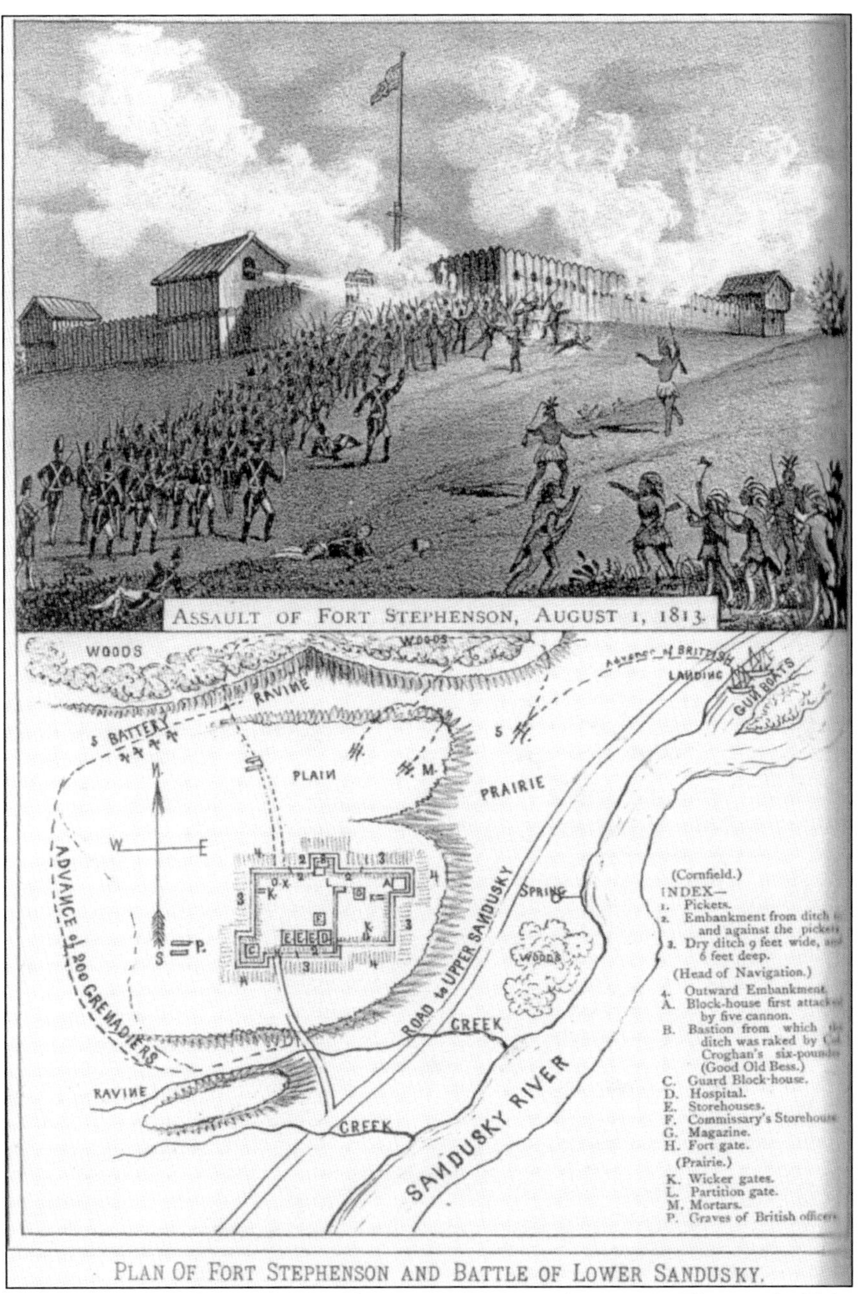

This drawing of the assault on Fort Stephenson was created in 1882. The top half depicts the artist's representation of the ill-fated main assault of the British 41st Infantry against the walls of the fort on August 2, 1813, after a heavy artillery bombardment the night before. When the British charged into the trench along the northwest wall, Major Croghan unleashed his only artillery piece, Old Betsy, and decimated the soldiers funneled into the narrow trench. Thus, the first major victory of the War of 1812 was complete, and after Commodore Perry's defeat of the British fleet a few weeks later in the Battle of Lake, the British threat to the Old Northwest ended. The map below shows the relationship of Fort Stephenson to the river. The spot marked "M" is near the grave of Uriah Drake, and the British gunboats were off Brady's Island.

Lower Sandusky [illegible] 13

Genl Harrison

Dear Sir

Mr Connor has just arrived with the Indians which were sent by you to Fort Meigs a few days since, to him I refer you for information from that quarter.

I have unloaded the boats which were brought from Cleaveland & shall sink them in the middle of the River (where it is 10 feet deep) about a half mile above the present landing. My men are engaged in making Cartridges, & will have in short time more than sufficient to answer any ordinary call.

I have collected all the most valuable stores in one house, should I be forced to ~~retire~~ evacuate the place they will be blown up.

Yours with Respect
G Croghan Majr
Comg L. Sandusky

Om780_1028727_008

In this letter written to Gen. William Henry Harrison, Croghan details his preparations for the British attack, including the securing of supplies and "rolling cartridges," which were small packages of black powder used to fire musket balls. Harrison originally ordered Croghan to retreat from the fort. However, risking treason, Croghan decided to stay, believing that his men could hold off an assault.

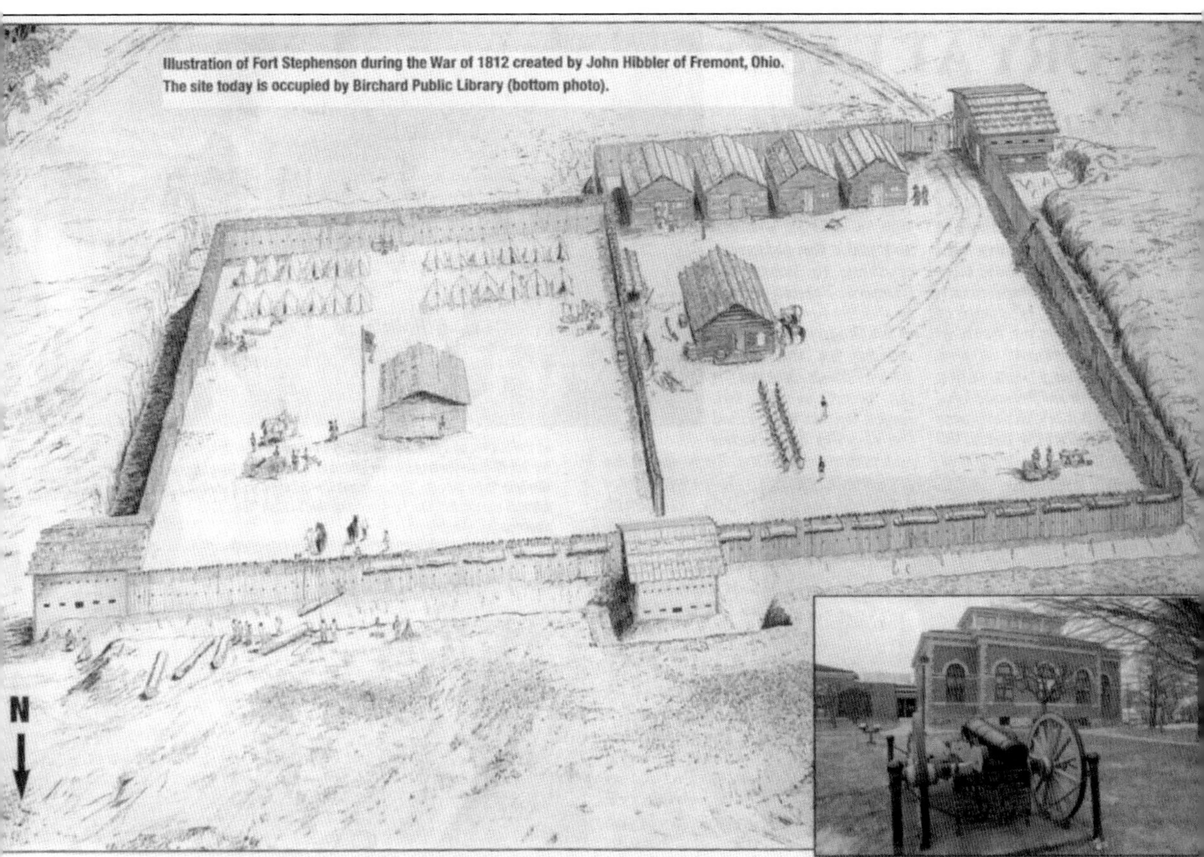

A detailed drawing of the fort, oriented toward the south, gives the location of the blockhouses, including the north-central blockhouse at the bottom from which Old Betsy shattered the British lines. The river is off the left side of this drawing. The inset is a picture of the 1879 Birchard Public Library, which is now on the grounds of Fort Stephenson, with Old Betsy still guarding the site.

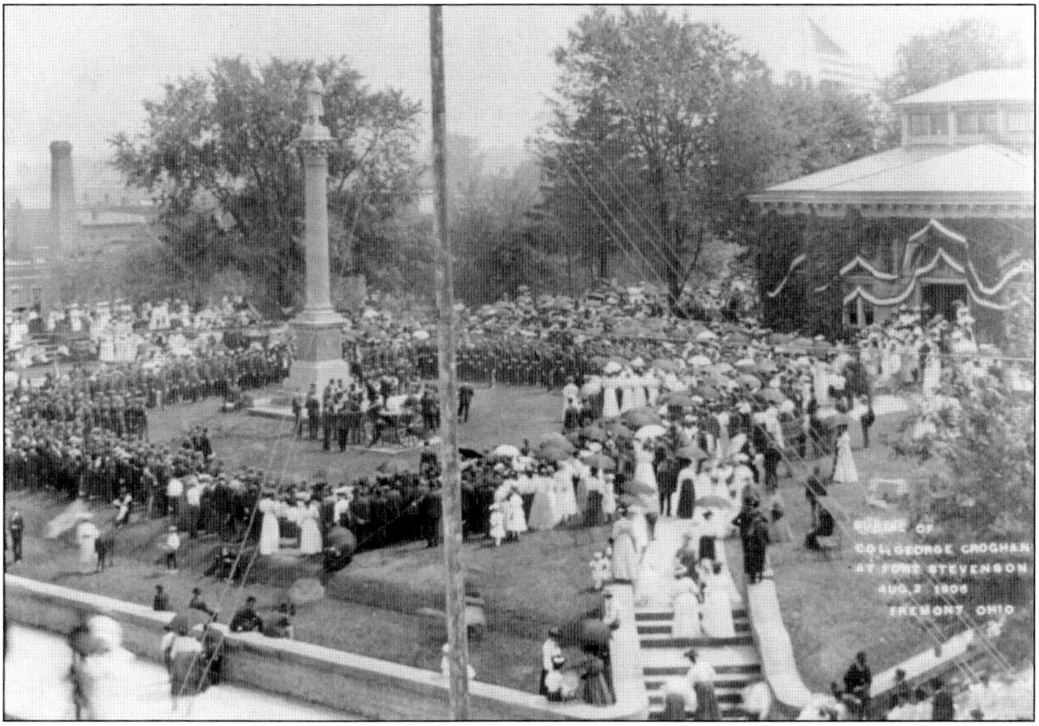

In 1906, the remains of Col. George Croghan were brought back to Fremont and reinterred beneath the 1885 Soldiers and Sailors Monument on the site of Fort Stephenson. The Birchard Public Library, which has a collection of artifacts from the battle, is at upper right, and Old Betsy stands beside the monument. This southeastward view shows a large crowd gathered for the ceremony on August 2, the 93rd anniversary of the battle. Croghan Street is in the foreground, and the river is behind the buildings at left.

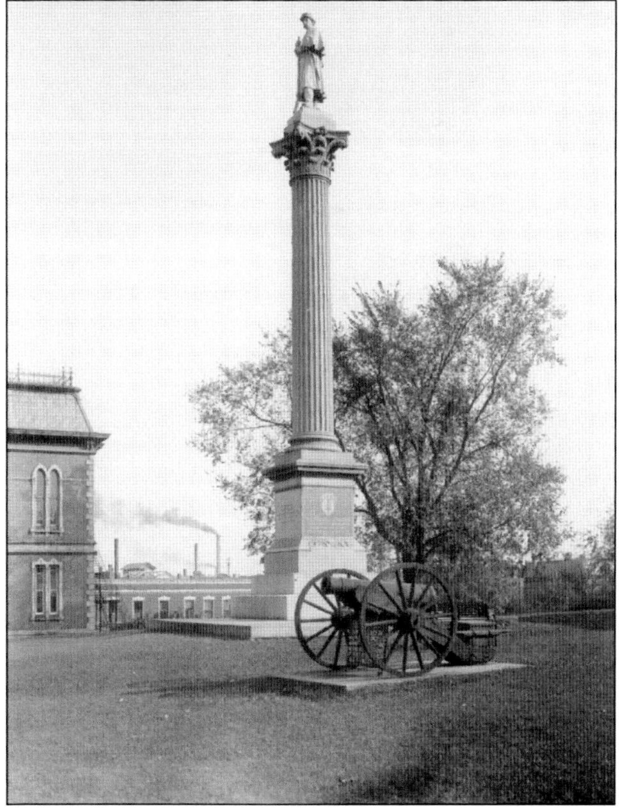

Here is an early photograph with a view looking southeast at Old Betsy and the Soldiers and Sailors Monument on Fort Stephenson Square. The back part of the Italianate Fremont municipal building, erected in 1877 and razed almost exactly a century later, stands at left. The British attack was almost right at the point from where this photograph was taken.

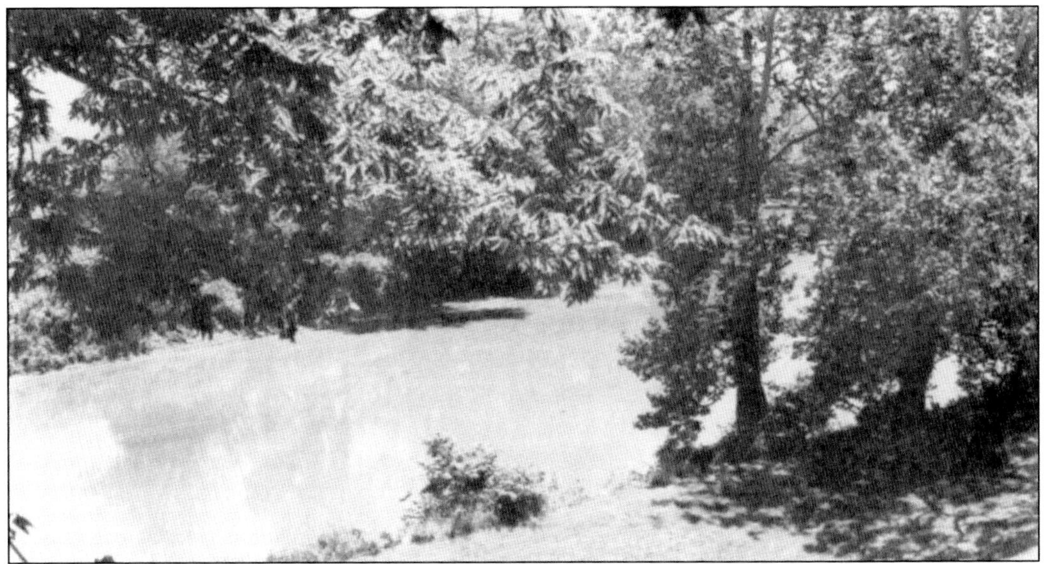

Fort Seneca was one of several forts built by General Harrison in northwest Ohio during the War of 1812. The main one was Fort Meigs on the Maumee River in Perrysburg, which withstood two heavy sieges. The others served mainly as supply depots, although Fort Stephenson was more strongly fortified before the battle. Harrison spent much of his time at centrally located Fort Seneca, about halfway between Fremont and Tiffin. There is a town on Route 53 called Fort Seneca, but the fort was actually on the river in Old Fort. The steep hill on which it was located can be seen in this photograph. (Courtesy of Ray Grob.)

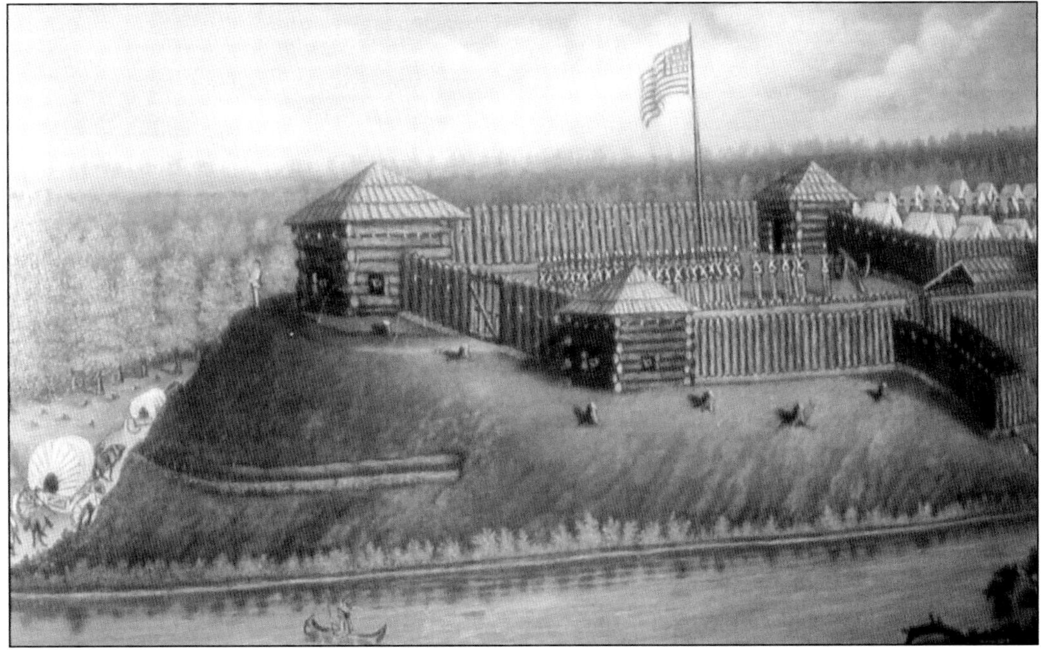

In the early 1900s, Tiffin lawyer Edward Lepper painted several of the historic sites along the Sandusky River. This painting is of Fort Seneca high above the river, complete with covered supply wagons and an Indian rowing past. The painting hangs at the Seneca County Museum in Tiffin.

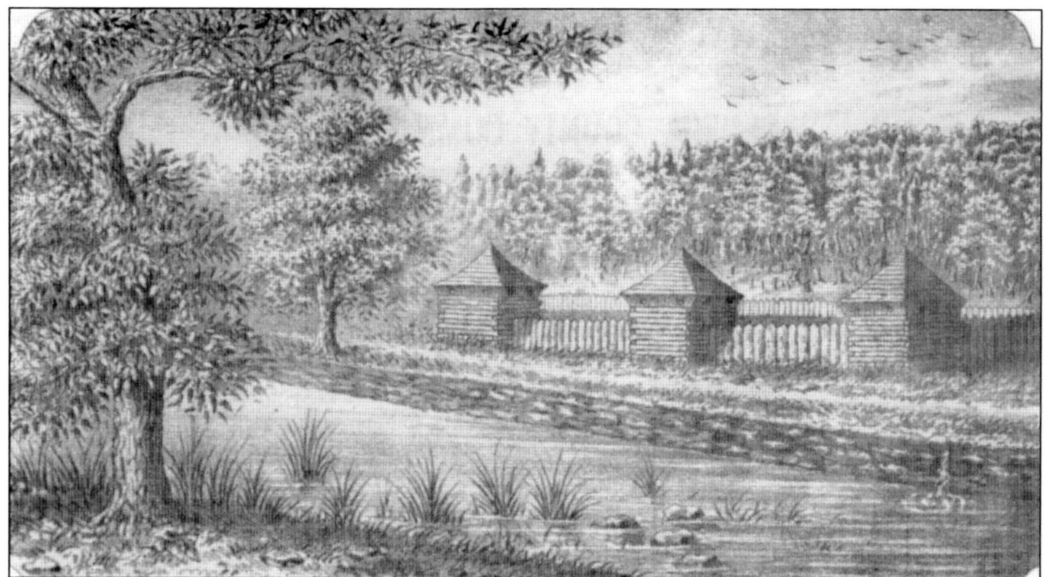

Fort Ball was another of General Harrison's supply forts on the river. It was located on the north bank between what are now North Washington and North Monroe Streets in Tiffin. It was constructed by Col. James V. Ball in 1913, and this sketch of the three blockhouses appears in William Lang's 1880 county history.

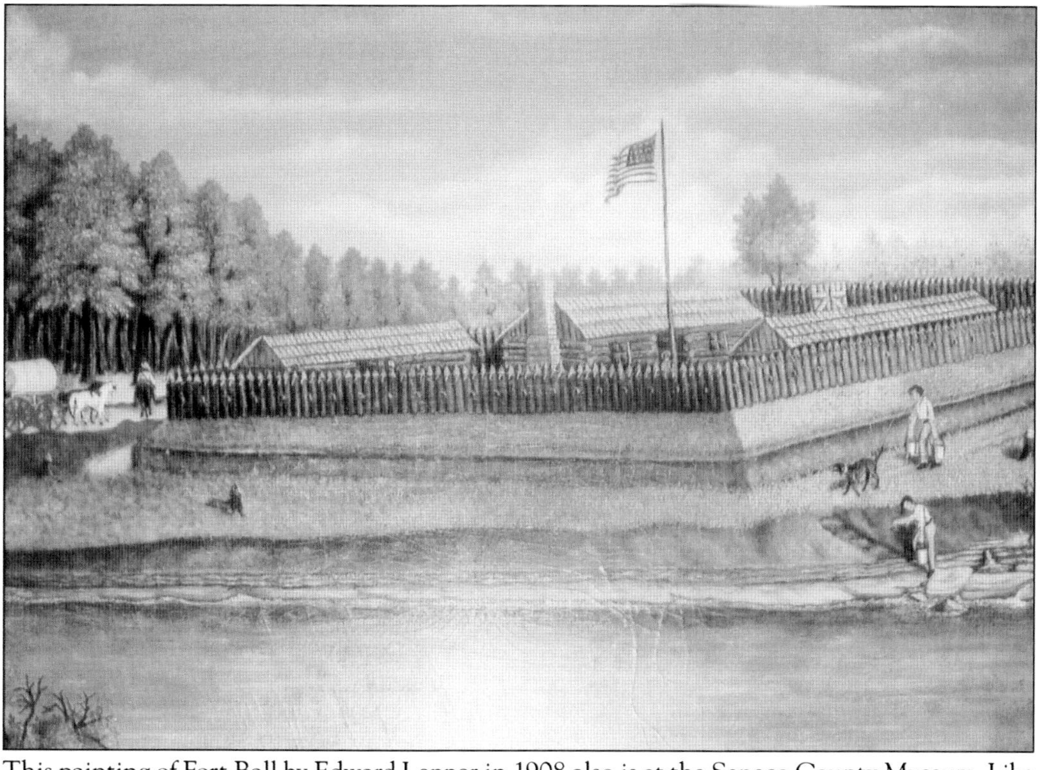

This painting of Fort Ball by Edward Lepper in 1908 also is at the Seneca County Museum. Like his painting of Fort Seneca, it is embellished with a wagon, people doing various tasks, and even a dog.

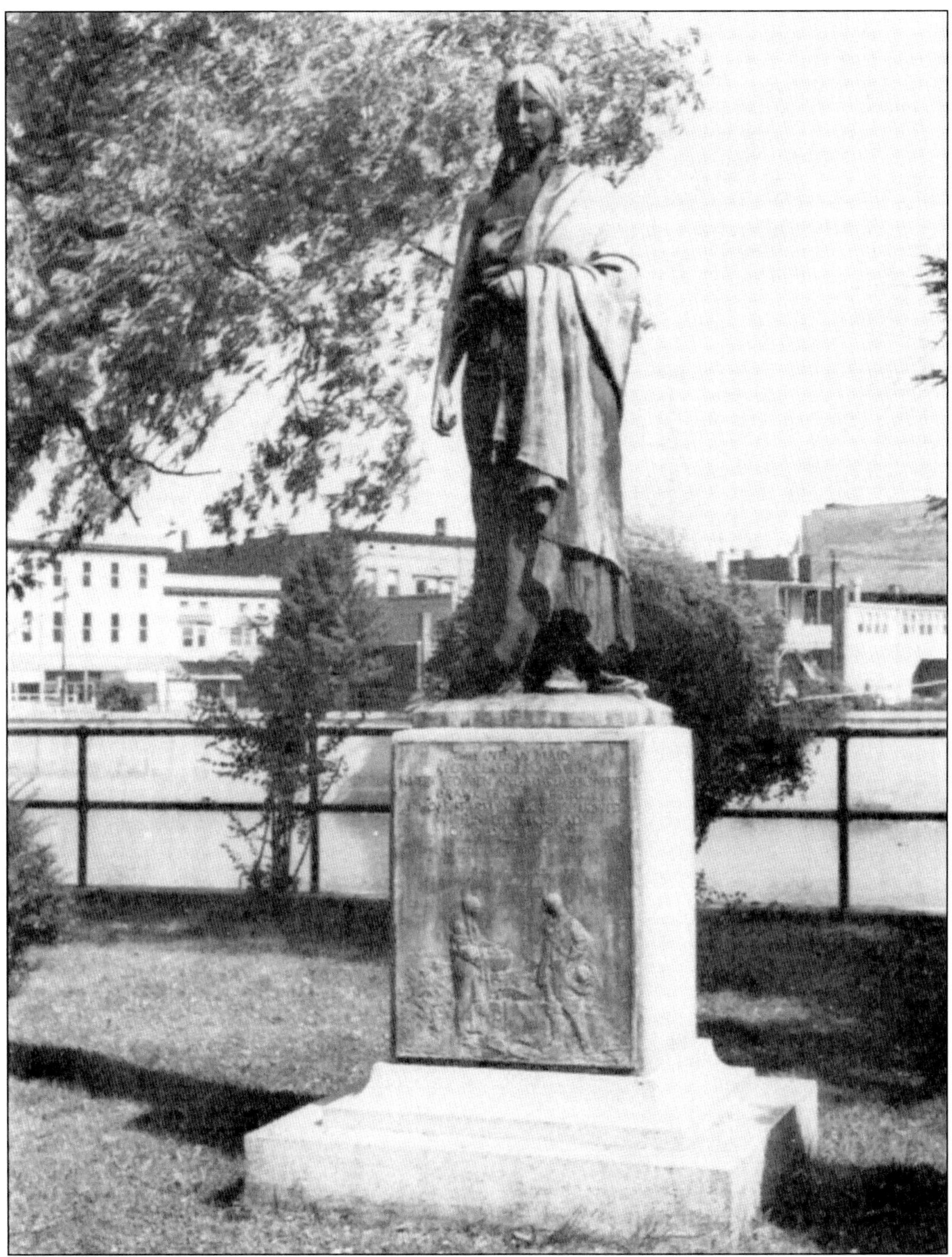

On the site of Fort Ball stands this *Indian Maid* statue, commemorating the location. It is said a spring of clear water flowed within the fort, possibly the reason the site was chosen. A beautiful park now runs all along the north shore, where the fort once stood between the river and Frost Parkway. The buildings in the background across the river are downtown on Washington Street. (Courtesy of Ray Grob.)

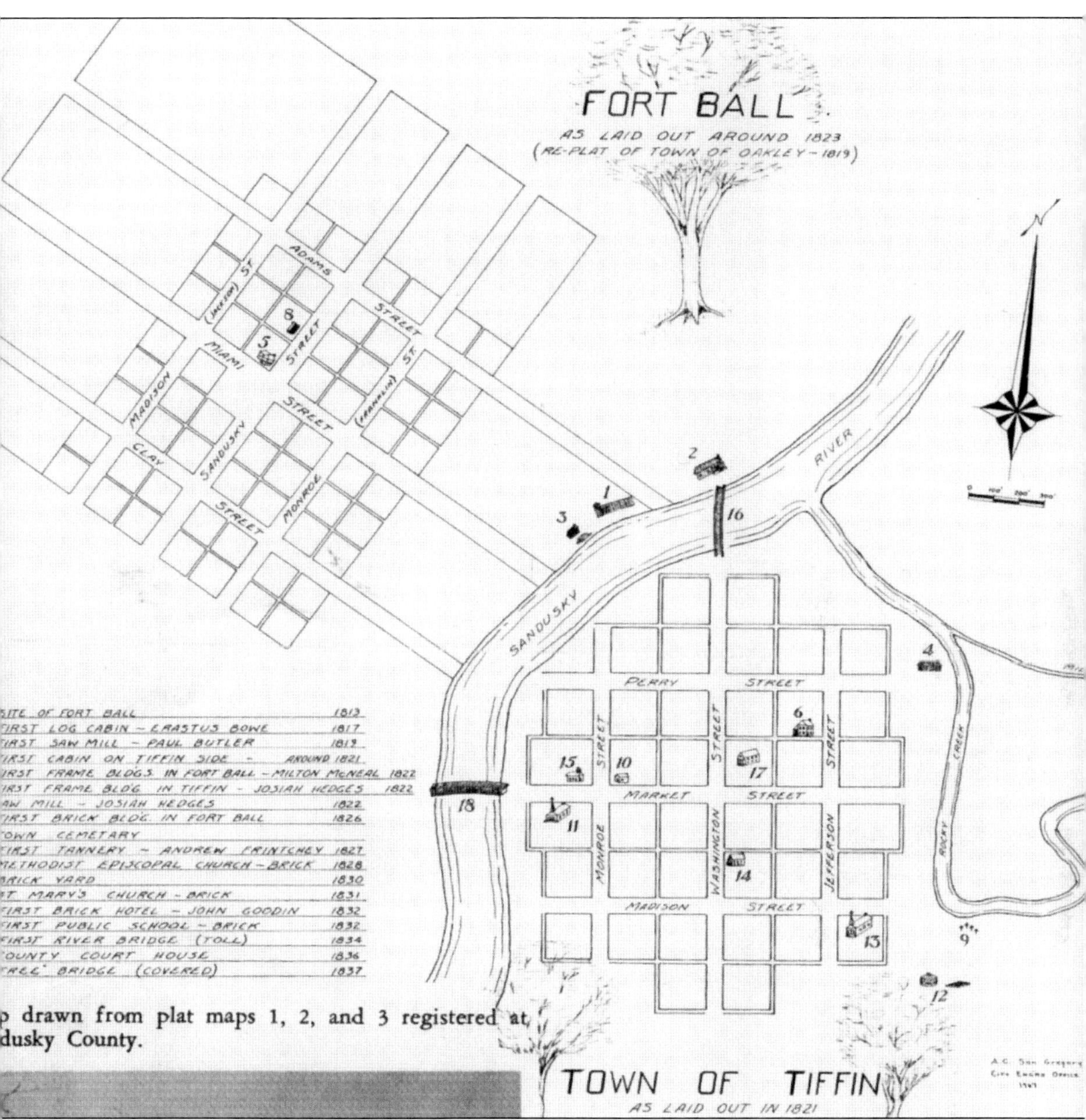

The city of Tiffin, as shown in this map, was originally platted as two communities. Fort Ball was first laid out northwest of the river as Oakley in 1819 but was replatted about 1823. Josiah Hedges platted the town of Tiffin, south and east of the river and named for the first governor of Ohio, in 1821. After some early squabbles, the town merged and now, nearly two centuries later, has become a city of over 17,000 people with a healthy economy, two universities, and a rich history.

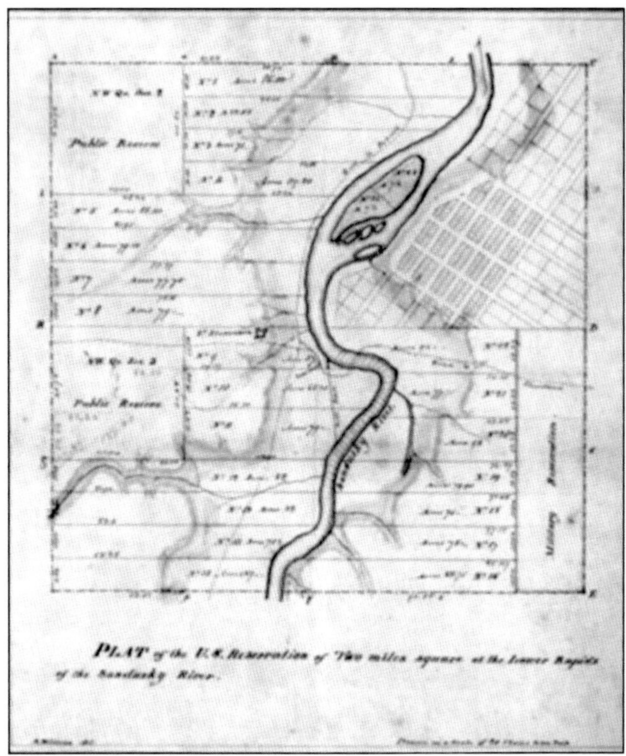

Like Tiffin's, Fremont's early history was tied to the Sandusky River, and it was first platted on both sides of the river. Croghansville was laid out on the east side in 1816, and the following year, the Kentucky Company laid out a larger tract on the west side called simply "Sandusky." Sandusky County was formed in 1820, and the courts moved west of the river two years later. Not long afterward, the two communities joined to become Lower Sandusky, named for the lower rapids of the river. To avoid confusion with the other towns called Sandusky, it was decided in 1849 to change its name to Fremont, in honor of the then-famous western "Pathfinder," John C. Frémont. The 1816 plat of Croghansville is plainly seen in this early map, on the east side of the river next to Brady's Island.

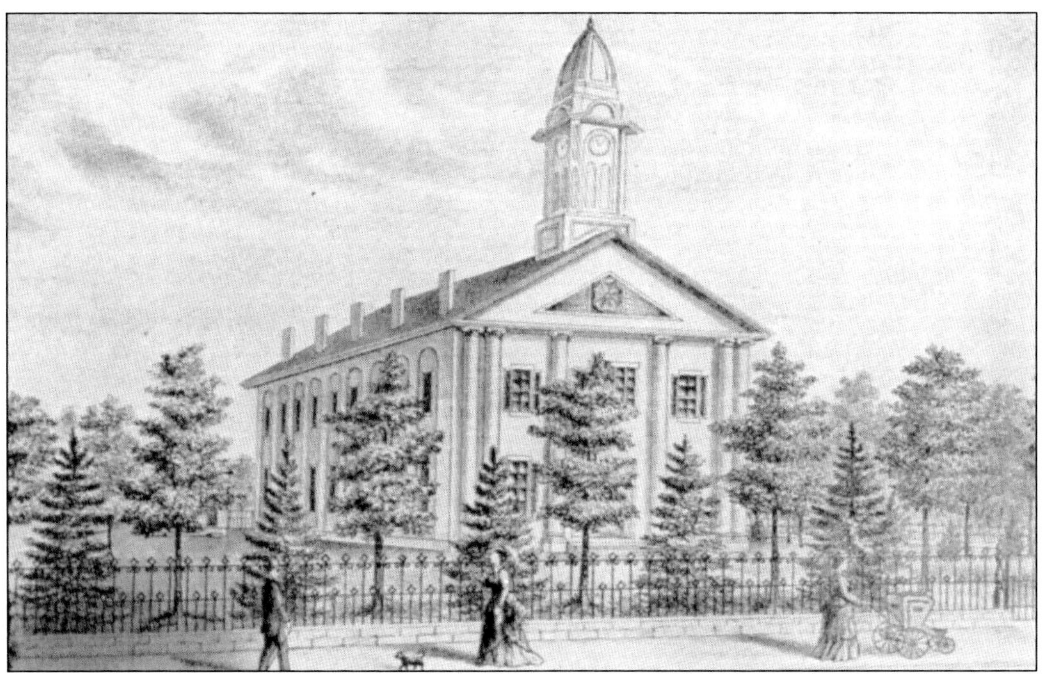

The second courthouse in Tiffin was built by John Baugher in 1841, using some of the walls from the 1834 building that was destroyed by fire. It stood on the site of the 1883 courthouse, unfortunately recently torn down for financial reasons, on the east side of Washington Street between Market and Perry Streets.

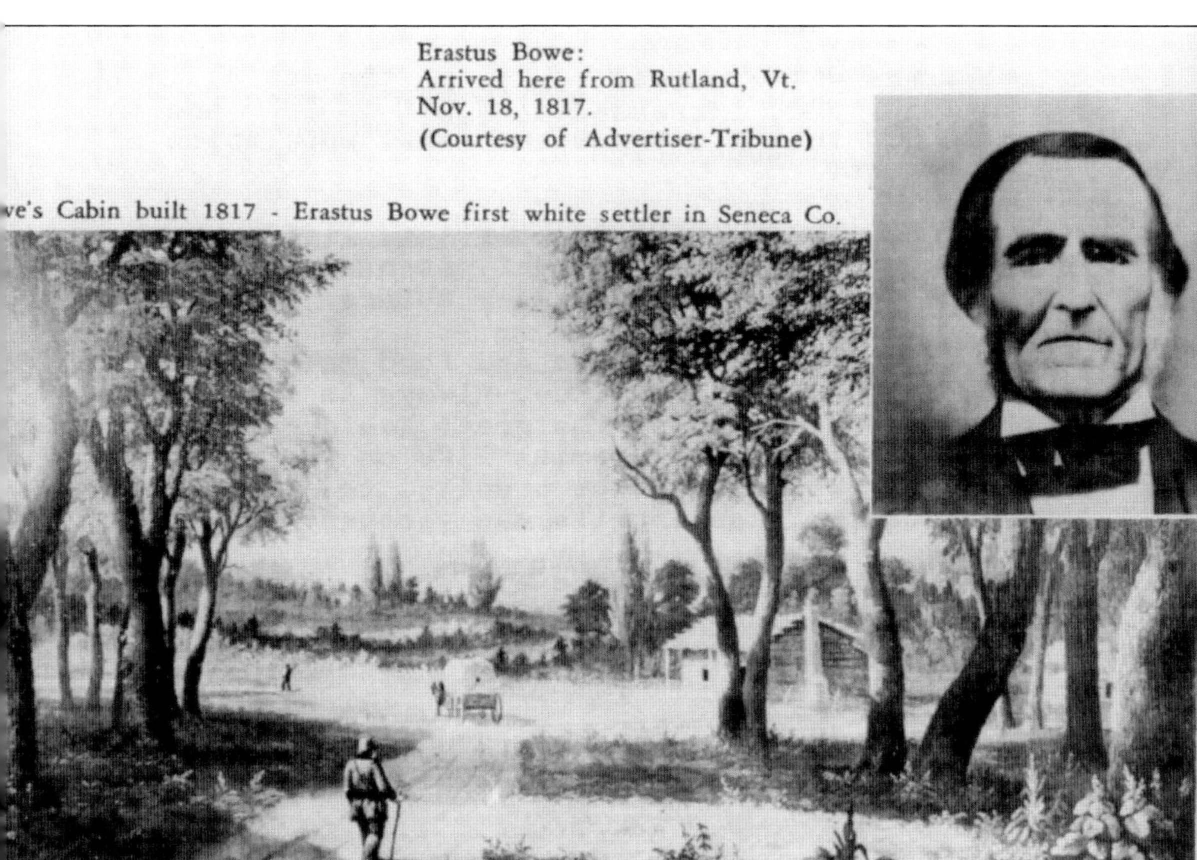

Near the site of Fort Ball, Erastus Bowe built a cabin on the north shore of the river in 1817, becoming the first white settler in the area. His cabin stood on what is now the middle of North Washington Street just north of the bridge.

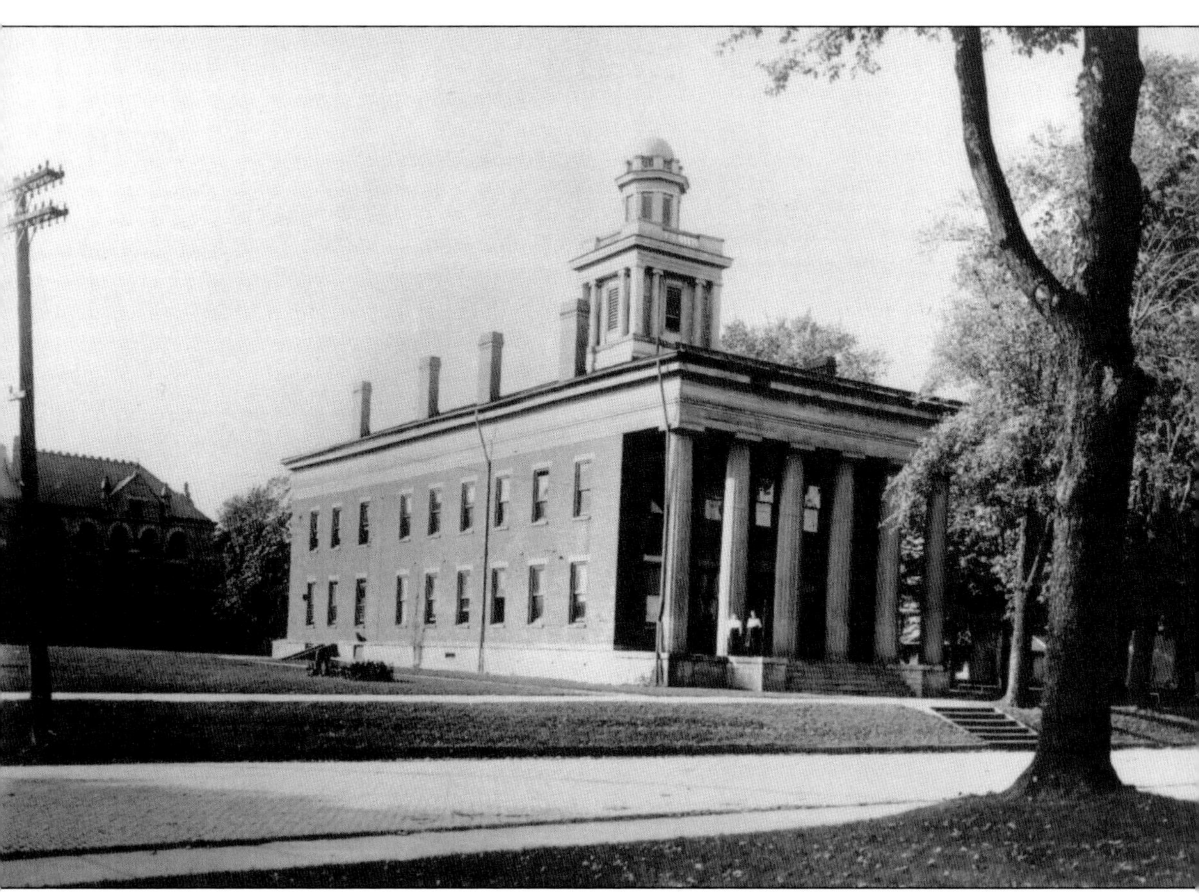

The Sandusky County Courthouse, built in 1843, is one of the oldest buildings in Fremont. The original structure is seen here on Park Avenue in this early-1900s photograph, with the 1890 jail standing behind it. The courthouse was tripled in size during the 1930s, but this northern third of the beautiful Greek Revival building still remains. The old jailhouse also still stands, now occupied by various county offices.

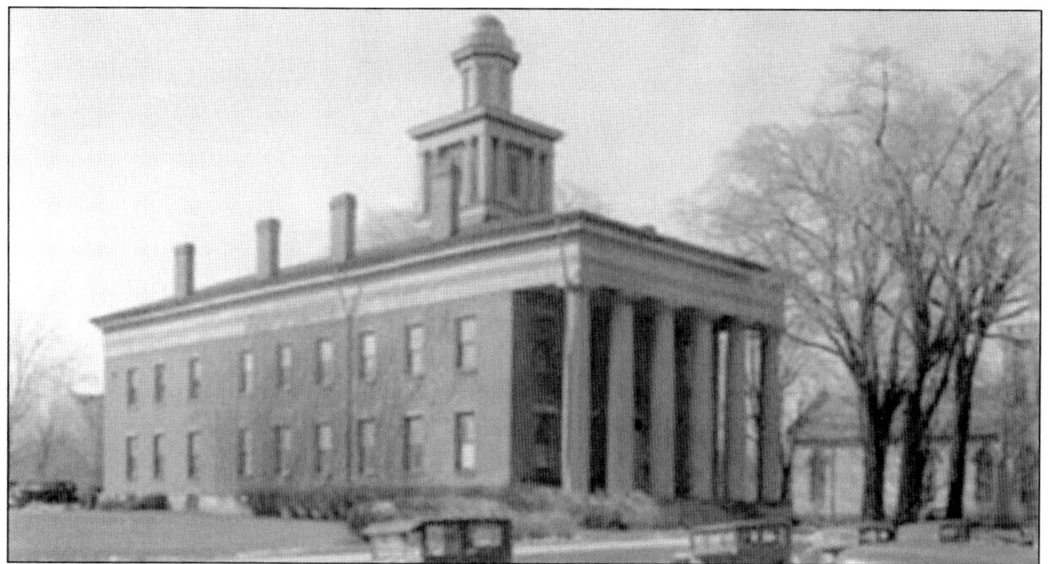

A 1934 picture of the county courthouse shows how little it changed in nearly a century. Soon after this photograph was taken, the building was tripled in size with two well-matched additions joined to the south. This original section, on the southwest corner of Park Avenue and Court Street, is pictured with St. Paul's Episcopal Church in the background. The church was also built in 1843.

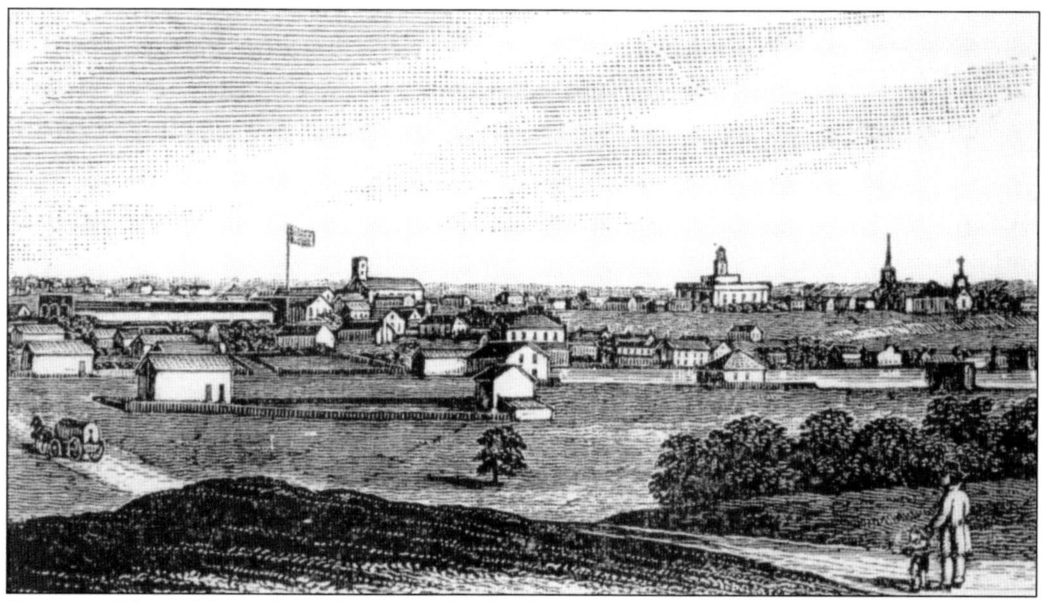

Historian Henry Howe drew this 1846 sketch of Lower Sandusky three years before it became Fremont. The view looks southwest from Croghansville hill near what is now North Sandusky Avenue. The river flows through the middle of the drawing, and the old covered bridge at State Street is at left. The flag to the right of the bridge designates the location of Fort Stephenson, and amid some church steeples at right stands the courthouse.

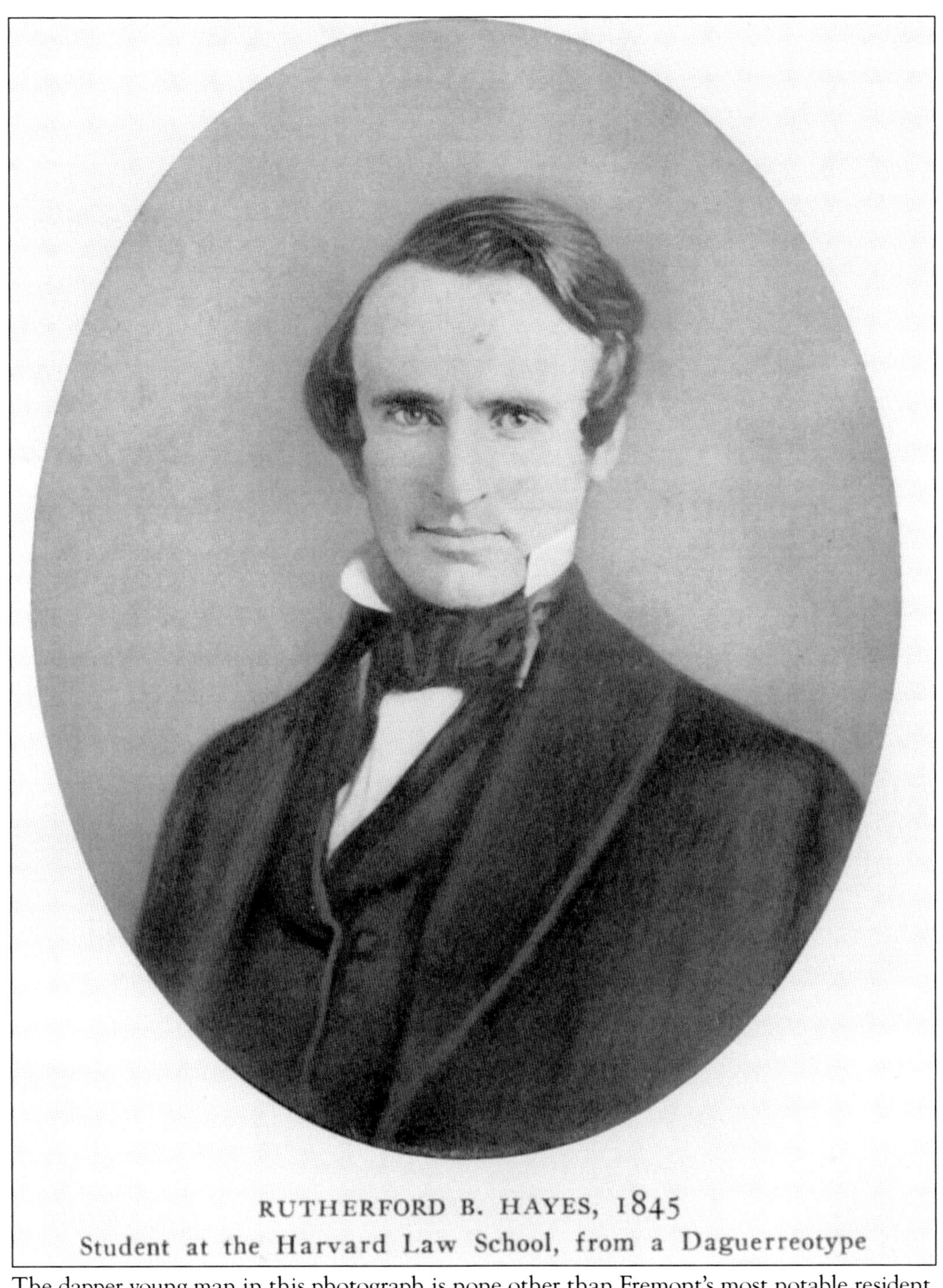

The dapper young man in this photograph is none other than Fremont's most notable resident, future president Rutherford B. Hayes. He is seen here as a new Harvard Law School graduate in 1845, the year he first settled in Lower Sandusky. His first stay as a young lawyer lasted only four years before he moved to Cincinnati to practice law in a larger city. He returned in the early 1870s, shortly before he was elected president in 1876. (Courtesy of the Hayes Presidential Center.)

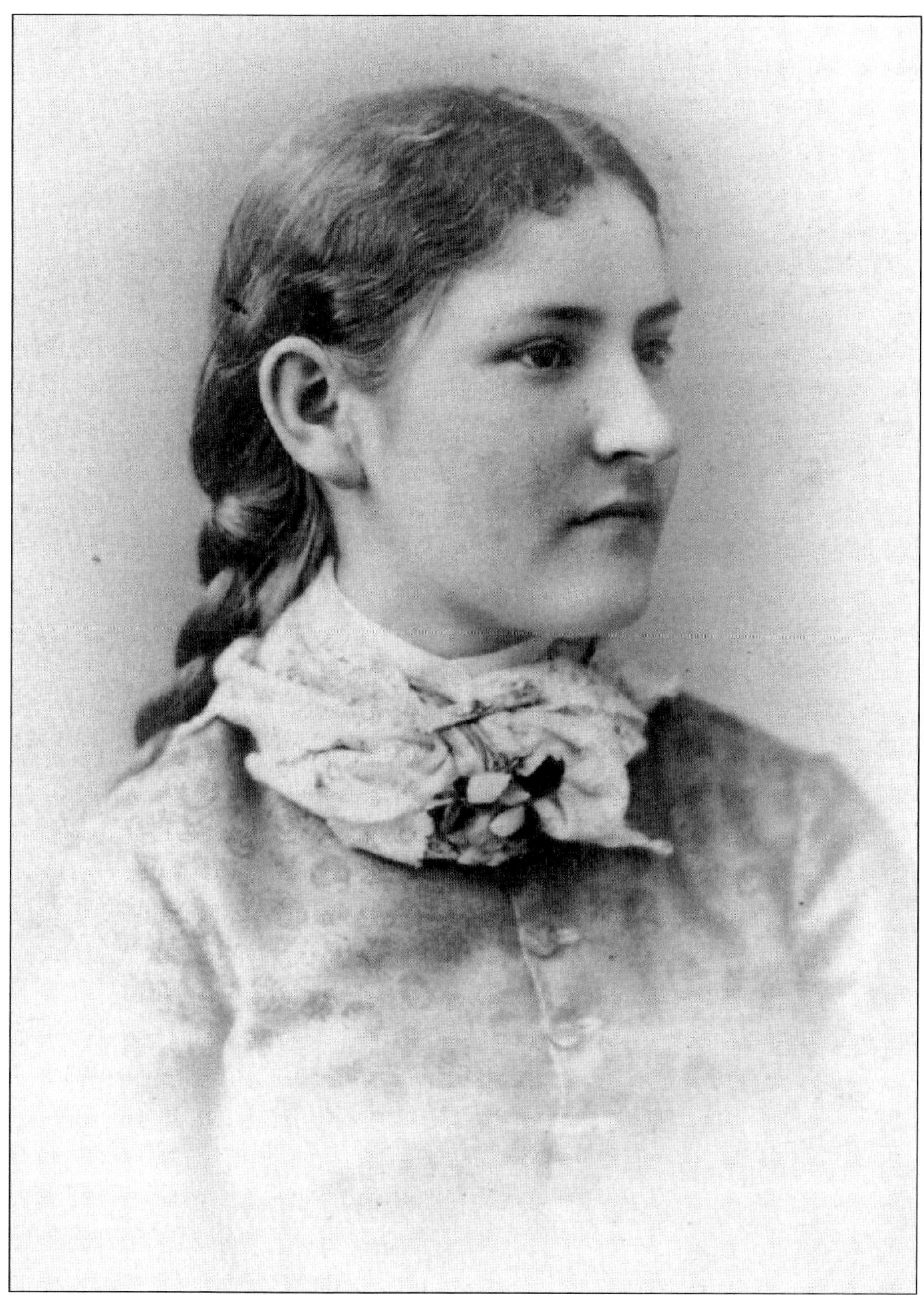

Lucy Keeler, a relative of the Hayes family, was the first prominent local historian of the Fremont area. An author of two works about the Sandusky River, Keeler was the 19th-century authority on the river. (Courtesy of the Hayes Presidential Center.)

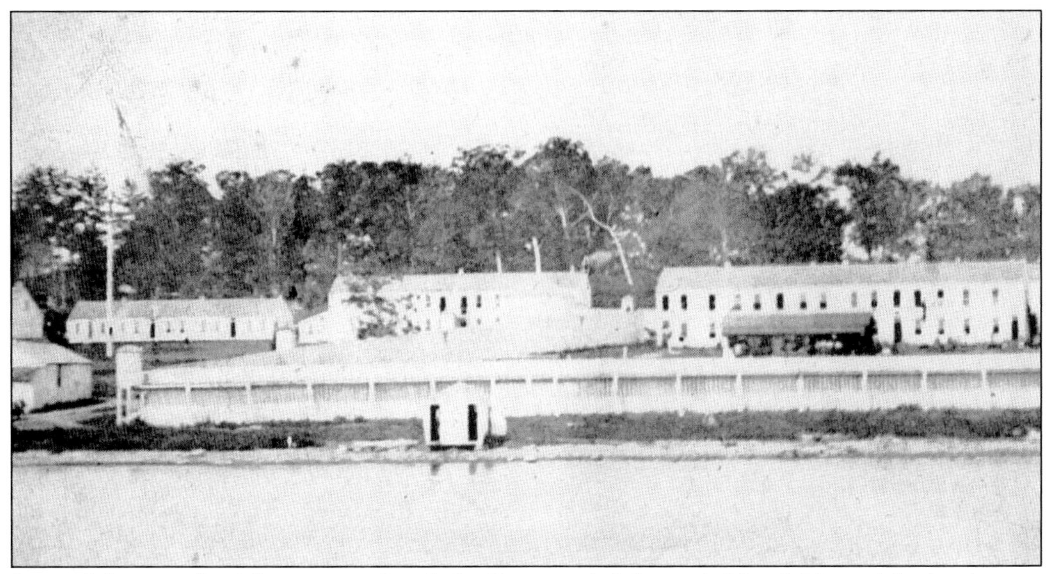

Beyond the mouth of the river in Sandusky Bay stands Johnson's Island. Named for landowner Leonard Johnson, it became the site of a Confederate prison during the Civil War. Because so many soldiers were captured during battles, there was a great need for prisons. In 1862, the prison camp for Confederate soldiers on Johnson's Island accepted its first inmates. Pictured is one of the guard barracks where Union soldiers were stationed, as well as the stockade wall and one of the 13 prison blocks.

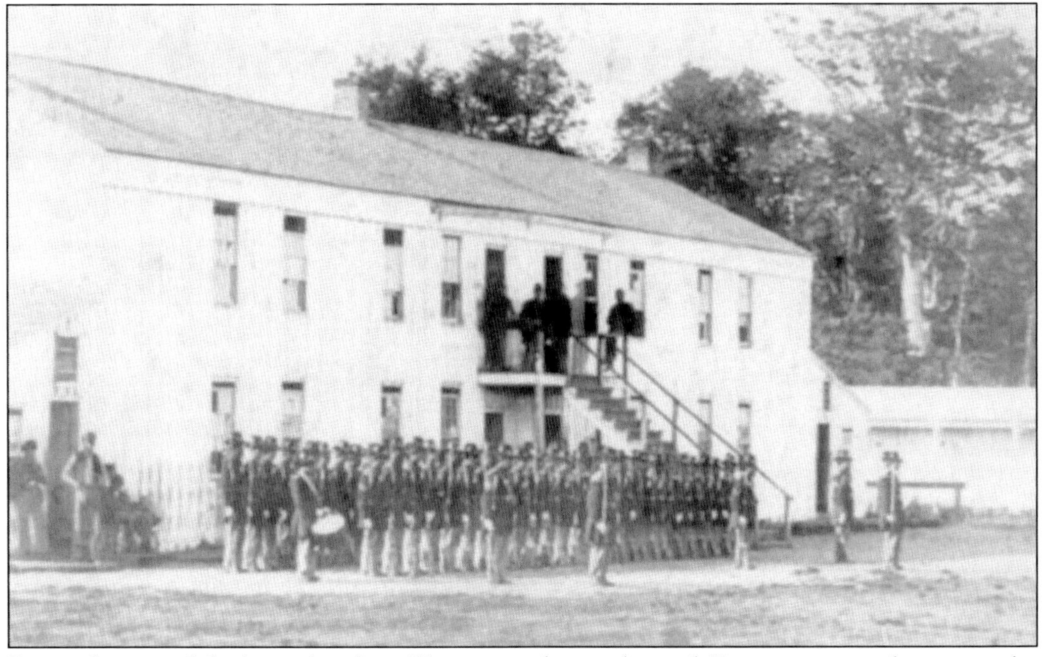

Pictured is one of the barracks where Union guards were housed. Four companies known as the Hoffman Battalion, named after prison commander Lt. Col. William Hoffman, were charged with guarding the prisoners. The guards were hated by the prisoners and were mostly men who had never tasted real combat. The camp had a "dead zone" between the outer wall and the prison, and guards would immediately shoot any prisoner who entered that area.

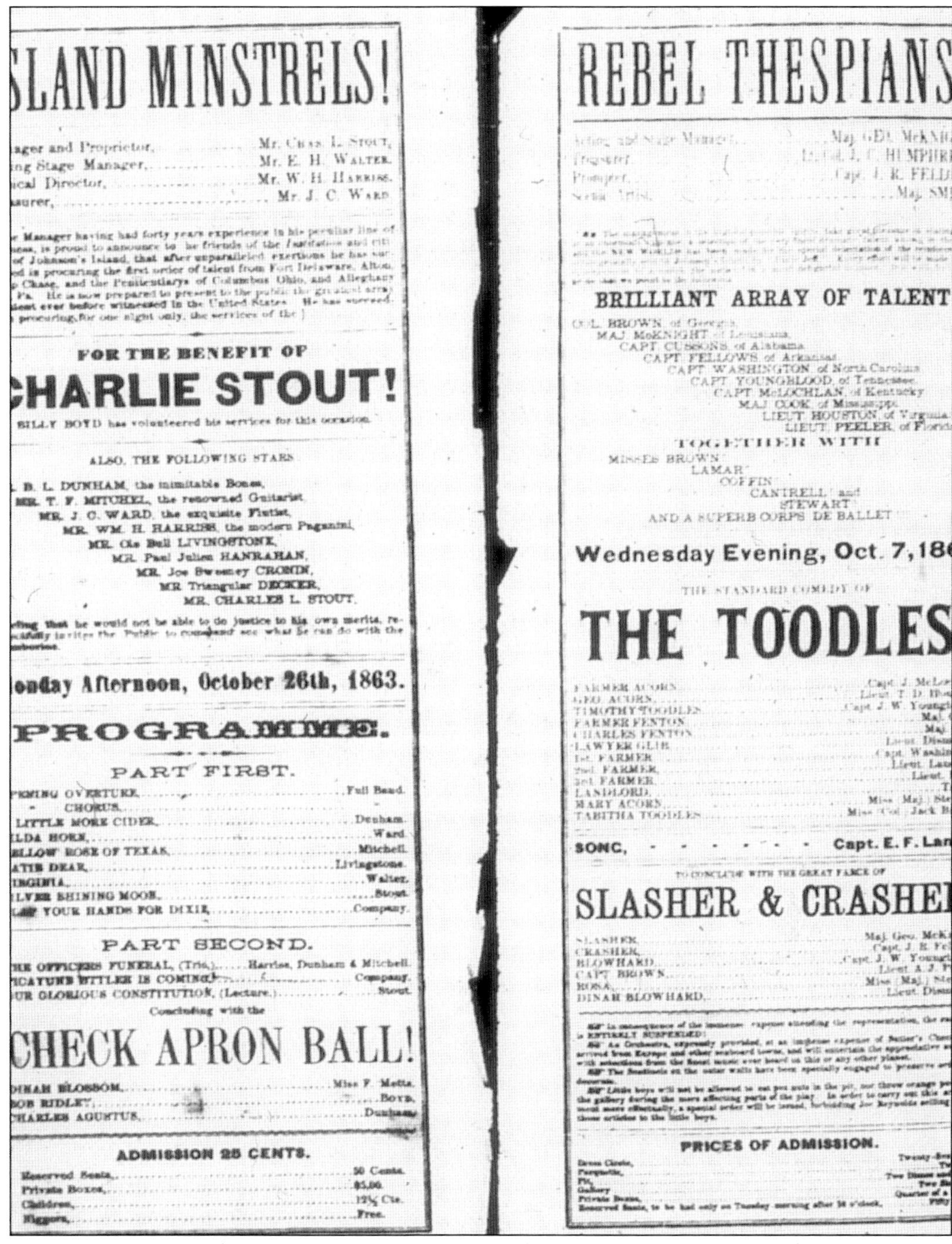

LAND MINSTRELS!

ager and Proprietor,	Mr. Chas. L. Stout,
ng Stage Manager,	Mr. E. H. Walter.
ical Director,	Mr. W. H. Harriss.
surer,	Mr. J. C. Ward.

e Manager having had forty years experience in his peculiar line of ness, is proud to announce to his friends of the Institution and citi of Johnson's Island, that after unparalleled exertions he has suc ed in procuring the first order of talent from Fort Delaware, Alton, Chase, and the Penitentiarys of Columbus Ohio, and Allegheny Pa. He is now prepared to present to the public the greatest array lent ever before witnessed in the United States. He has succeed procuring, for one night only, the services of the

FOR THE BENEFIT OF

HARLIE STOUT!

BILLY BOYD has volunteered his services for this occasion.

ALSO, THE FOLLOWING STARS

B. L. DUNHAM, the inimitable Bones,
MR. T. F. MITCHEL, the renowned Guitarist,
MR. J. C. WARD, the exquisite Flutist,
MR. WM. H. HARRISS, the modern Paganini,
MR. Ole Bull LIVINGSTONE,
MR. Paul Julien HANRAHAN,
MR. Joe Sweeney CRONIN,
MR Triangular DECKER,
MR. CHARLES L. STOUT.

ing that he would not be able to do justice to his own merits, re ully invites the Public to come and see what he can do with the mboriens.

onday Afternoon, October 26th, 1863.

PROGRAMME.

PART FIRST.

ening OVERTURE,	Full Band.
CHORUS,	
LITTLE MORE CIDER,	Dunham.
LDA HORN,	Ward.
LLOW ROSE OF TEXAS,	Mitchell.
ATIE DEAR,	Livingstone.
IRGINIA,	Walter.
LVER SHINING MOON,	Stout.
YOUR HANDS FOR DIXIE,	Company.

PART SECOND.

HE OFFICERS FUNERAL, (Trio,)	Harriss, Dunham & Mitchell.
ICAYUNE BUTLER IS COMING,	Company.
UR GLORIOUS CONSTITUTION, (Lecture.)	Stout.

Concluding with the

CHECK APRON BALL!

DINAH BLOSSOM,	Miss F. Metts.
BOB RIDLEY,	Boyd.
CHARLES AGUSTUS,	Dunham.

ADMISSION 25 CENTS.

Reserved Seats,	50 Cents.
Private Boxes,	$5.00.
Children,	12½ Cts.
Niggers,	Free.

REBEL THESPIANS

Acting and Stage Manager,	Maj. GEO. McKNI
Treasurer,	Lt. Col. J. C. HUMPHR
Prompter,	Capt. J. R. FELD
Scenic Artist,	Maj. SM

BRILLIANT ARRAY OF TALENT

COL. BROWN of Georgia.
MAJ. McKNIGHT of Louisiana.
CAPT. CUSSONS of Alabama.
CAPT. FELLOWS of Arkansas.
CAPT. WASHINGTON of North Carolina.
CAPT. YOUNGBLOOD of Tennessee.
CAPT. McLOCHLAN of Kentucky.
MAJ. COOK of Mississippi.
LIEUT. HOUSTON of Virginia.
LIEUT. PEELER of Florida.

TOGETHER WITH

MISSES BROWN,
LAMAR,
COFFIN,
CANTRELL and
STEWART.
AND A SUPERB CORPS DE BALLET

Wednesday Evening, Oct. 7, 18

THE STANDARD COMEDY OF

THE TOODLES

FARMER ACORN,	Capt. J. McLo
GEO. ACORN,	Lieut. T. D. Hou
TIMOTHY TOODLES,	Capt. J. W. Youngb
FARMER FENTON,	Maj.
CHARLES FENTON,	Maj.
LAWYER GLIB,	Lieut. Dism
1st. FARMER,	Capt. Washin
2nd. FARMER,	Lieut. Lau
3rd. FARMER,	Lieut.
LANDLORD,	T
MARY ACORN,	Miss (Maj.) Ste
TABITHA TOODLES,	Miss (Col.) Jack B

SONG, - - - - - - - Capt. E. F. Lan

TO CONCLUDE WITH THE GREAT FARCE OF

SLASHER & CRASHE

SLASHER,	Maj. Geo. McK
CRASHER,	Capt. J. R. Fe
BLOWHARD,	Capt. J. W. Youngb
CAPT. BROWN,	Lieut. A. J. F
ROSA,	Miss (Maj.) Ste
DINAH BLOWHARD,	Lieut. Dism

PRICES OF ADMISSION.

Dress Circle,
Parquette,
Pit,
Gallery,
Private Boxes,
Reserved Seats, to be had only on Tuesday morning after 10 o'clock,

Once prisoners passed muster in the morning, they often had much idle time on their hands. This playbill tells of a performance by the Rebel Thespians, a theater group of Confederate prisoners who would put on shows for each other. To pass the time, prisoners would engage in all sorts of activities, including baseball, furniture and jewelry making, autograph collecting, journaling, and attending YMCA meetings.

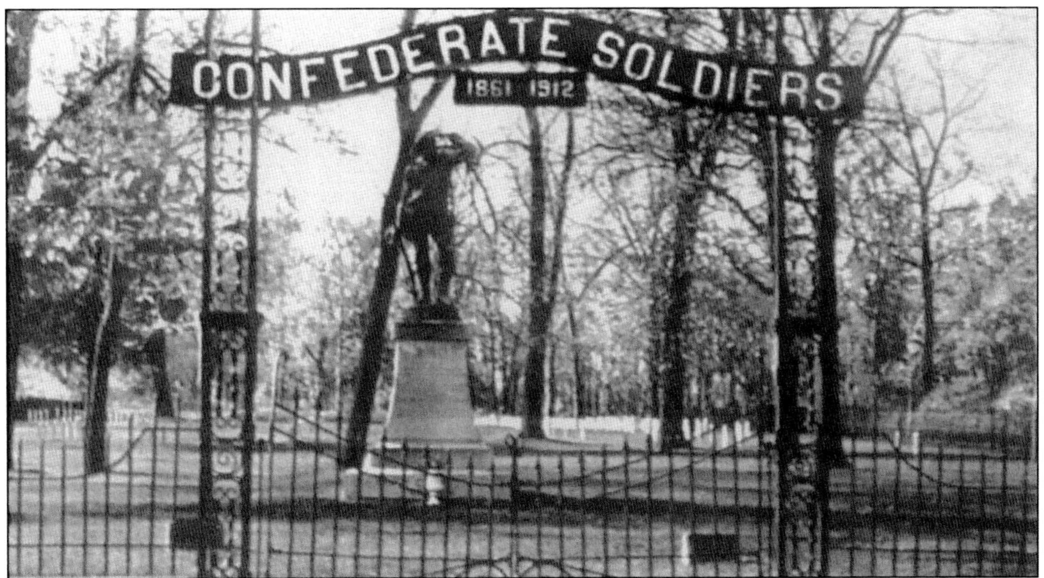

Here is an early view of the cemetery on Johnson's Island where 206 Confederate prisoners were buried—which is all that remains of the large Civil War prison camp that was on the island. The tall soldier monument was given by the Daughters of the Confederacy and dedicated in 1910. It still looks toward the south, waiting for the rescue that never came.

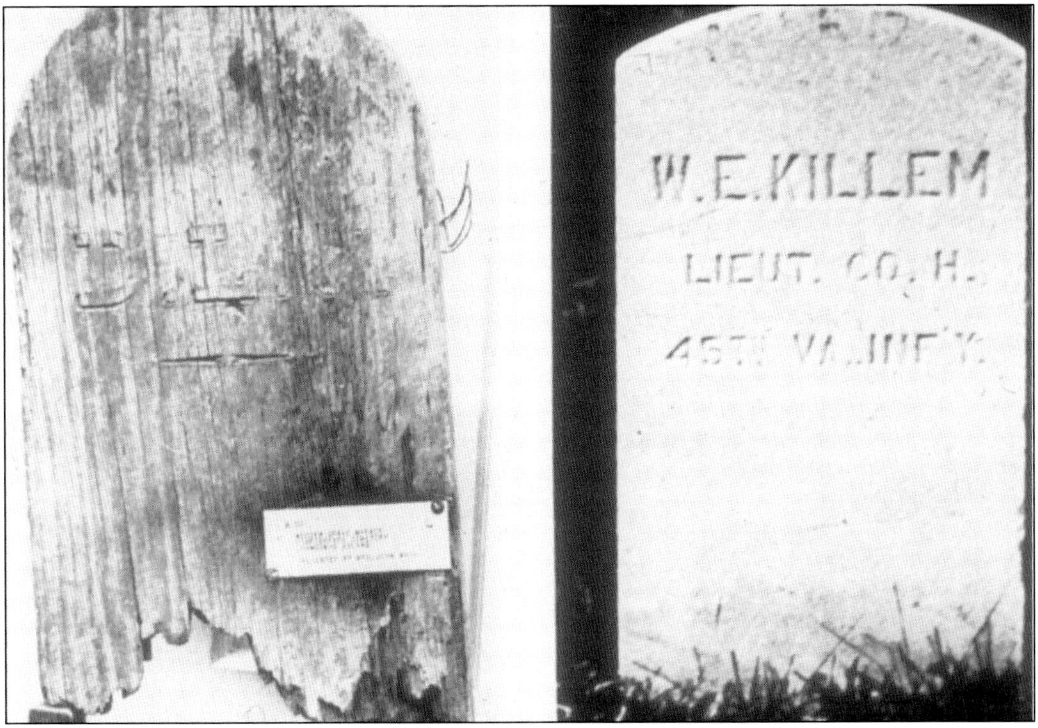

This interesting photograph compares the original grave markers with the government-issued ones that replaced them in the early 1900s. Over time, some of the newer ones have been destroyed and replaced again. The stone on the right features a name that is rather enlightening as to the reason why he was imprisoned.

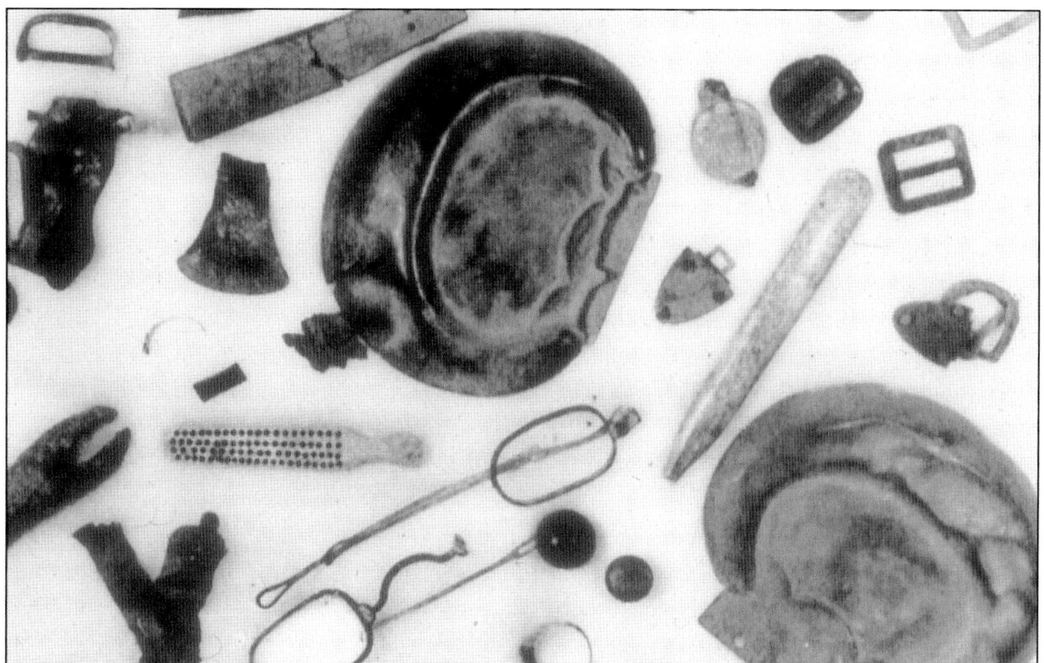

Many archaeological excavations have been done over the years at Johnson's Island. Pictured are some of the uncovered artifacts, including a hat, broken eyeglasses, buckles, buttons, tools, and a bent chamber pot.

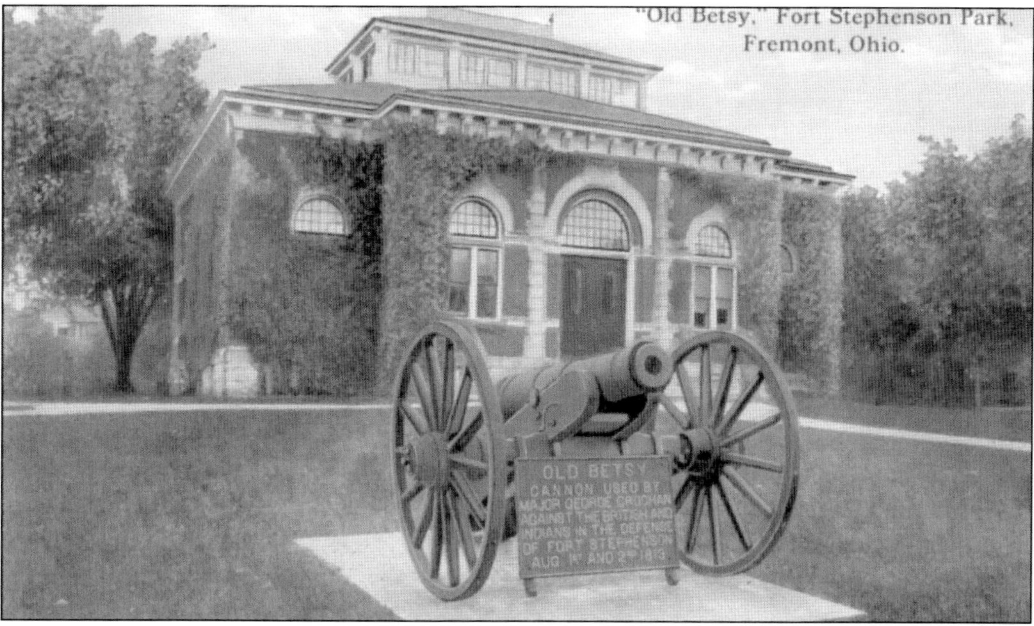

For those interested in further exploring the history of the Sandusky River, there are many excellent places to conduct research, such as museums in Bucyrus and Upper Sandusky, as well as the Sandusky County Historical Society in Fremont. Birchard Public Library in Fremont, pictured before several additions, not only sits on the site of Fort Stephenson but also has several artifacts from the battle.

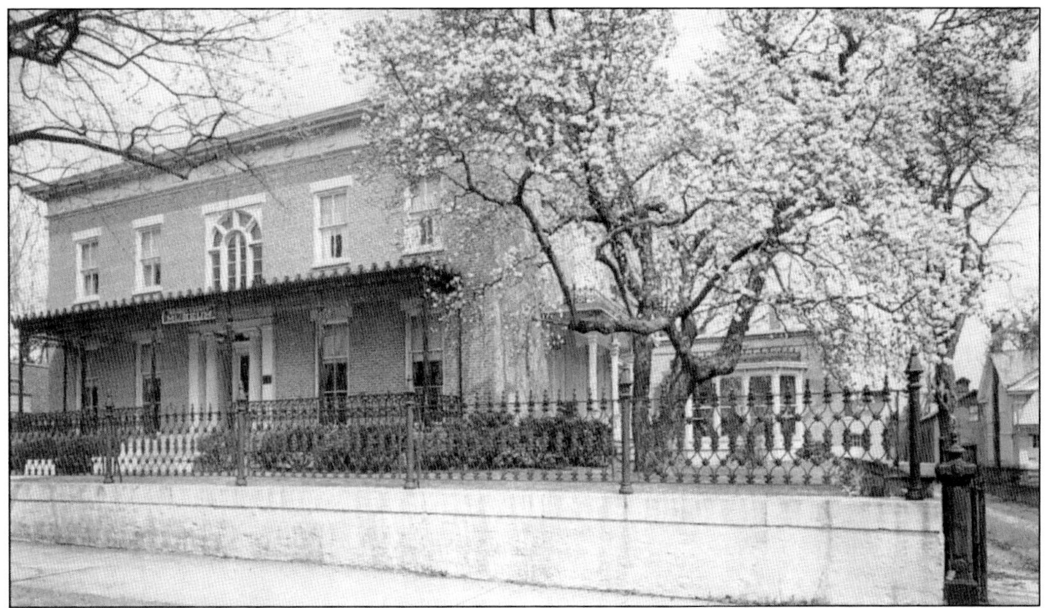

The two most comprehensive collections of local history can be found in the Seneca County Museum in Tiffin and the Hayes Presidential Museum and Library in Fremont. The Shawhan mansion, pictured, is the home of the Seneca County Museum at 28 Clay Street, which has a large collection of photographs, especially of the 1913 flood, along with many artifacts and other research materials. (Courtesy of the Seneca County Museum.)

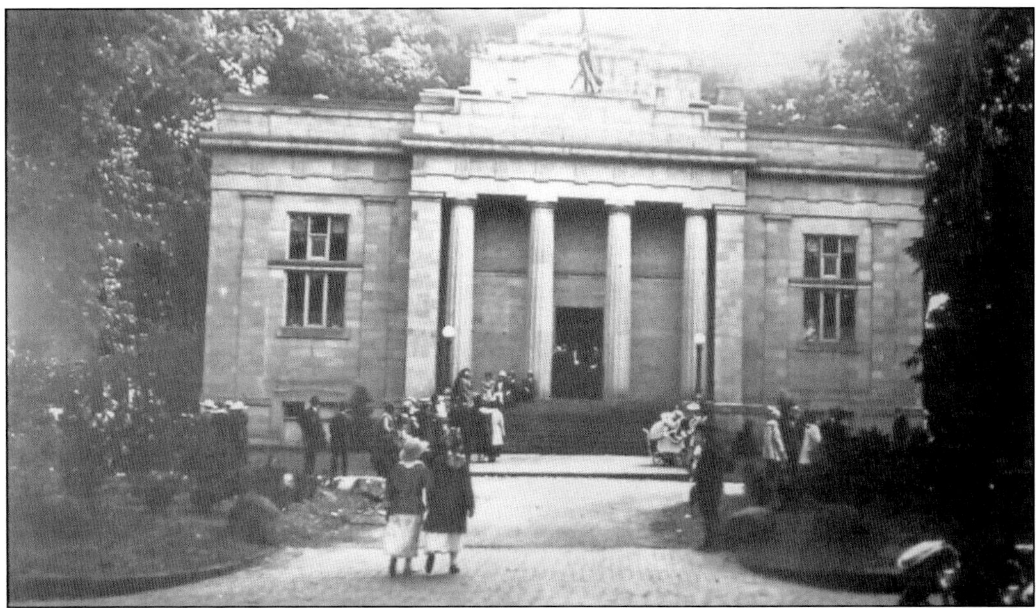

The Hayes Library at the Hayes Presidential Center in Fremont was the first presidential library in the country. Located on the top floor of the Hayes Museum in Spiegel Grove, it is perhaps the most extensive research library for the whole period of the Gilded Age. It is both a national treasure and an excellent resource for local history. The original section of the museum and library, now greatly expanded, is pictured shortly after it opened in 1916. Next year, it will celebrate its 100th anniversary.

Two

A Scenic River

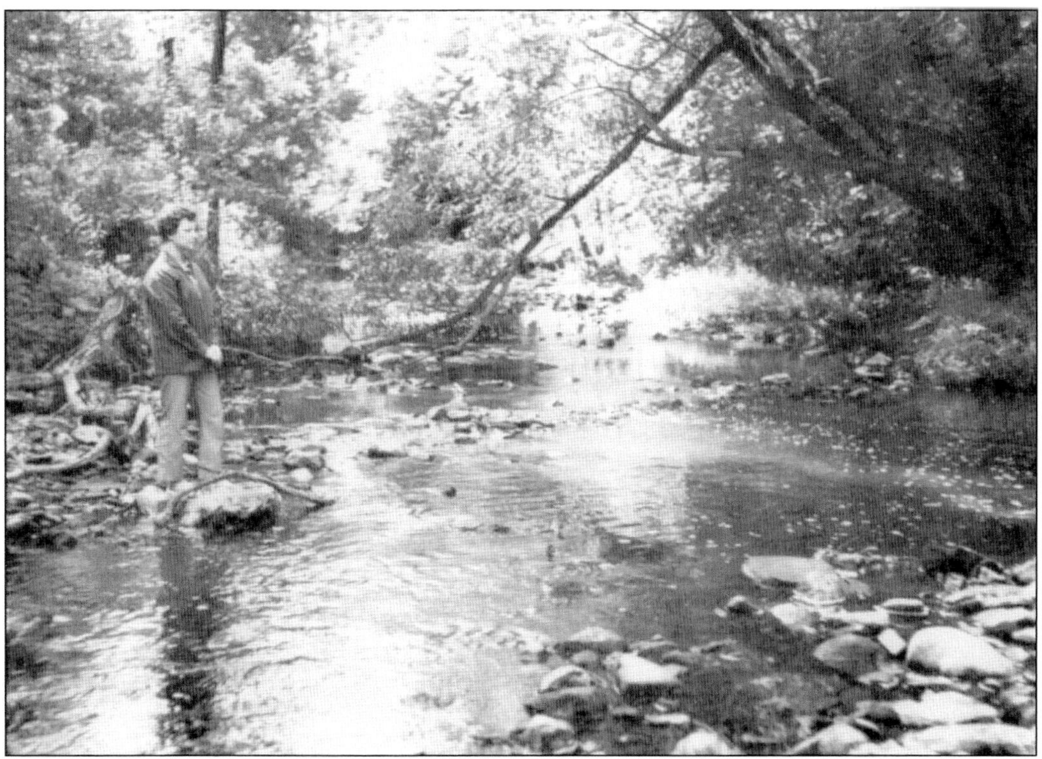

The shallow waters of Paramour Creek, pictured, flow past Leesville and Crestline in Richland County and join with Allen Run by Lake Galion, the true source of the Sandusky River. (Courtesy of Ray Grob.)

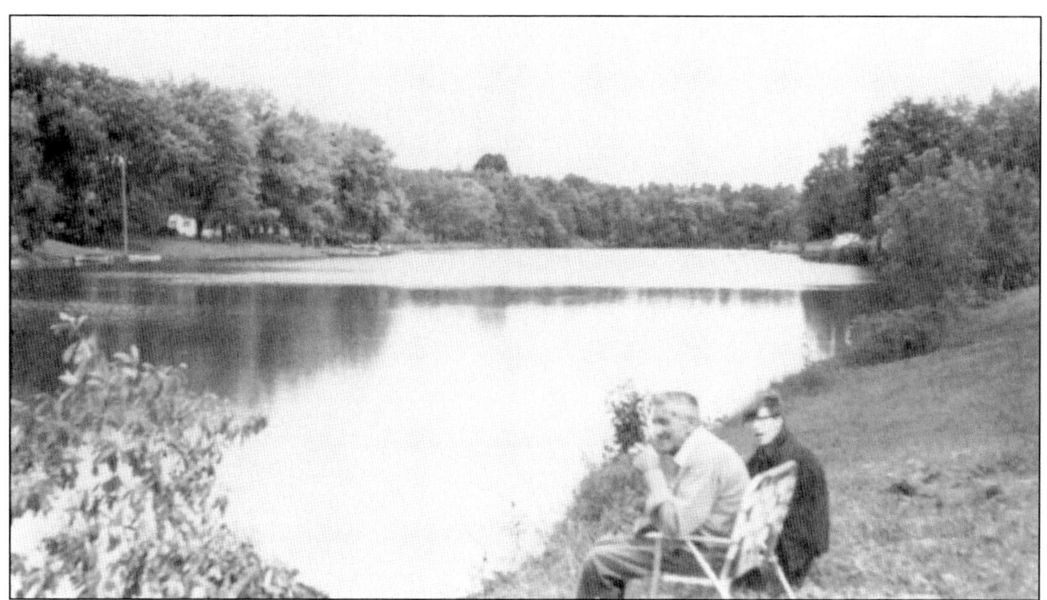

Lake Galion, pictured, is one mile southwest of the village of Leesville, and at the northern tip of the lake is a spillway, where the overflow meets with Paramour Creek. (Courtesy of Ray Grob.)

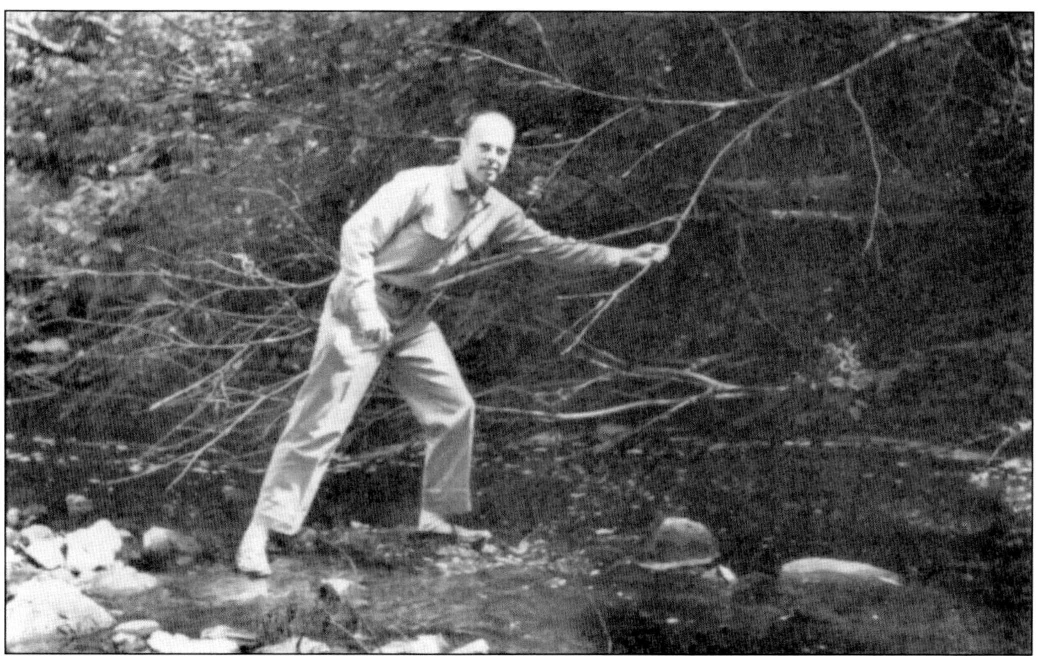

Ray Grob, fourth generation of a Fremont family-photography business and a frequent writer about the Sandusky River, steps across the shallow river near its source. (Courtesy of Ray Grob.)

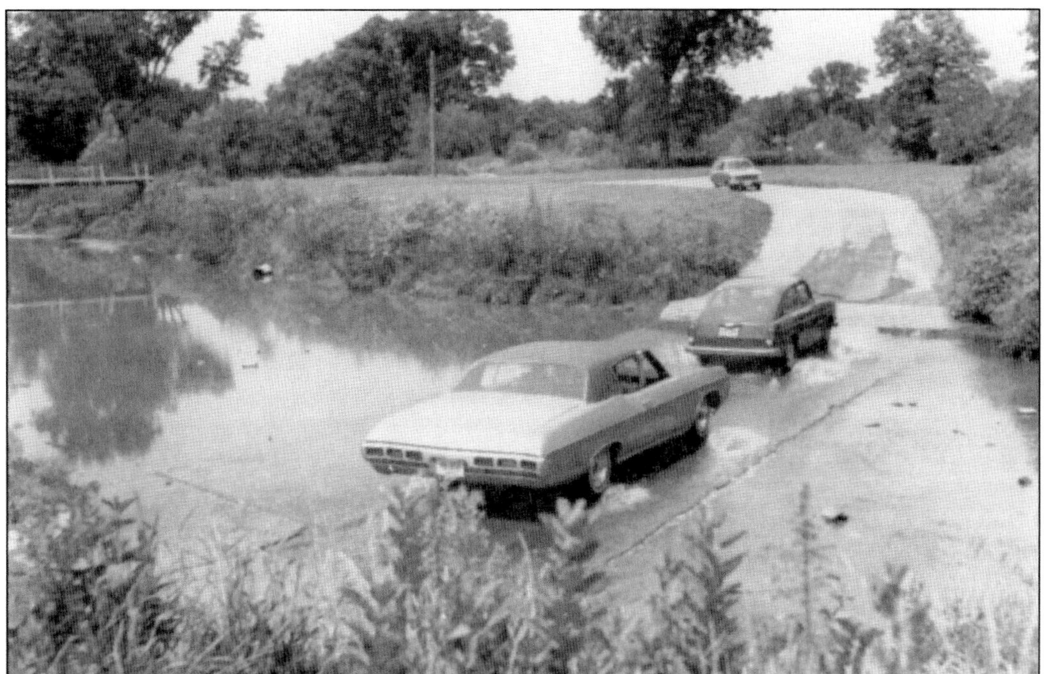

In Bucyrus, the river flows past Aumiller Park, land donated to the city by the Daniel Aumiller family in 1925. In shallow water, cars can actually drive through the Sandusky River to enter the park. (Courtesy of Ray Grob.)

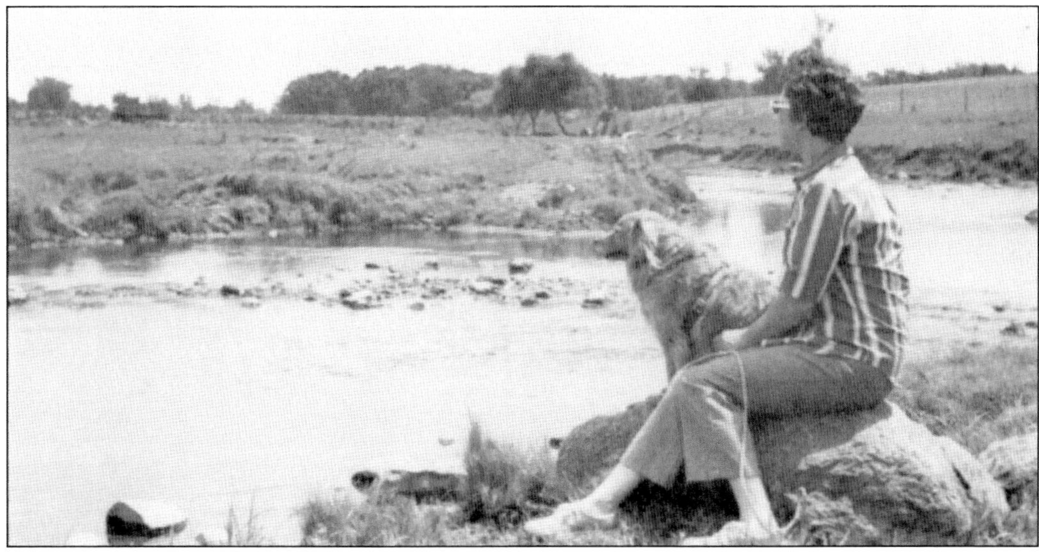

Southwest of Bucyrus, the young river winds through open farmland near where Colonel Crawford's army was badly defeated by Indian warriors led by a chief called "The Pipe." Also near here, Broken Sword Creek, the first major tributary, joins the Sandusky. The creek got its name from the victory over Crawford's army. (Courtesy of Ray Grob.)

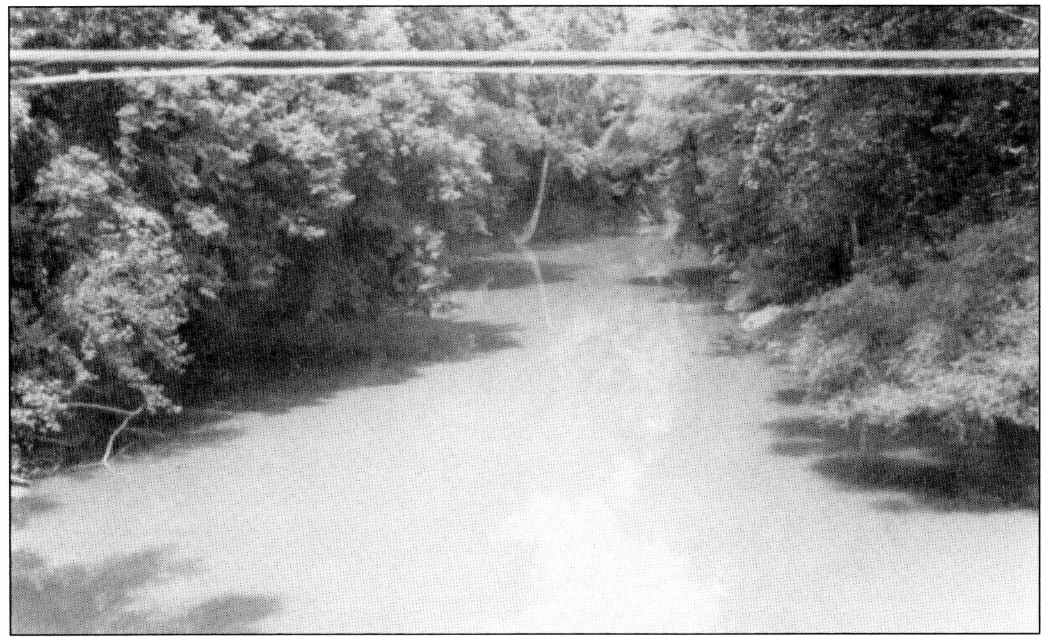

This view looks downstream from the highway bridge on Route 30 at Upper Sandusky, which was named for the location of the upper rapids of the river. General Harrison built Fort Ferree nearby during his War of 1812 campaign. Also near Upper Sandusky stand the Indian Spring where Colonel Crawford's men stopped to drink on June 4, 1782, and the Overland Inn where novelist Charles Dickens ate in 1842. (Courtesy of Ray Grob.)

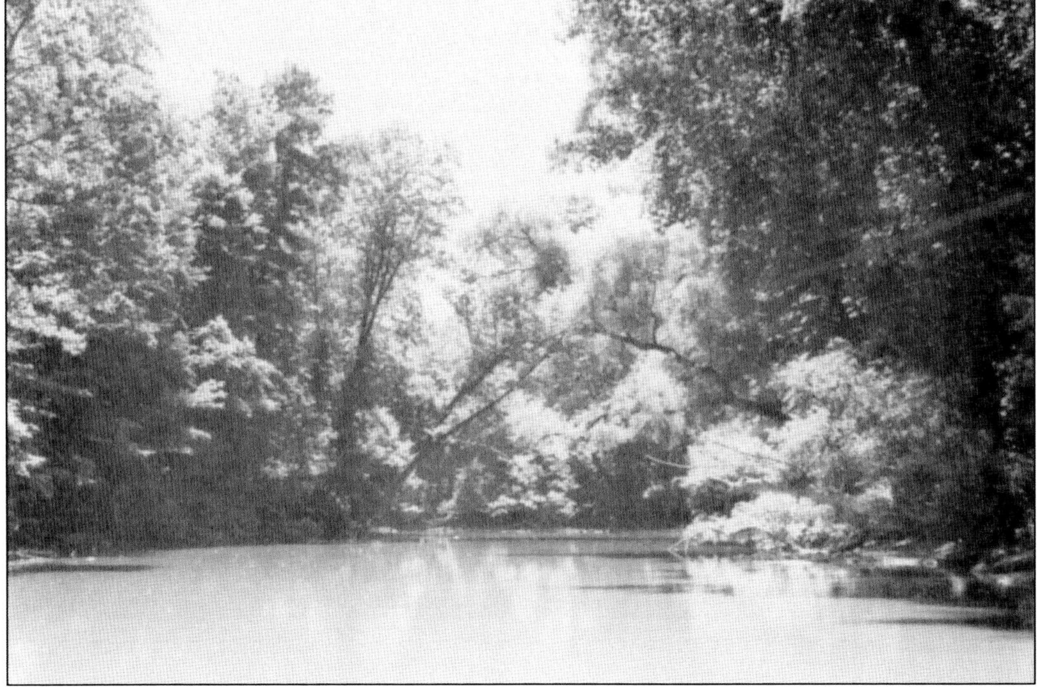

North of Upper Sandusky, the river widens and travels through a beautiful stretch of forest. (Courtesy of Ray Grob.)

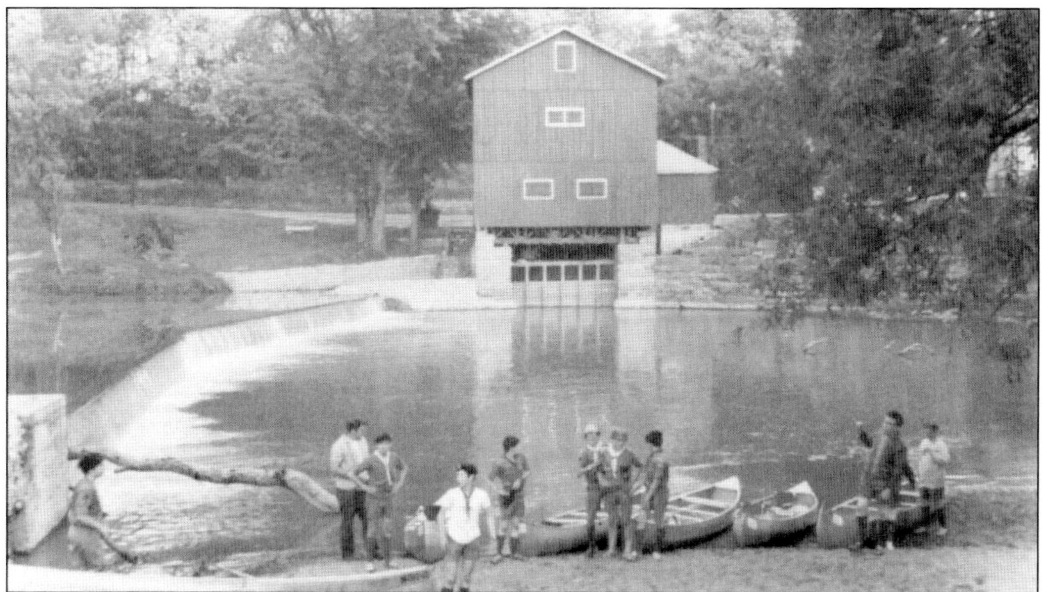
A spillway spans the river at Indian Mill, a popular historic site across from a public park and picnic grounds. Below the spillway is a good fishing spot and excellent place to begin a canoe trip. (Courtesy of Ray Grob.)

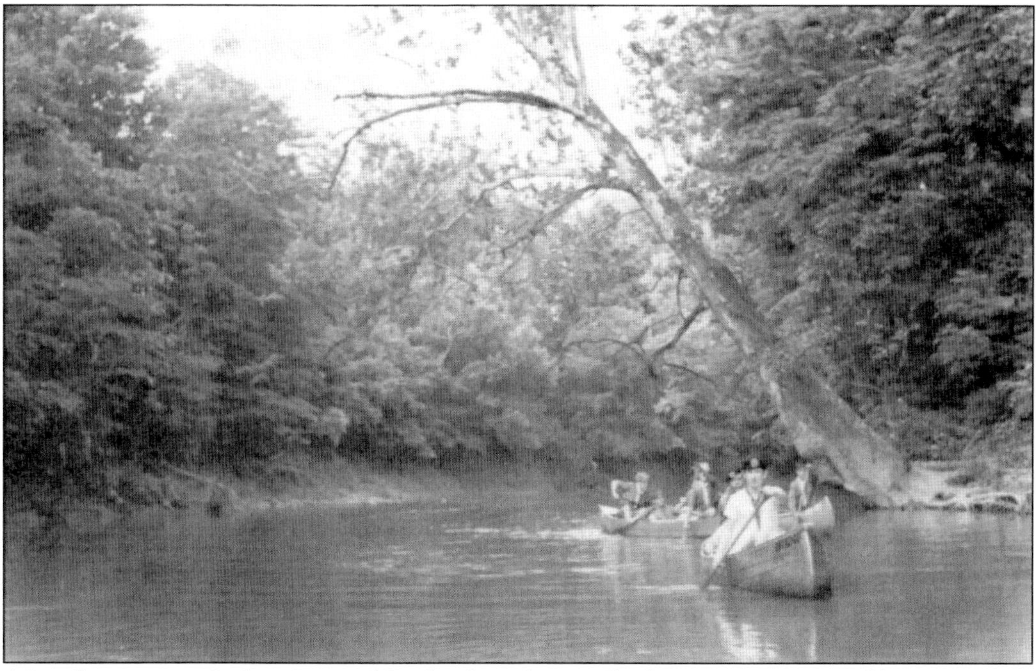
After flowing past Parker Covered Bridge (see chapter 3), the river narrows and becomes more isolated. Canoeists are photographed enjoying the remote beauty of their surroundings as they paddle leisurely downstream. (Courtesy of Ray Grob.)

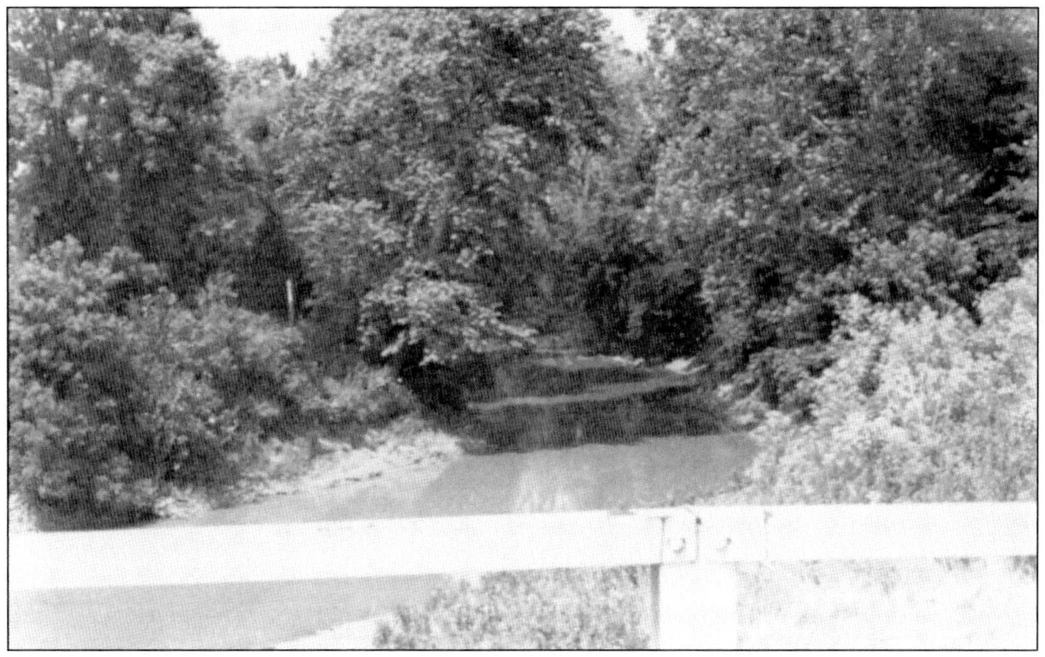

Route 103 crosses the river just east of the tiny village of Tymochtee in northern Wyandot County. This view from the bridge shows the river winding its way among willows and cottonwoods. (Courtesy of Ray Grob.)

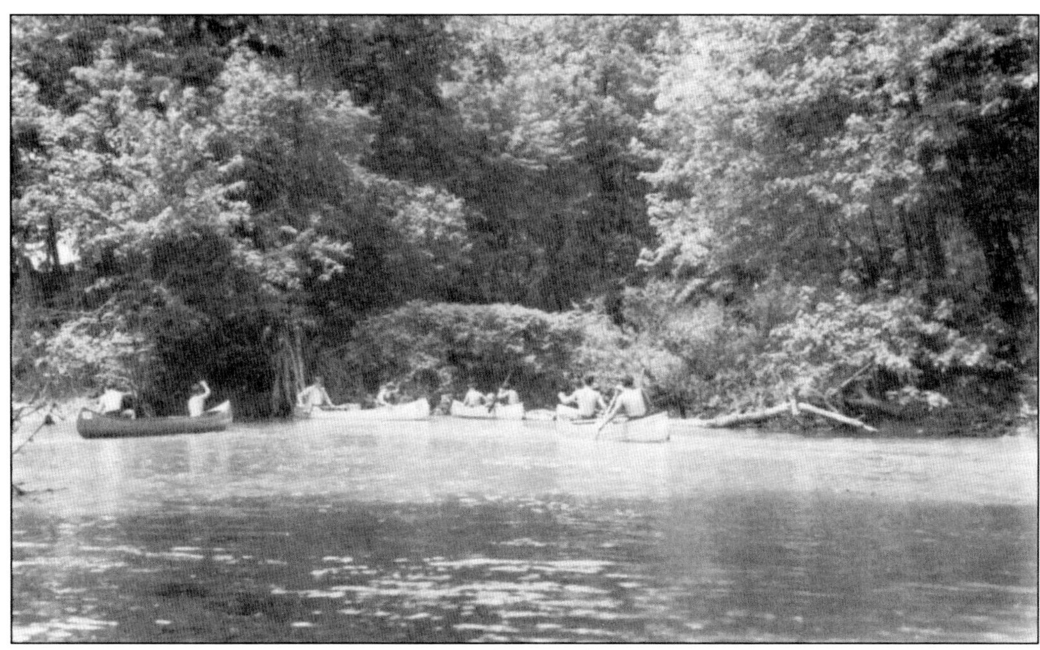

In this photograph, Boy Scouts canoe near the mouth of Tymochtee Creek, exploring some of the dense vegetation where the creek merges with the Sandusky. (Courtesy of Ray Grob.)

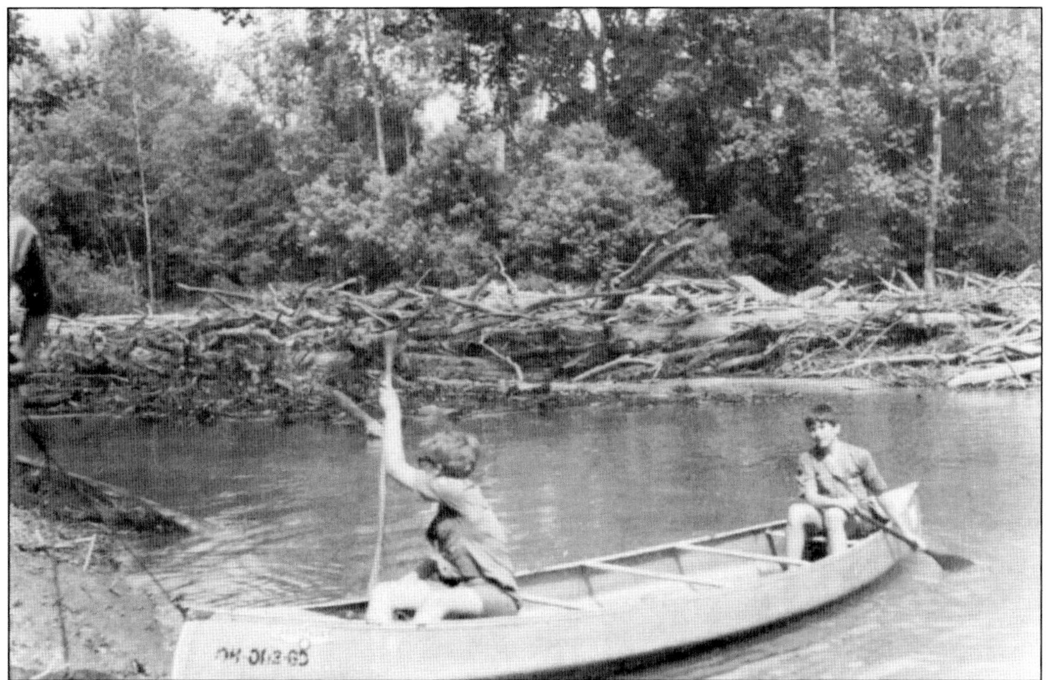

Two Boy Scouts are pictured in their canoe rowing past a huge logjam that had been accumulating for about 30 years at this bend in the river, which is southeast of McCutchenville, a small town on the Wyandot-Seneca county line. (Courtesy of Ray Grob.)

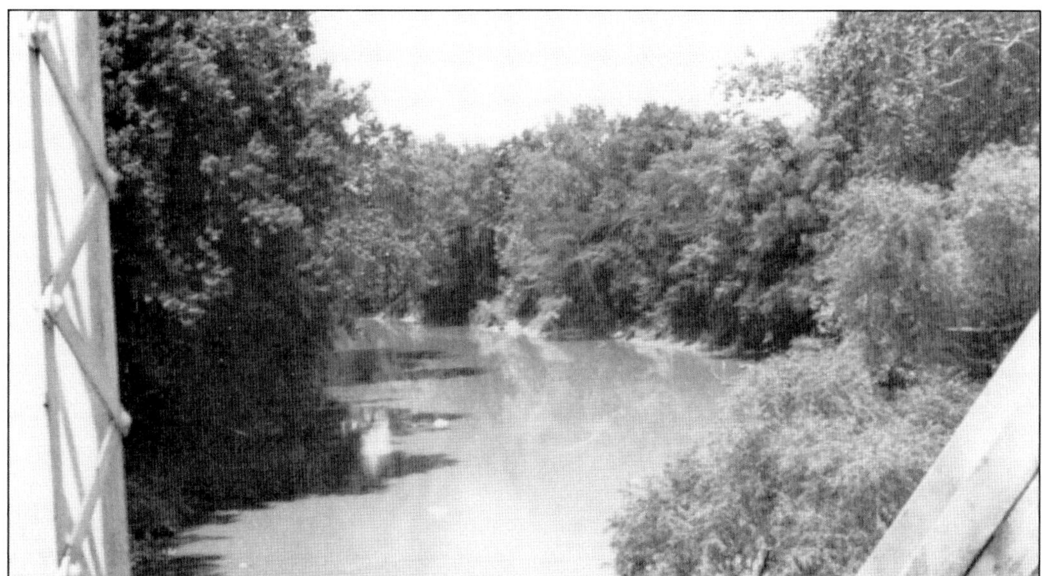

Photographed from Scott Bridge on Seneca CR 90, the Sandusky River begins to wind through a remote and wild stretch of beech, oak, maple, and walnut trees with almost no sign of civilization on either shore. (Courtesy of Ray Grob.)

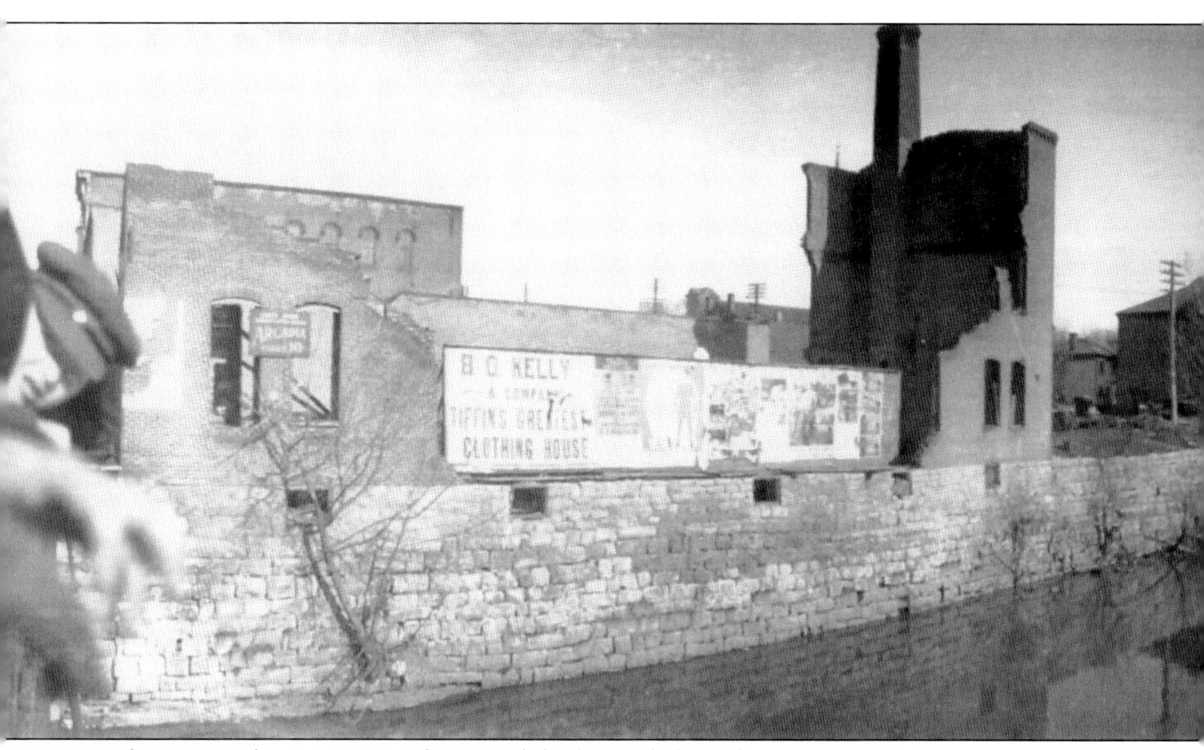

The view in this panoramic photograph looks south from the Market Street iron bridge in Tiffin about 1906. The stone embankment along the east shore would soon prove to be inadequate during

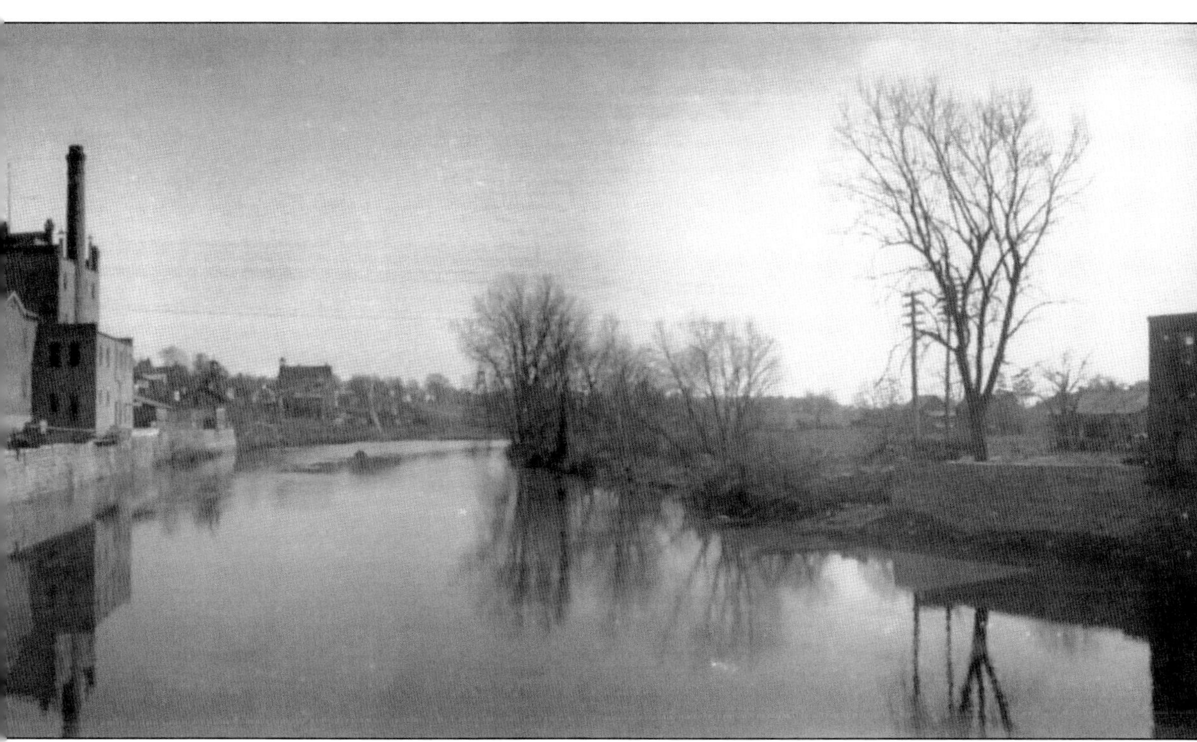

the 1913 flood. The Hubach Brewery stands at center beyond the old buildings in disrepair. At far left, a young boy leans over the bridge railing to be in the photograph.

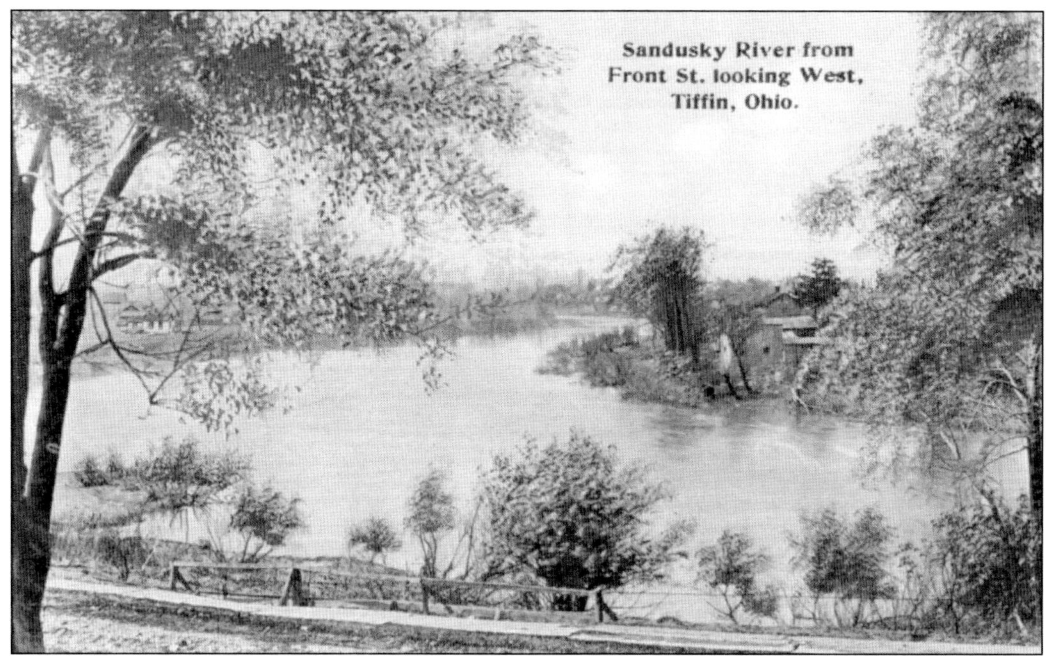

An early postcard view west from Front Street shows the river winding though Tiffin at a time when only the beginnings of settlements were along the shores in that area. (Courtesy of the Seneca County Museum.)

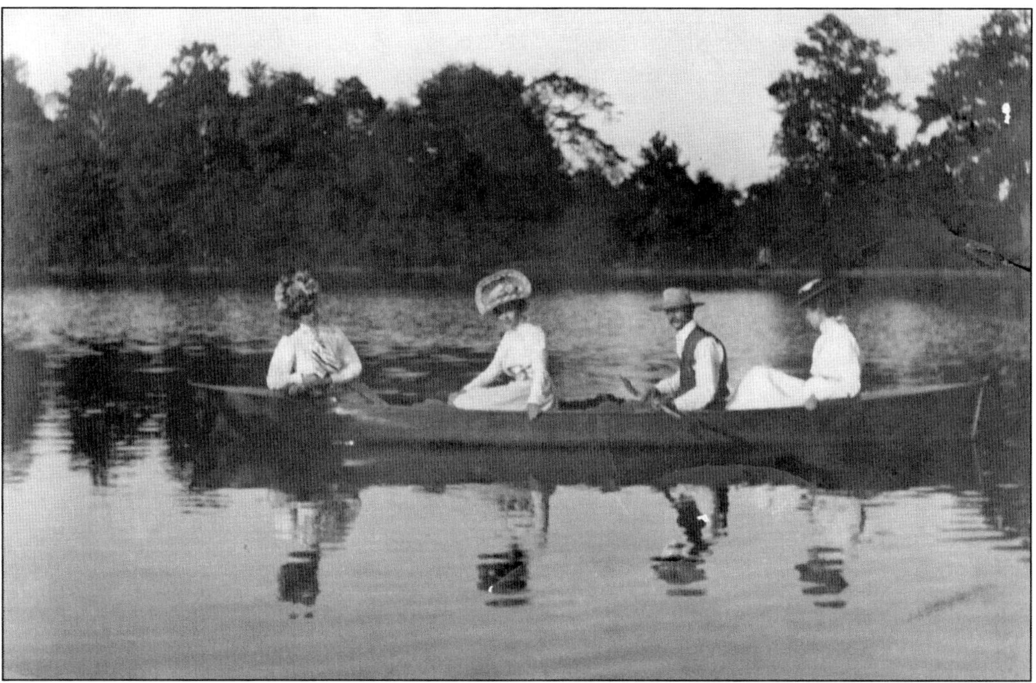

Camp Mosquito was the name given to a campground along the river near Tiffin. In this 1890s photograph, three well-dressed young ladies and a lucky gentleman visiting the campground pose in a canoe on the river. Only the young man is holding a paddle. (Courtesy of the Seneca County Museum.)

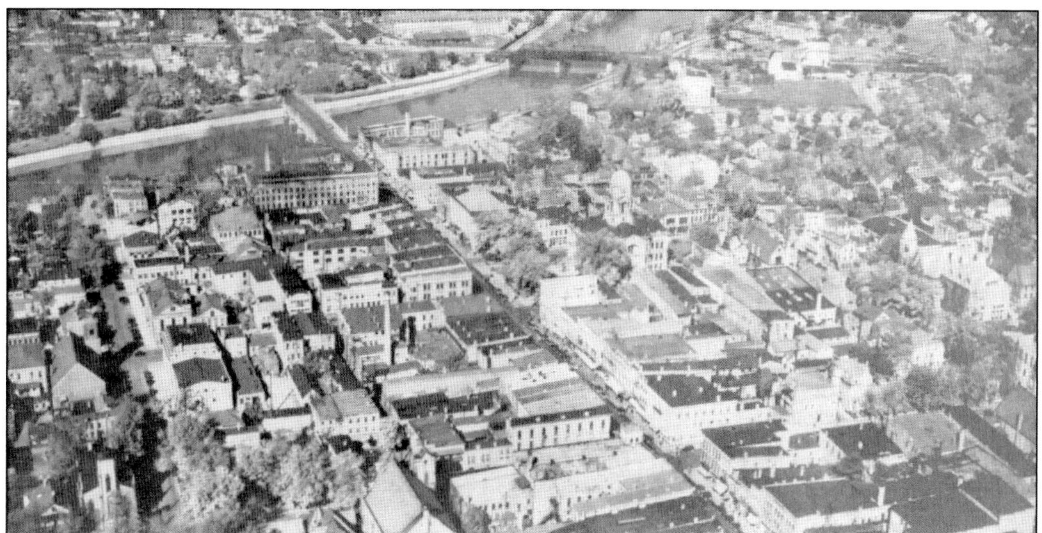

An aerial photograph of downtown Tiffin taken in May 1929 shows the river flowing northeast past the Washington Street Bridge and the railroad trestle bridge at the top. Landmarks include the massive Shawhan Hotel below the Washington Street Bridge, the courthouse near the center, and the old Columbian High School at right.

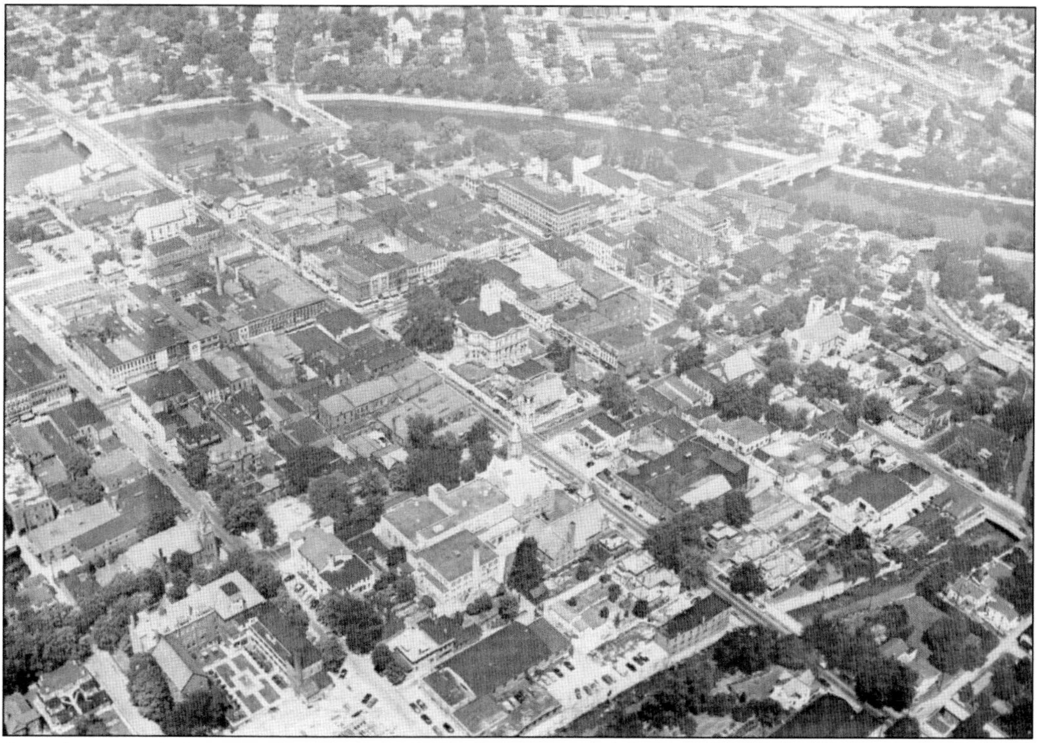

Another aerial photograph from June 1953 has a view that looks down on the Sandusky River bending from north to northeast at top. In this northwest view, the Market Street and Perry Street bridges are seen at left and the Washington Street Bridge at right. The courthouse again appears in the center, above the Columbian High School building.

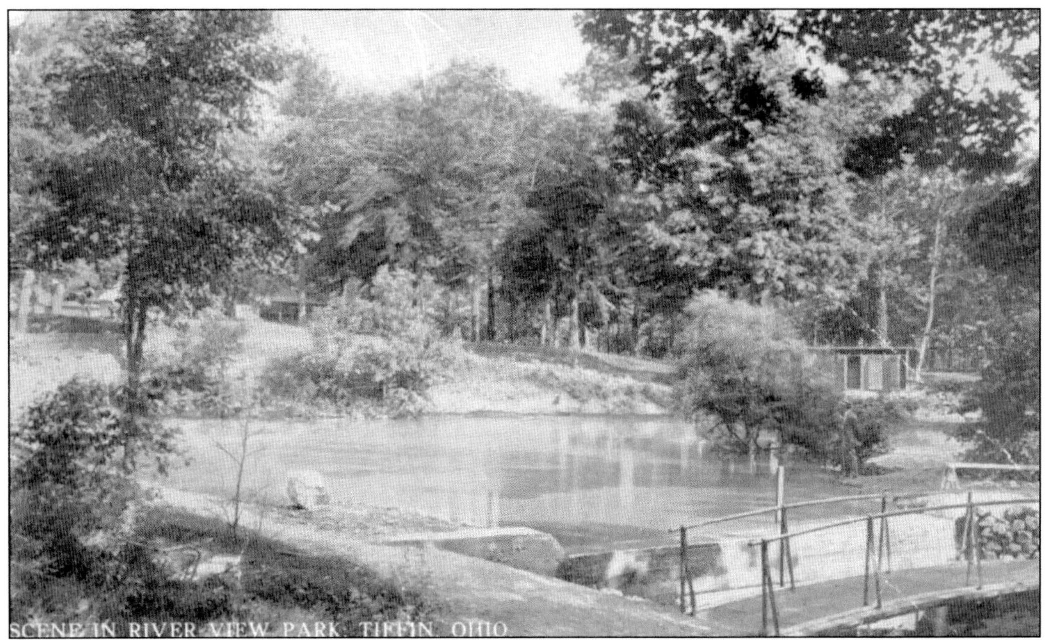

North of Tiffin, located near Huss Street on the east side of the Sandusky, Riverside Park was a popular place in the early 20th century. This postcard captures the quiet beauty of the park along the river. (Courtesy of the Seneca County Museum.)

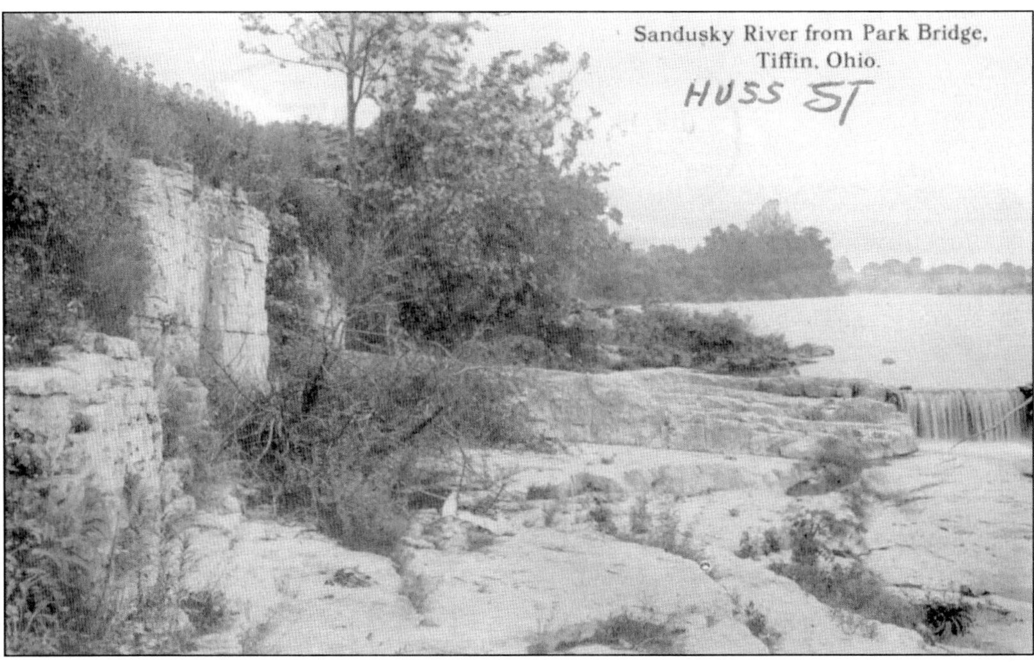

Another postcard view shows the spillway from the Park Bridge along the shore in the early 1900s.

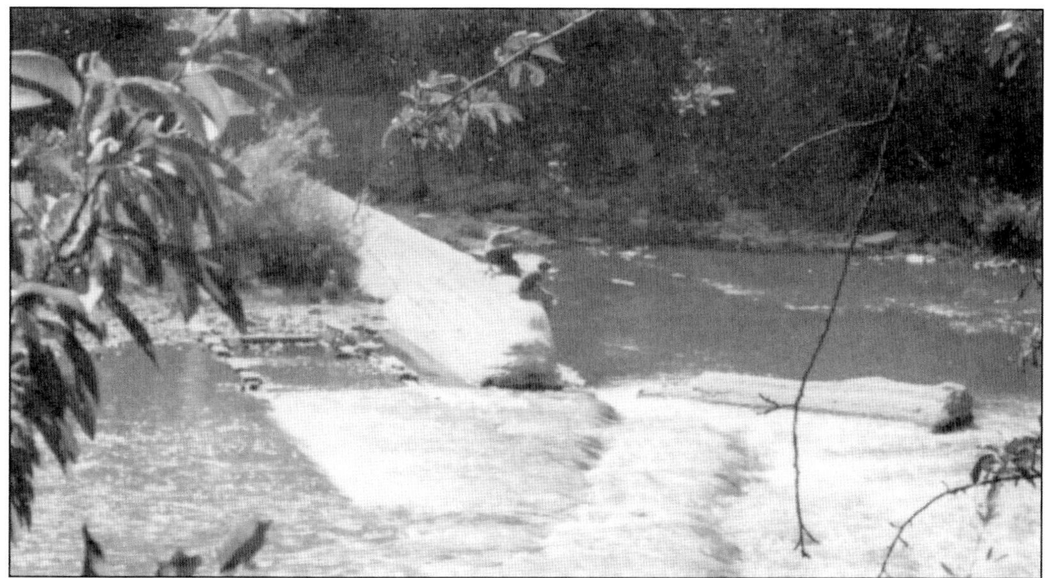

Many years of floods and high water have gradually washed away Speck's dam near Huss Street, which is a reminder of the time when many small dams and mills lined the river. In this photograph, a boy is fishing from the ruins. (Courtesy of Ray Grob.)

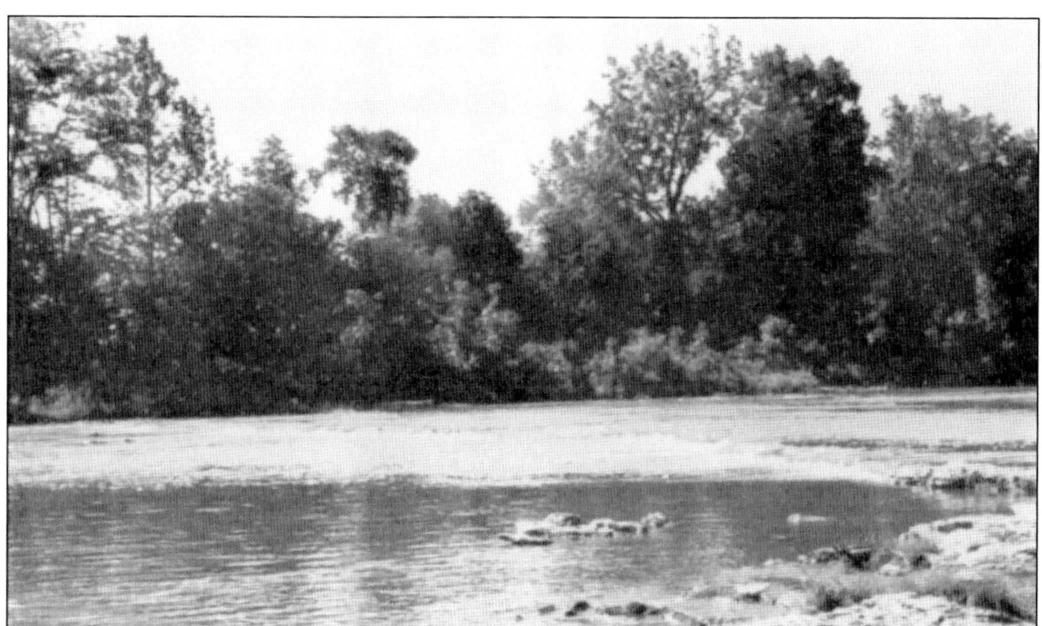

North of the old dam, the river begins to rapidly run over the shallow limestone and gravel bottom. The many dams and shallow water in the area make it necessary for canoeists to portage around Tiffin. (Courtesy of Ray Grob.)

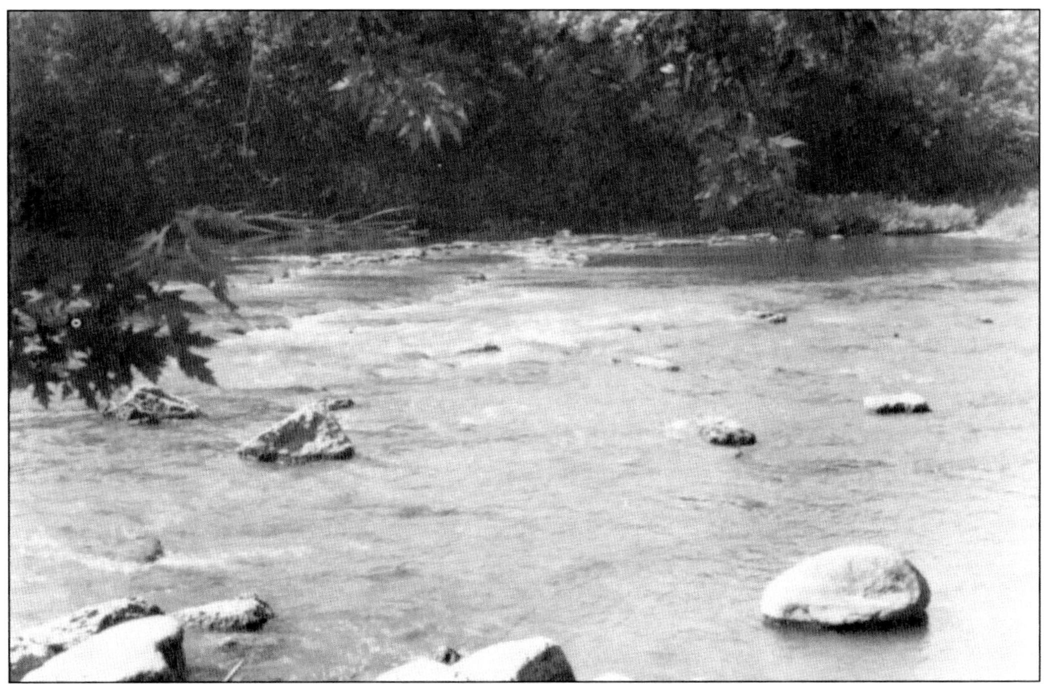

As the river flows north out of Tiffin, many boulders are scattered around in the shallow water on the limestone ledges. (Courtesy of Ray Grob.)

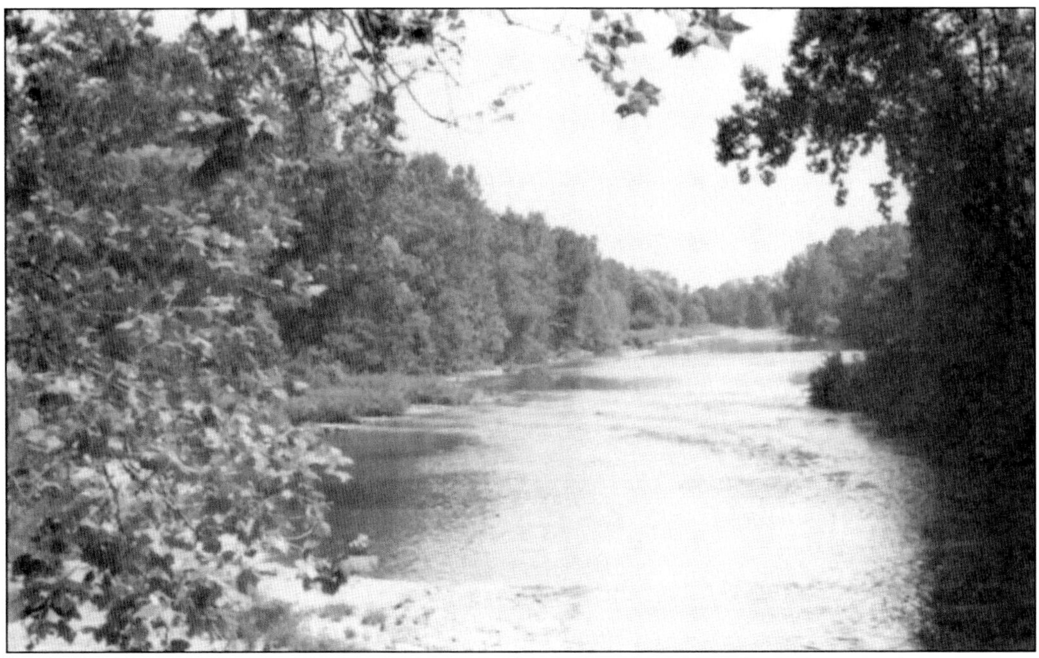

In spite of the rock ledges and shallow water that make travel hard for canoeists, the scenery is beautiful, with trees lining both shores of the river. (Courtesy of Ray Grob.)

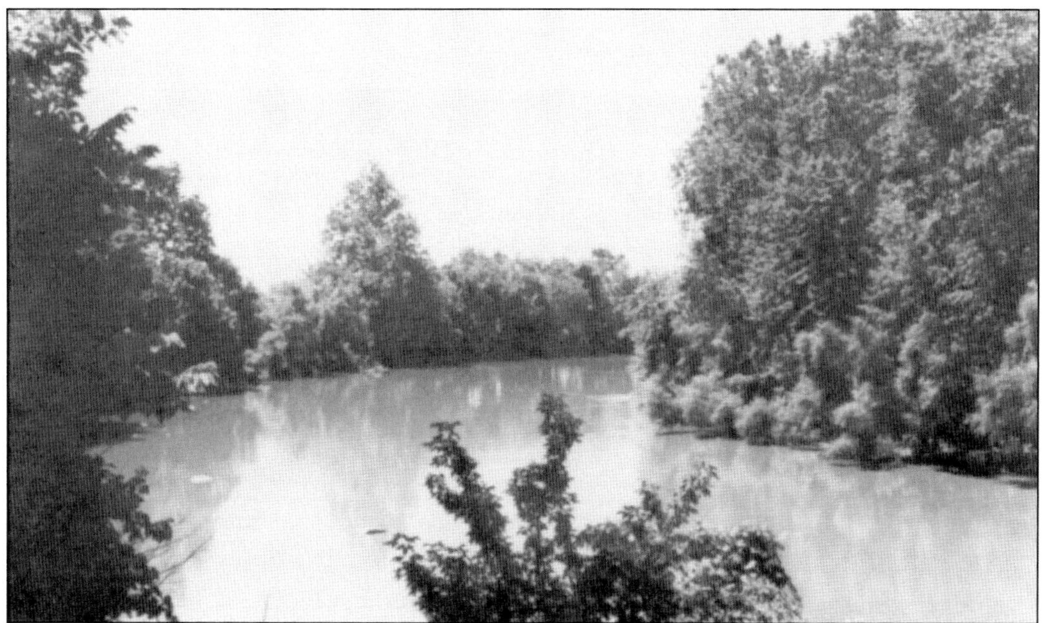

Past the site of Fort Seneca on the west bank of the river in Old Fort, the river again provides beautiful scenery for travelers, as seen in this summer photograph of the winding river approaching a bend. (Courtesy of Ray Grob.)

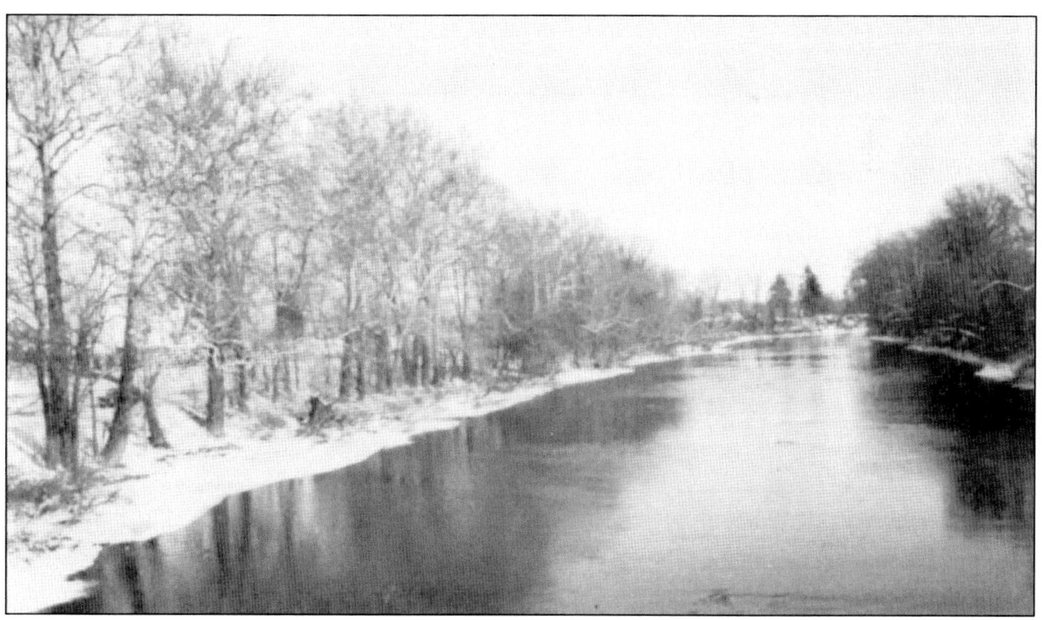

Even in winter, great beauty can be found on the river. In this photograph, light snow lines the banks and sparkles in the trees along the shore as the river continues its way north toward Fremont. (Courtesy of Ray Grob.)

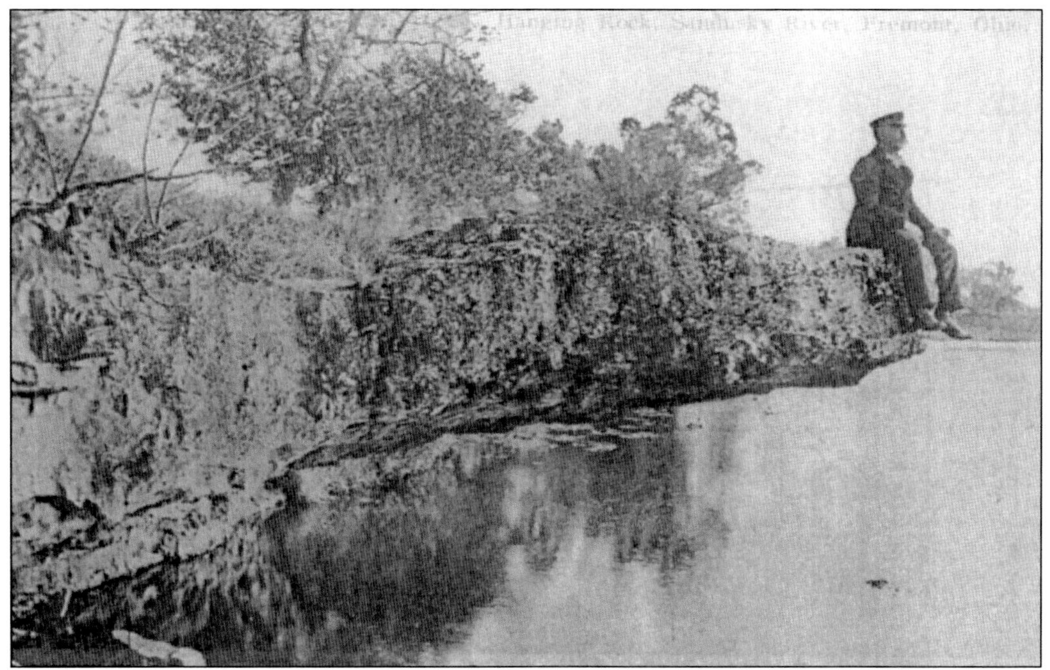

This unusual rocky outcropping near Fremont called Hanging Rock does not deter this man from enjoying a view from his precarious perch out over the water.

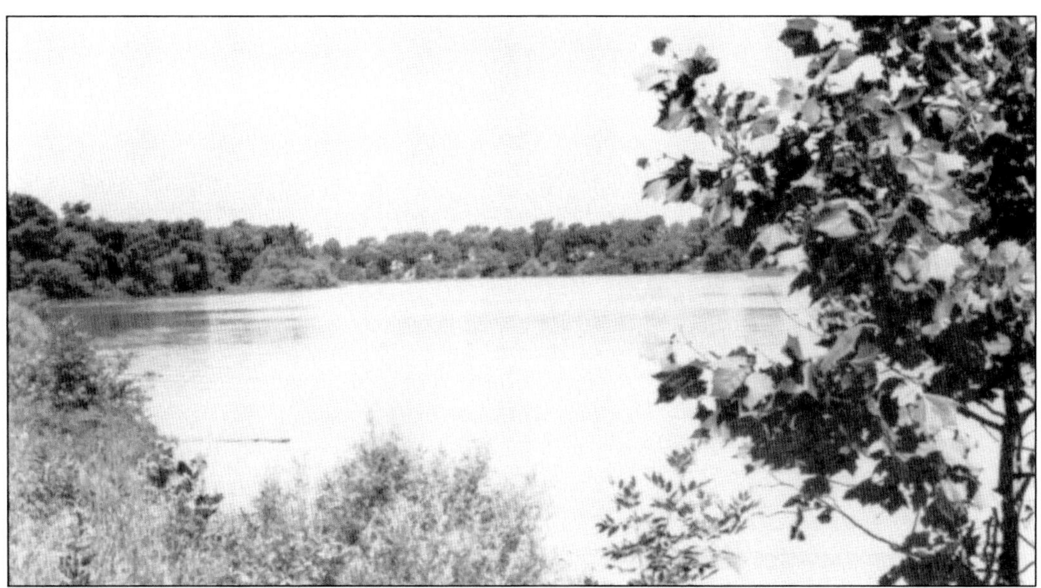

As the Sandusky approaches Fremont from the west, the Ballville Dam creates a placid area with a wooded shoreline. Along the shore west of the dam is Chief Tarhe Park, from which this photograph of the river was taken. The calm water, as wide as a lake, is a popular area for fishing, canoeing, sailing, and ice-skating. (Courtesy of Ray Grob.)

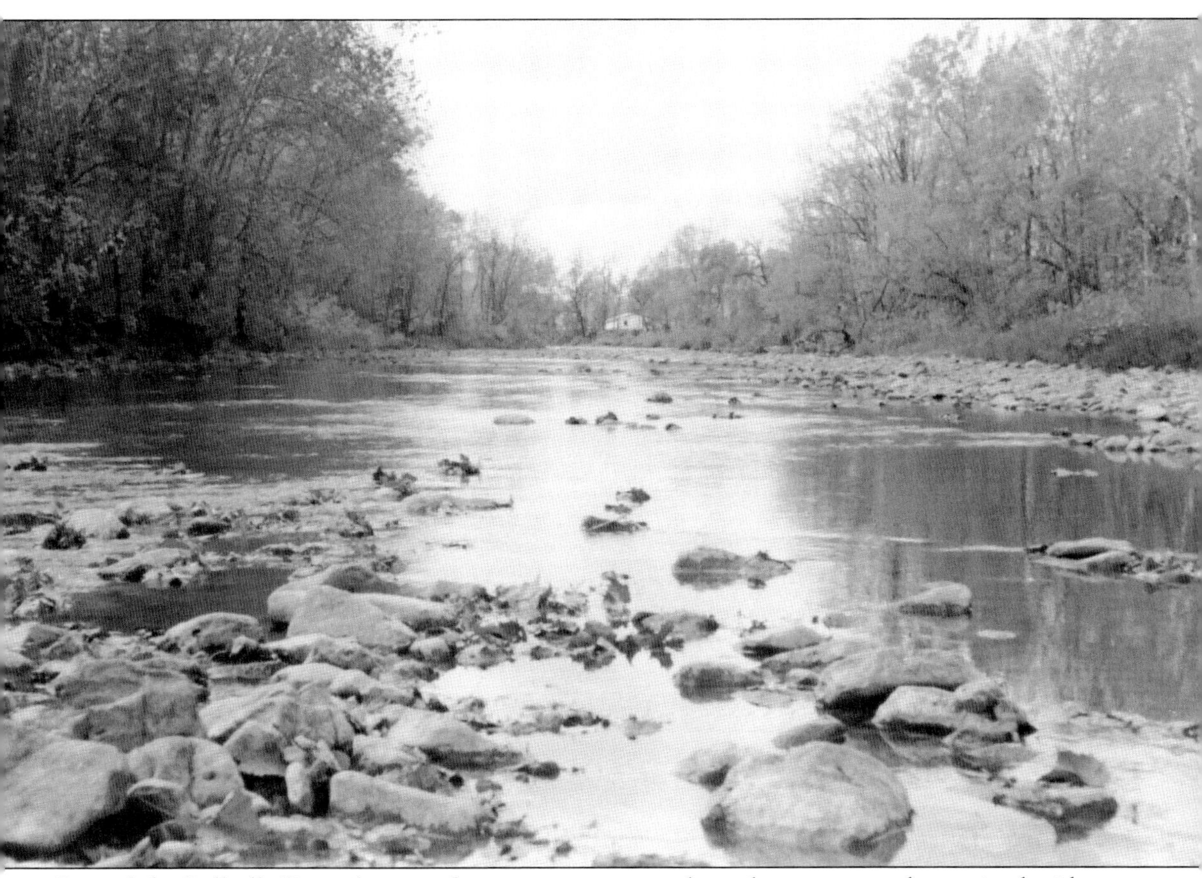

Beyond the Ballville Dam, the ever-changing river passes through a narrow rocky section beside the River Cliff Golf Course (formerly Thornwood) down one of its most beautiful stretches.

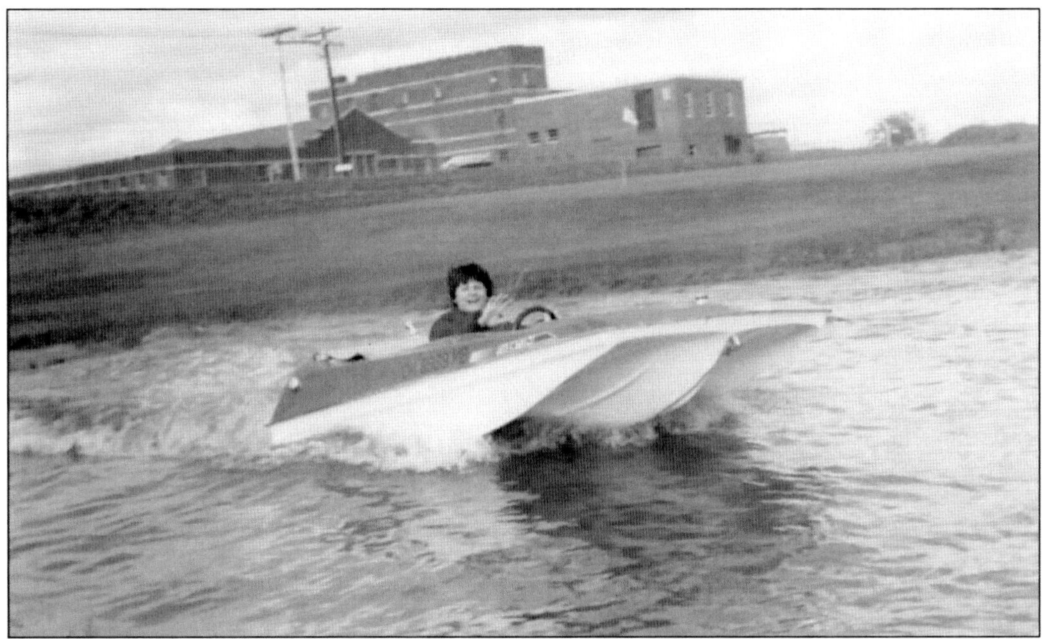

Along the shore south of the water treatment plant and Rodger Young Park, the river becomes wider and can be used even for motorboating. The water plant is seen here in the background of this picture. (Courtesy of Krista Michaels.)

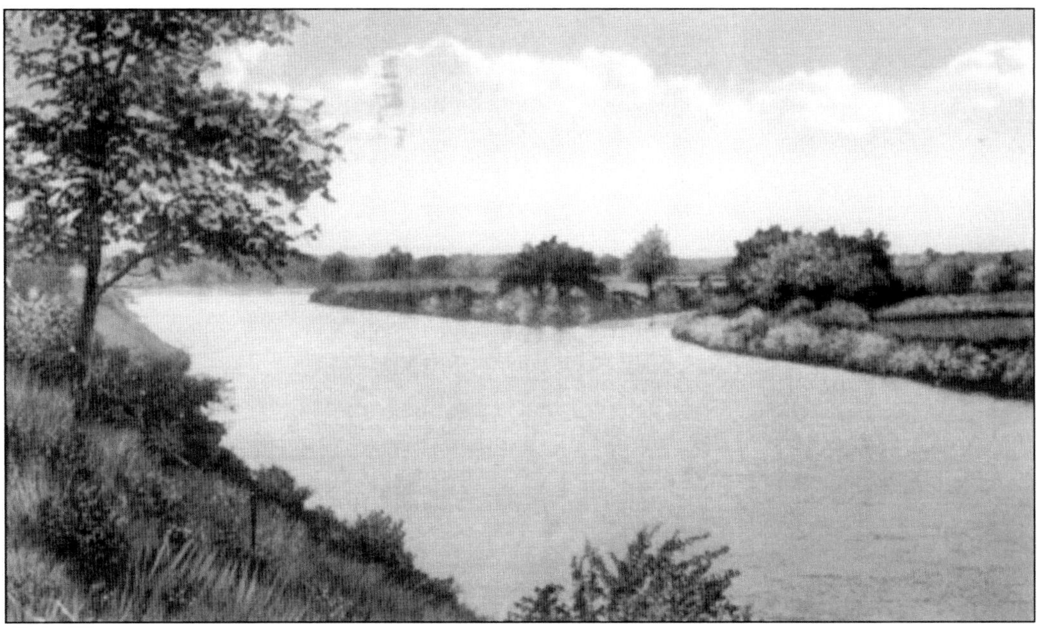

The river, which flows east along the southern boundaries of Fremont, suddenly turns north near Sharps Island to travel through the city. In this early postcard, Sharps Island is distinctly separated from the shore, but many years of filling and changes in the river have connected the little island to the shoreline.

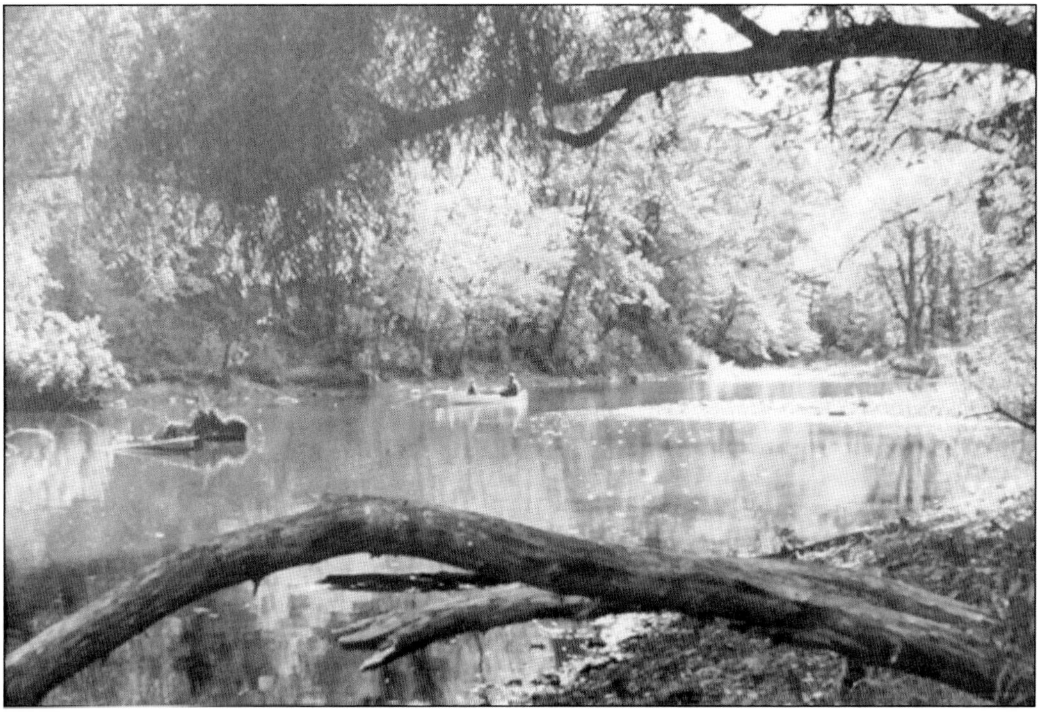

Two people in a canoe appear through the trees in this later view from now-overgrown Sharps Island. (Courtesy of Krista Michaels.)

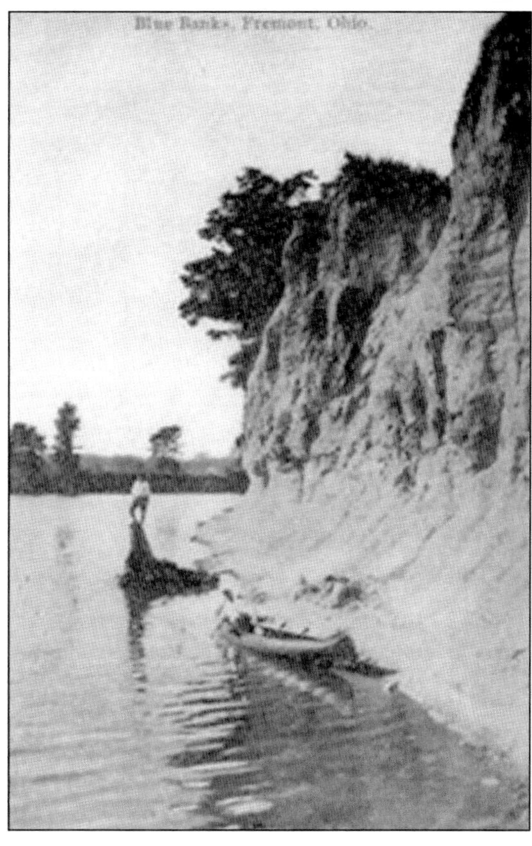

As the river begins to flow north toward Fremont, it passes the landmark Blue Banks. Compared to a man balancing on the little pinnacle in the river, the height of the cliffs is apparent in this early postcard view. Indian burial sites have been found at the top of the cliffs, an indication of the prominent role the Blue Banks played in the lives of the early tribes that lived along the Sandusky River.

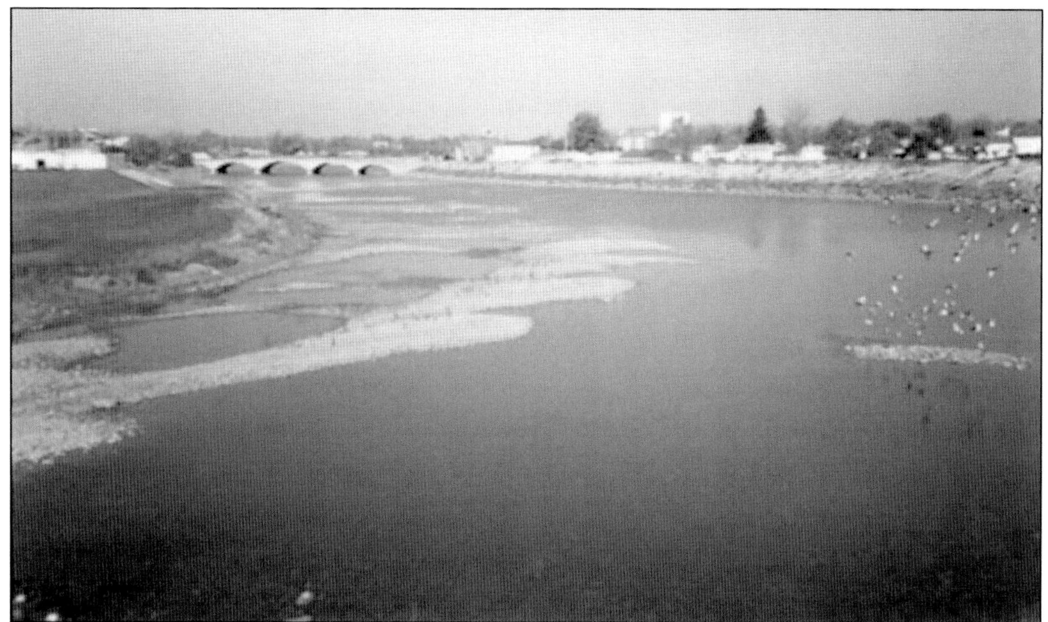

As the river passes through Fremont, a flock of birds ascends from an outcropping in the shallow water between the Miles Newton Bridge and the State Street Bridge seen in the distance. Here, the river once made a wide loop to the right, creating a peninsula that was called the "Oxbow." When the floodwall was constructed, the river was channeled straight north, as seen in this photograph, through the base of the Oxbow.

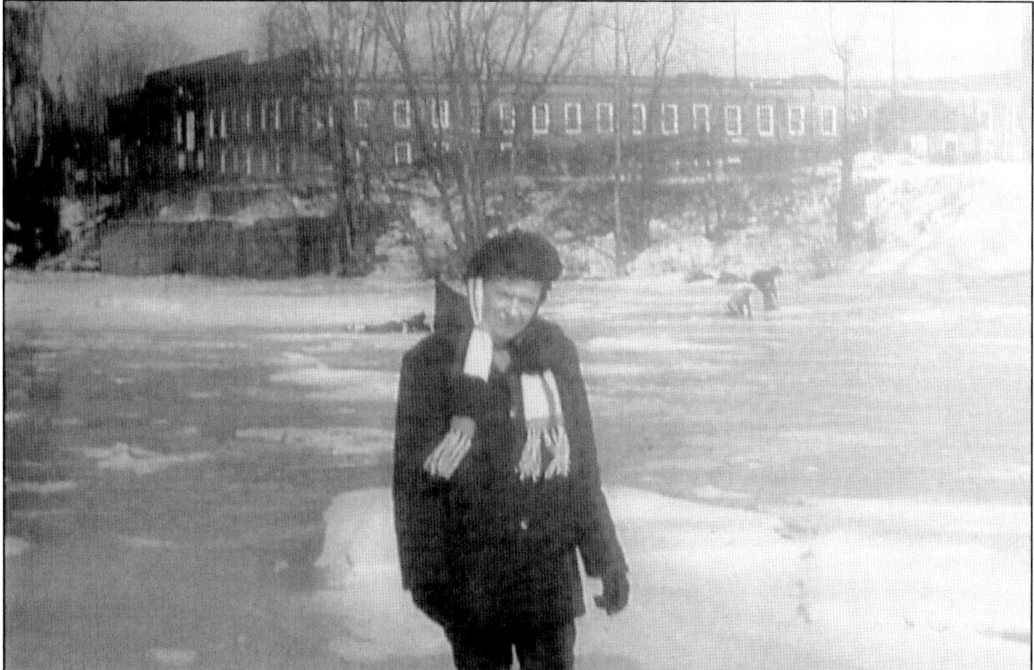

The eastward loop of the Oxbow created calm water that more easily froze over for ice-skating. Judy Michaels is pictured skating on the river about 1948. The large Lake Shore Electric carbarns are behind her on the shore of the river, where a modern Kroger store is located today.

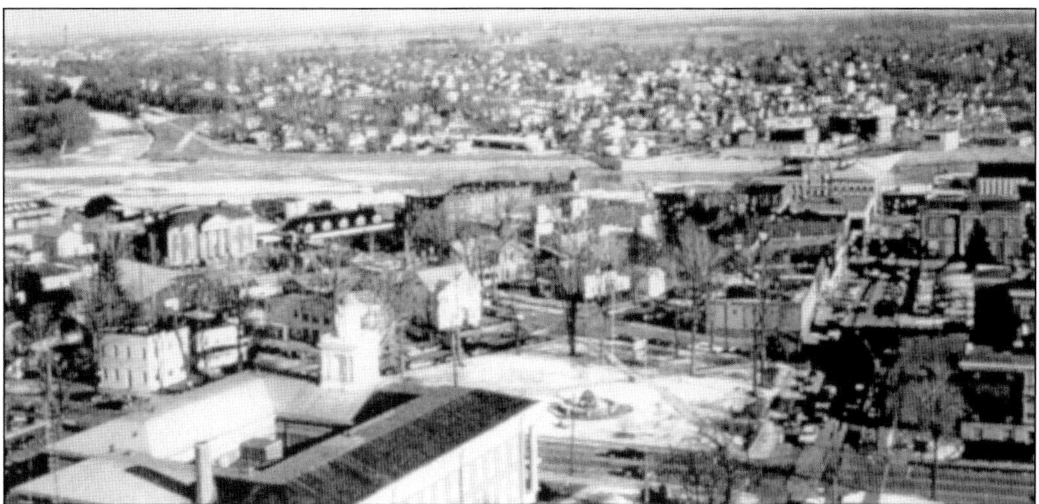

The Sandusky River stretches across the center of this 1977 aerial view, which looks northeast from the steeple of St. Joseph's Catholic Church, the highest point in Fremont. The Sandusky County Courthouse is in the left foreground, facing Flag Park. Fort Stephenson stood on the south side of Croghan Street at the right of the photograph. (Courtesy of Fred Durnwald.)

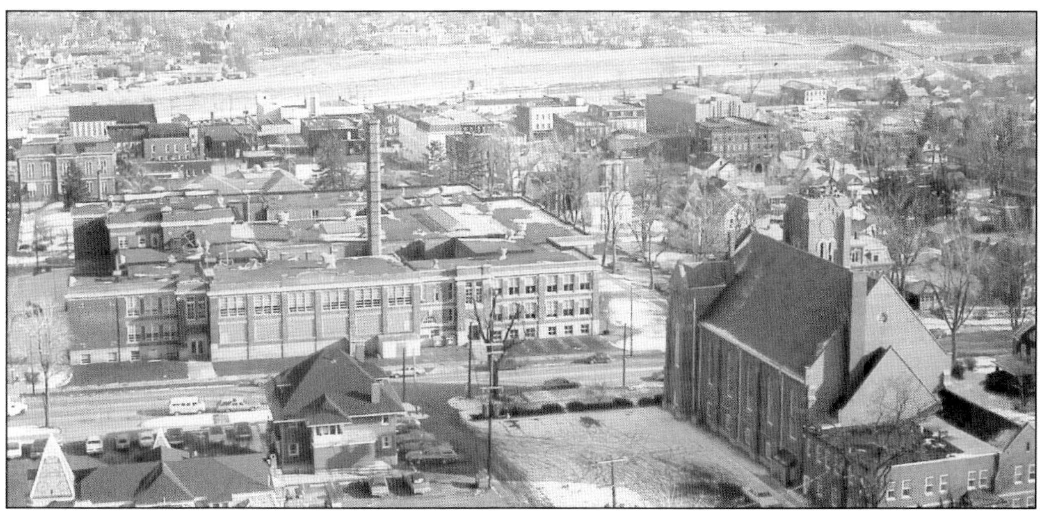

Taken at the same time as the previous photograph, this southeast view from the steeple of St. Joseph's shows the river, with its floodwall only a few years old, in the distance. The Miles Newton Bridge, built in 1970, appears at upper right, and First Presbyterian Church is at lower right, its steeple lost in the tornado that came through Fremont on June 30, 1977. (Courtesy of Fred Durnwald.)

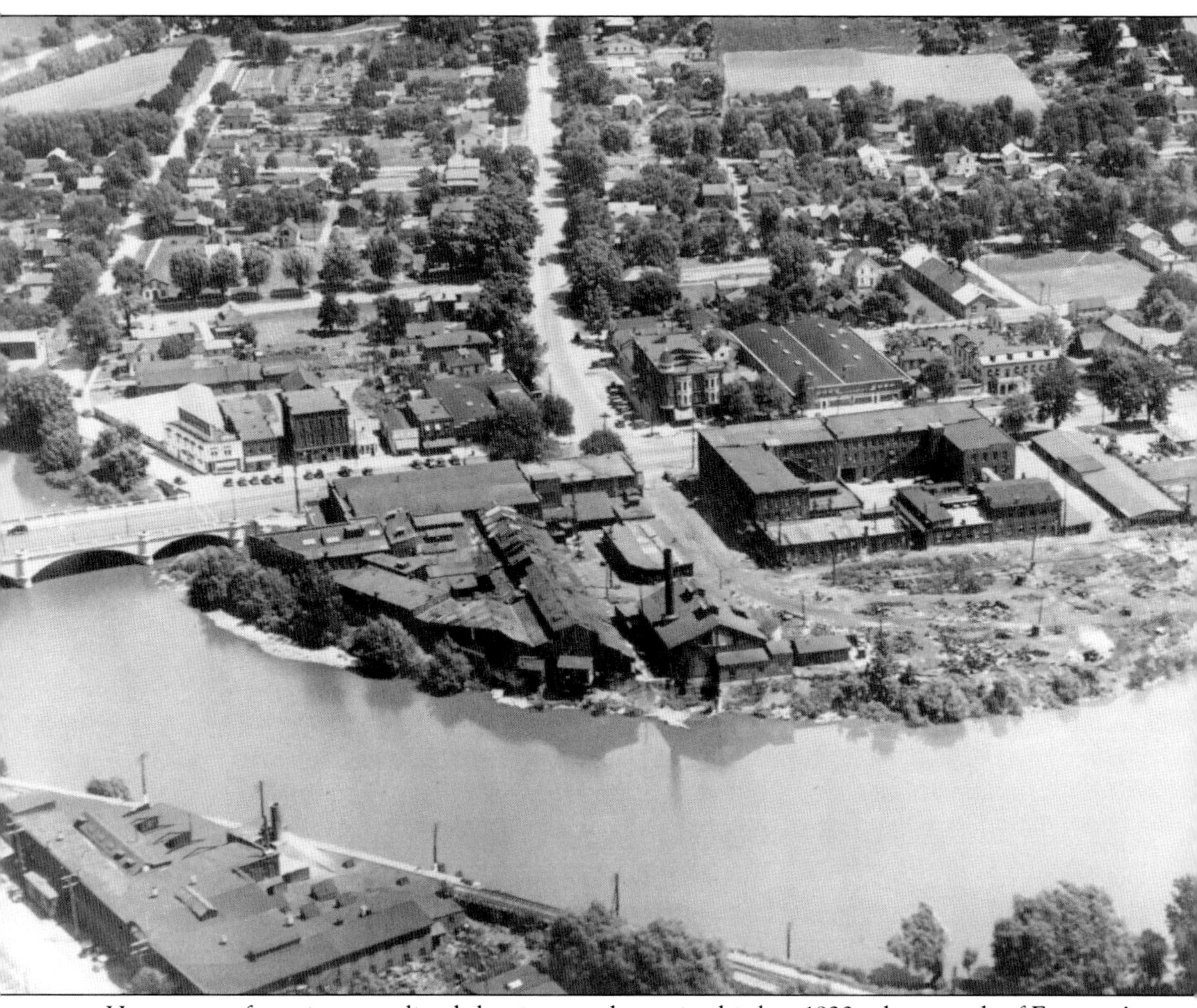

Heavy manufacturing once lined the river, as shown in this late-1920s photograph of Fremont's east side with a view that looks north up Sandusky Avenue in the center. David June Engine Works appears at lower left next to the railroad tracks that have run along the west side of the river since 1882.

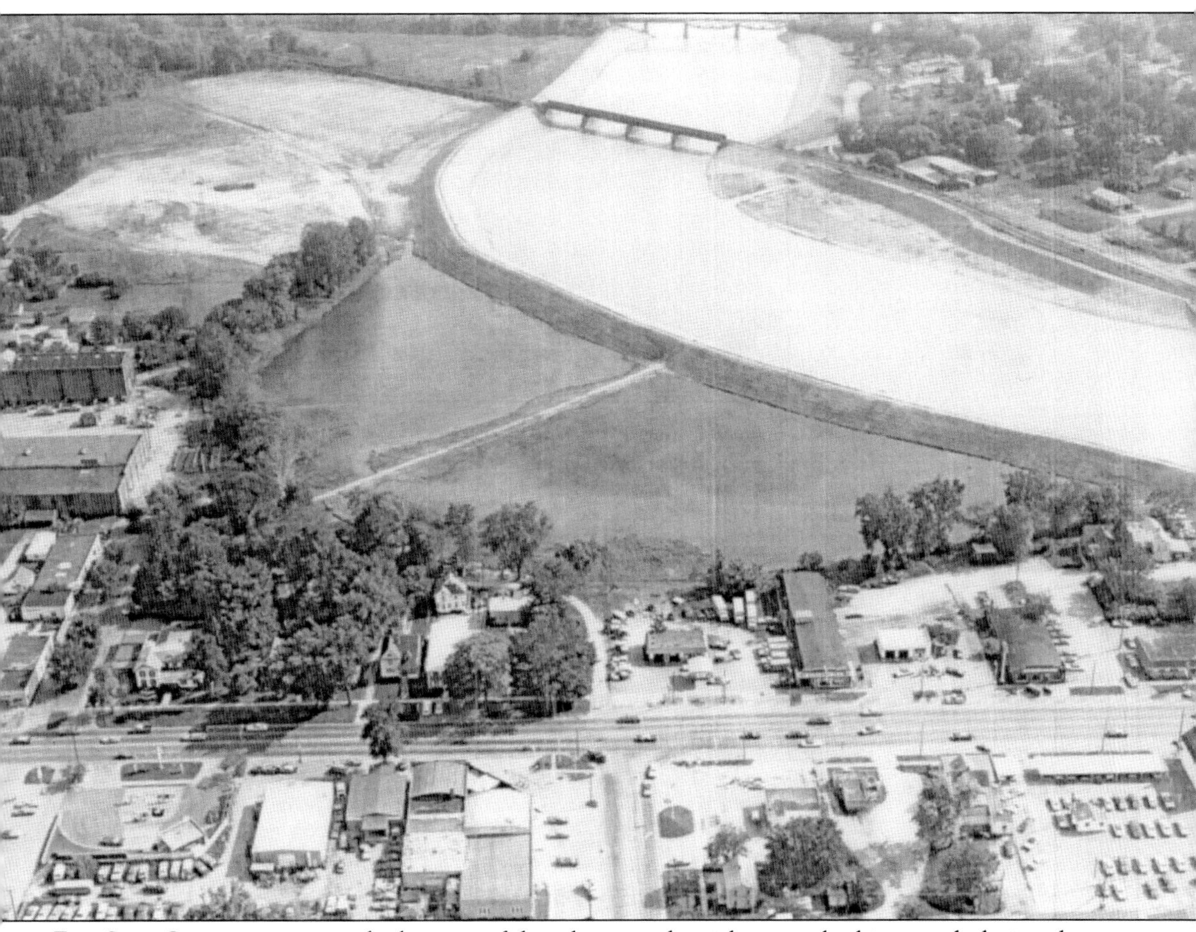

East State Street runs across the bottom of this photograph, with a view looking south during the construction of the floodwall about 1970. The outlines of the Oxbow peninsula can still clearly be seen in the center, even as the river flows straight down its new course between the boundaries of the floodwall. The old carbarns and power plant that once backed the river still stand at far left on Fifth Street. The Newton Bridge was built soon after this picture was taken, near where the railroad bridge connects with the west bank of the river.

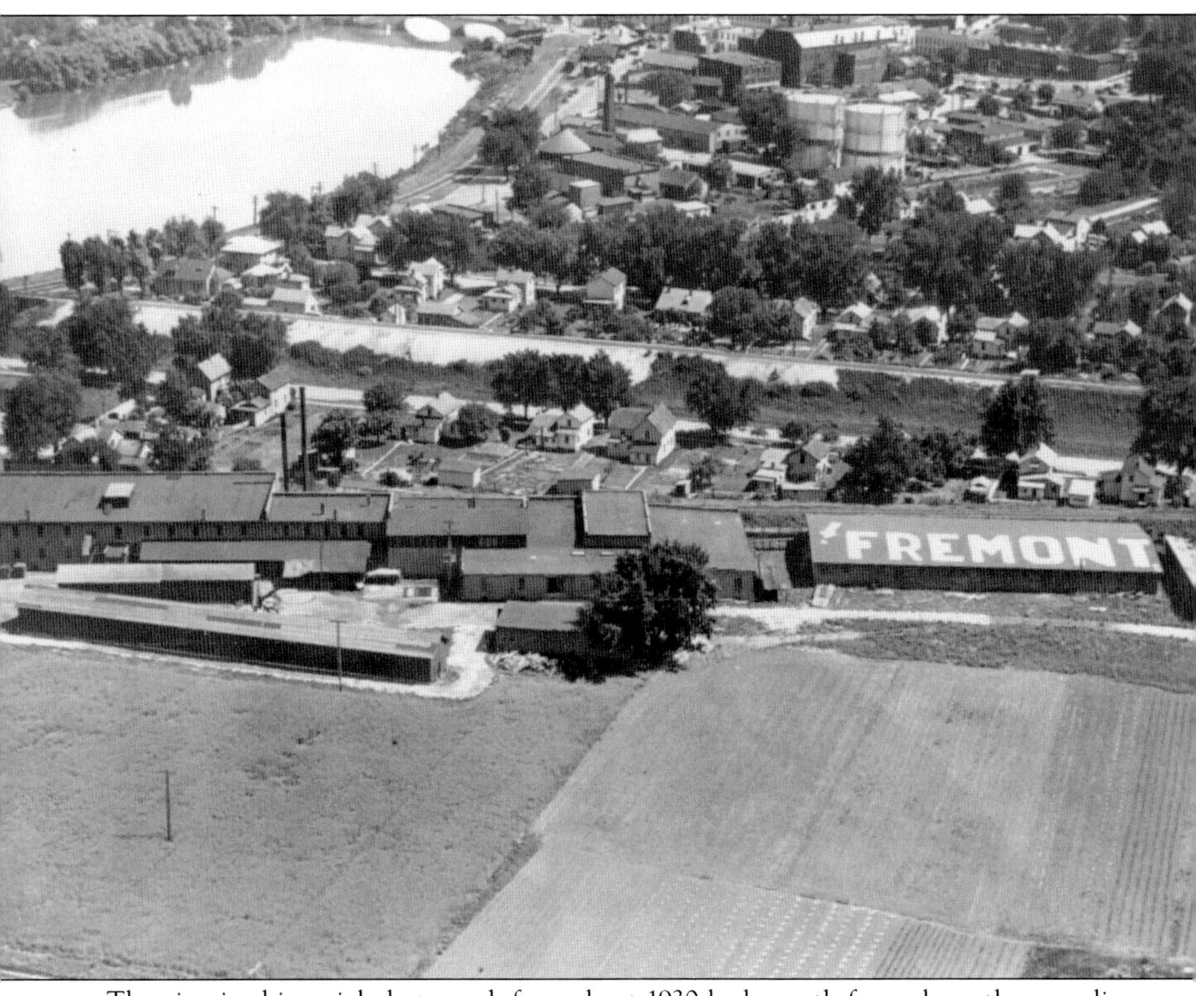

The view in this aerial photograph from about 1930 looks south from above the sprawling Fremont Kraut Company in the foreground. The State Street Bridge appears at upper left. Since the early days of Fremont, the river has fostered the economic growth of this largely industrial section of the city.

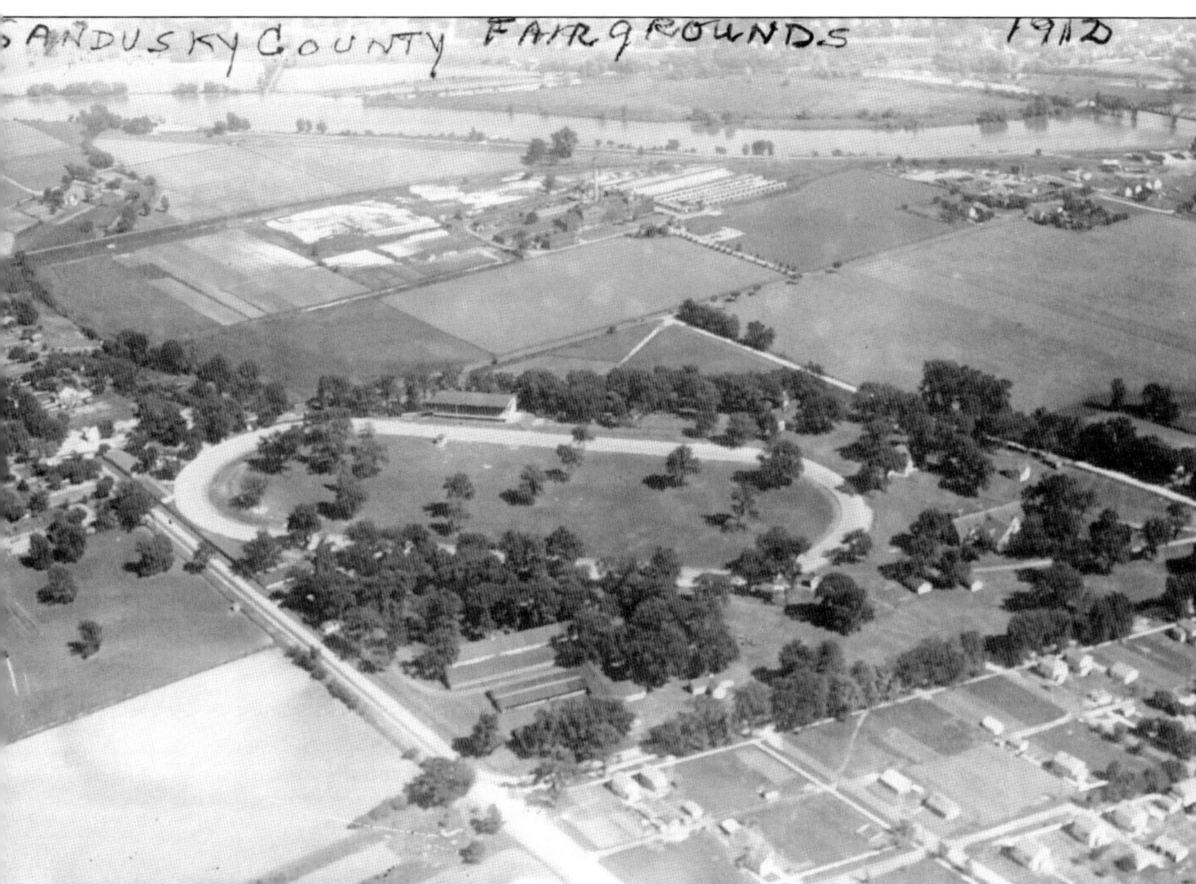

The large oval racetrack of the Sandusky County Fairgrounds dominates the center of this 1930s photograph, with a view looking southeast toward the river. Between the river and fairgrounds is the recently closed sugar beet factory, which spread its aroma around the city for 100 years, beginning about 1900. North Street is seen at lower left, and the railroad trestle bridge to Brady's Island appears at upper right.

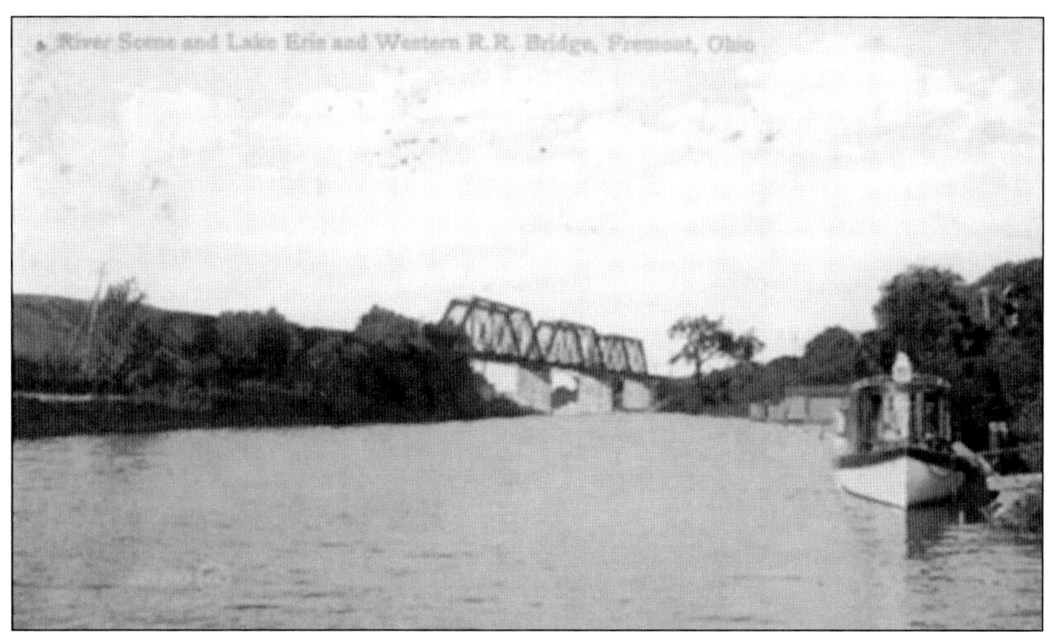

A side channel of the river runs east of Brady's Island to pass under a section of the old Lake Erie & Western Railroad trestle seen in the distance. The boat docked at right would now be tied to the present-day docks located in front of the well-known Tackle Box restaurant.

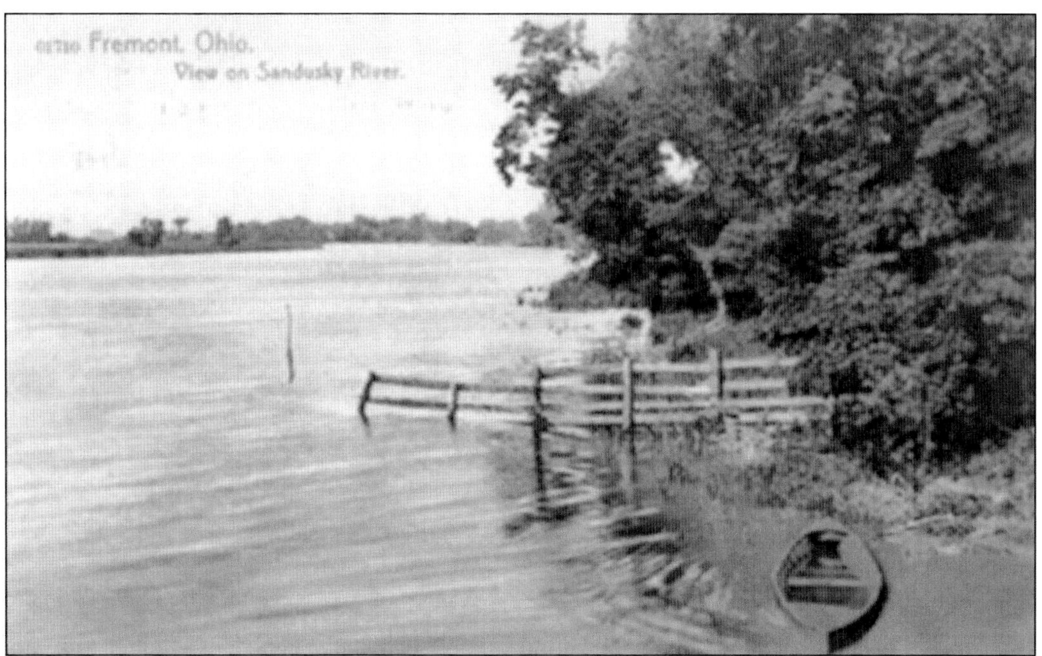

The river north of Fremont is wide, with a negligible fall toward Lake Erie, letting boaters peacefully glide downstream. In this postcard view, a rowboat waits by the shore to make a pleasant trip.

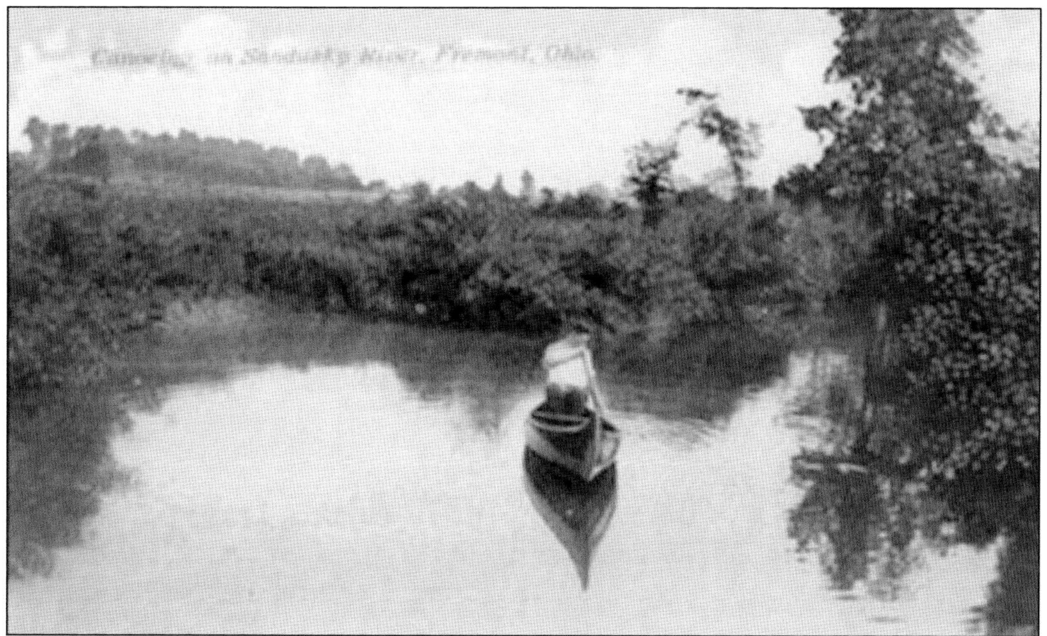

Typical of many early-1900s postcards, this image shows a journey down the river along wooded shorelines being enjoyed in a solitary canoe.

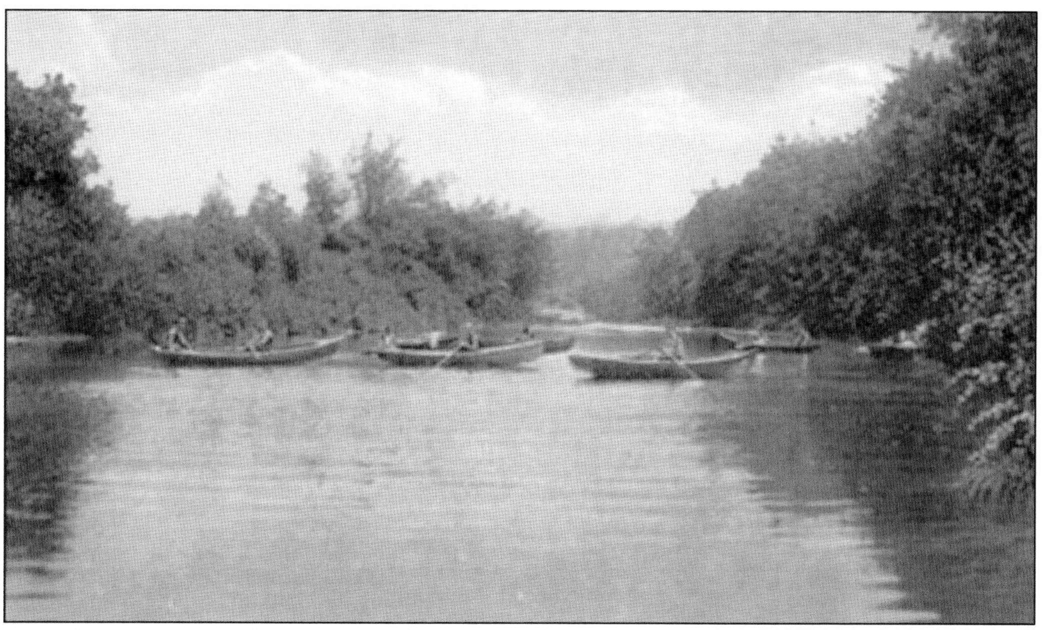

Several canoes are in formation on the river in this postcard dated 1917. It is not known if the boaters wanted to stay together or just had trouble steering their canoes.

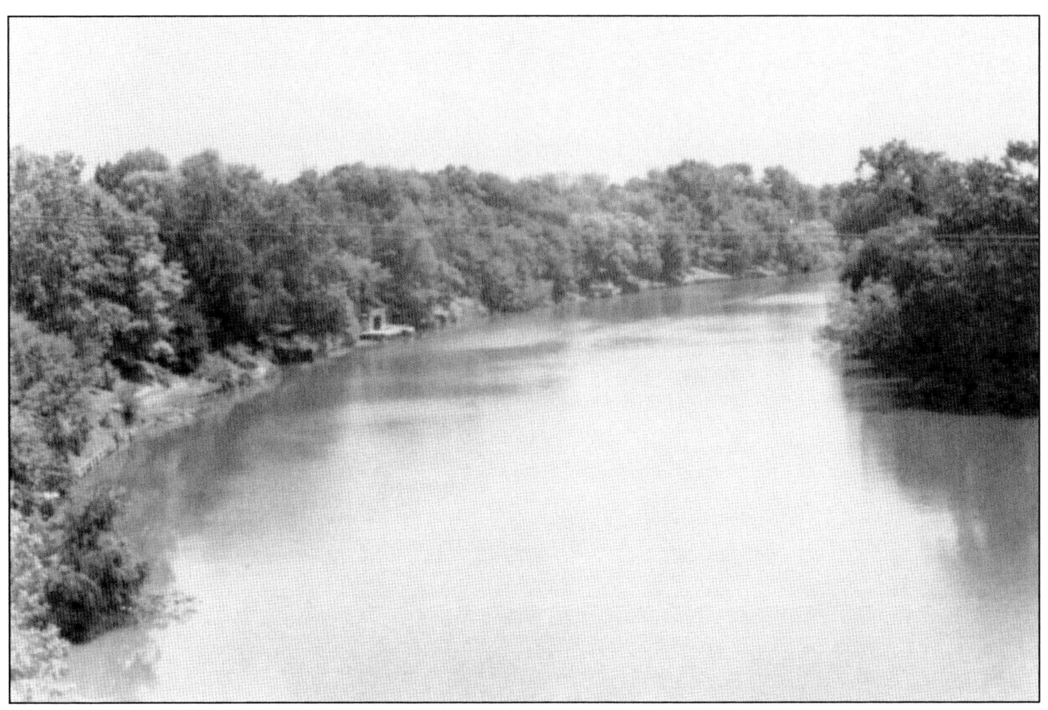

This section of the river passes the Whitaker Reserve along the west bank at left. Not far from here, the British brought their gunboats upriver for the Battle of Fort Stephenson. (Courtesy of Ray Grob.)

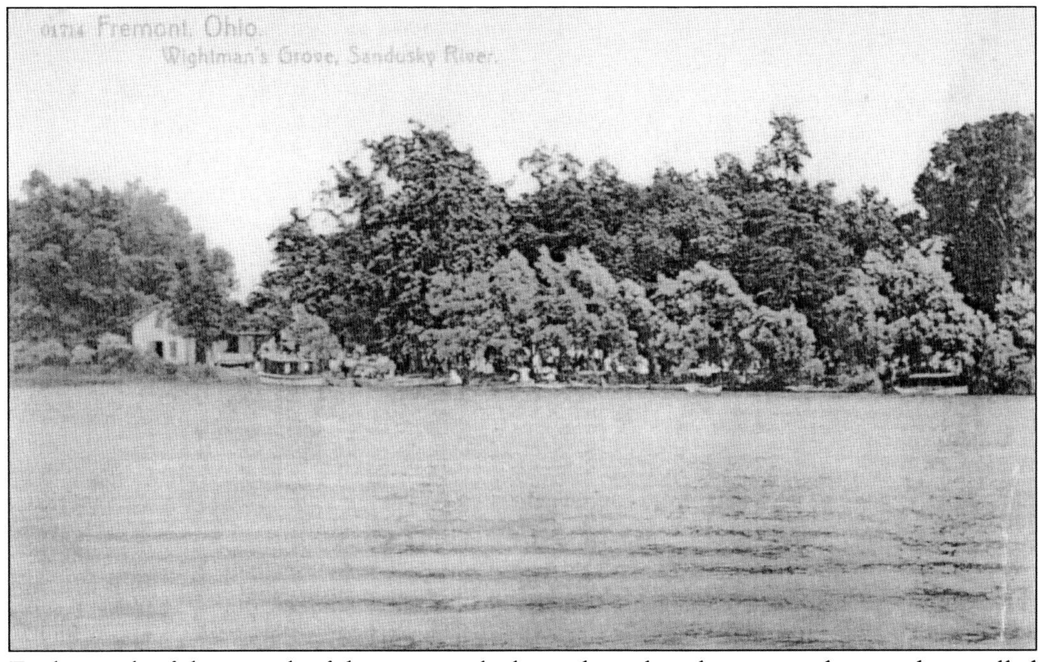

To the north of this stretch of the river is a little residential settlement on the east shore called Wightman's Grove, pictured in this early-20th-century postcard. (Courtesy of Ray Grob.)

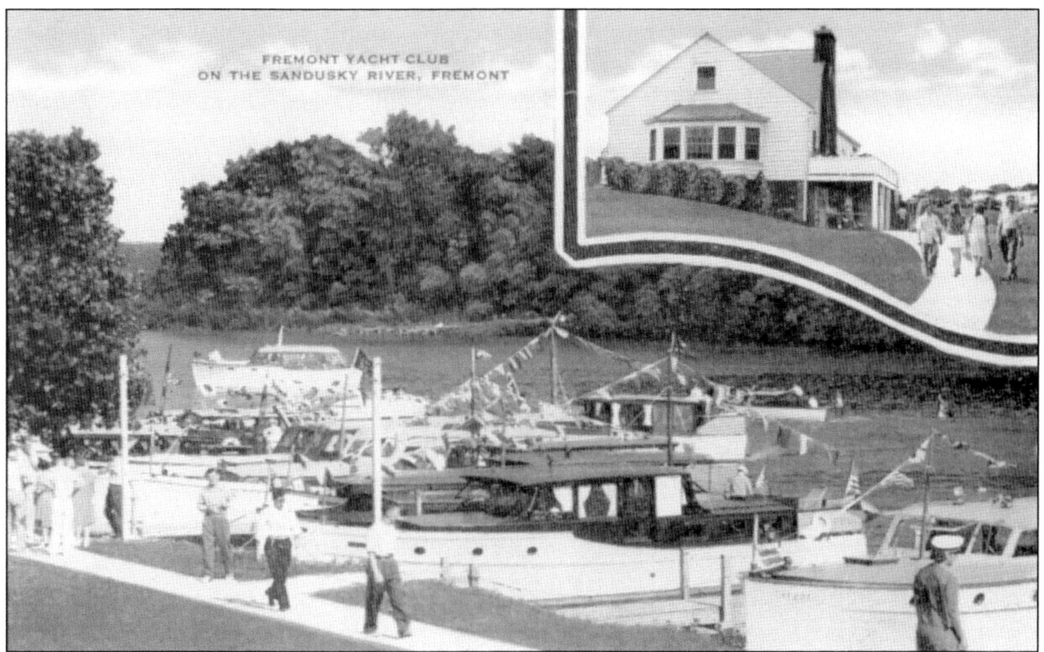

The Fremont Yacht Club is also located in this area. Many fine boats are docked in this mid-century postcard view with an inset of the clubhouse at upper right.

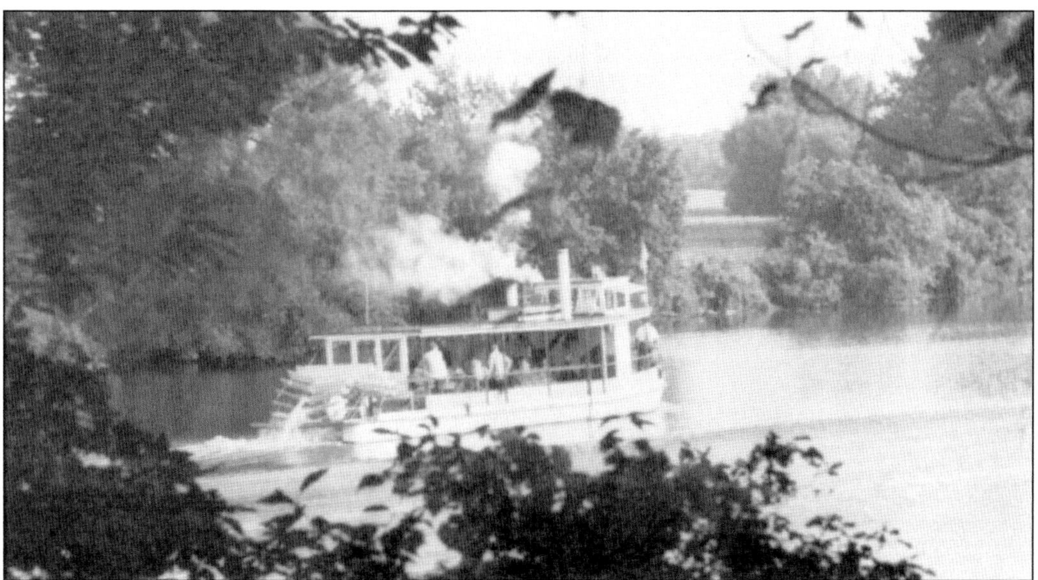

At one time, the SS *Fascination*, which was an authentic steam-powered paddle wheeler, carried passengers up and down the river between Fremont and Sandusky Bay, reminiscent of earlier days of river travel in America. (Courtesy of Ray Grob.)

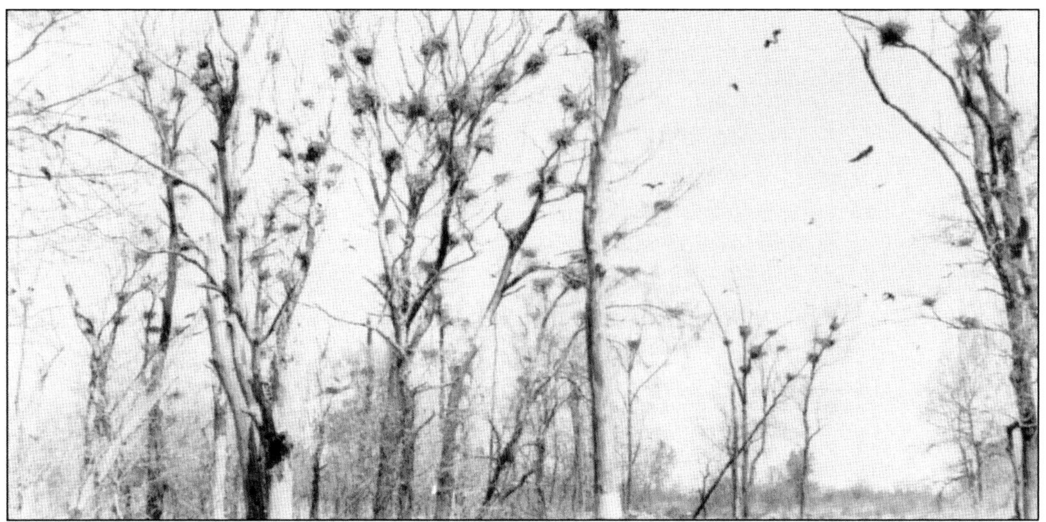

This photograph shows many nests in the largest rookery of the great blue heron in Ohio, located across from the mouth of the Sandusky River on private land owned by the Winous Point Shooting Club at Muddy Creek Bay. (Courtesy of Ray Grob.)

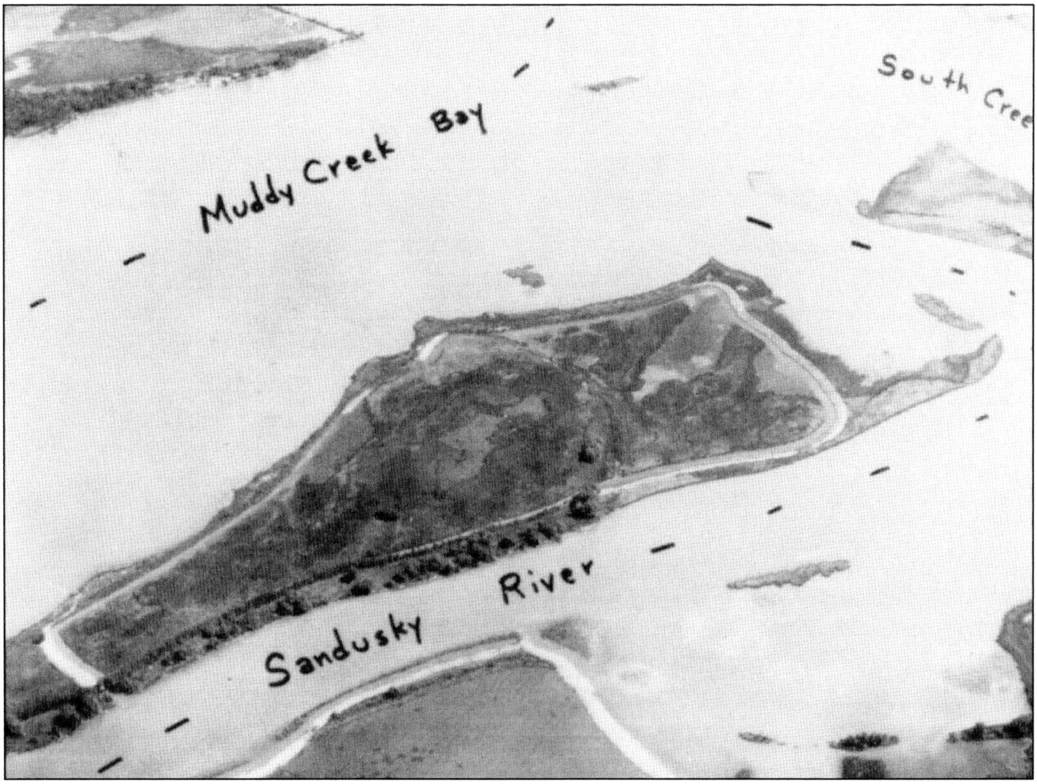

This aerial photograph depicts the place where the river empties into Muddy Creek Bay. Muddy Creek, which flows northeast through western Sandusky County, past Creek Bend Farm near Lindsey, and then out to the bay, got its name from the substantial amount of silt it carries along the way. Its waters merge and flow through Sandusky Bay to Lake Erie, completing the Sandusky River's scenic journey through northwest Ohio.

Three

Bridges, Dams, and Other Sites on the River

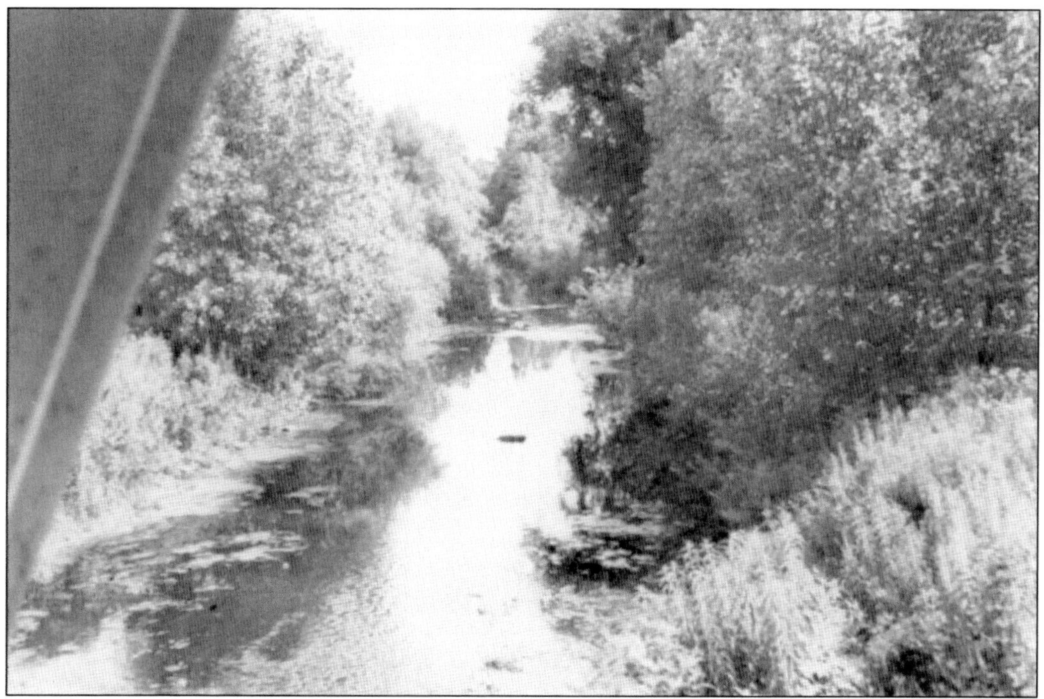

The still-narrow Sandusky River, pictured only two miles from its source, flows under its first bridge at Leesville Road just south of US Route 30. (Courtesy of Ray Grob.)

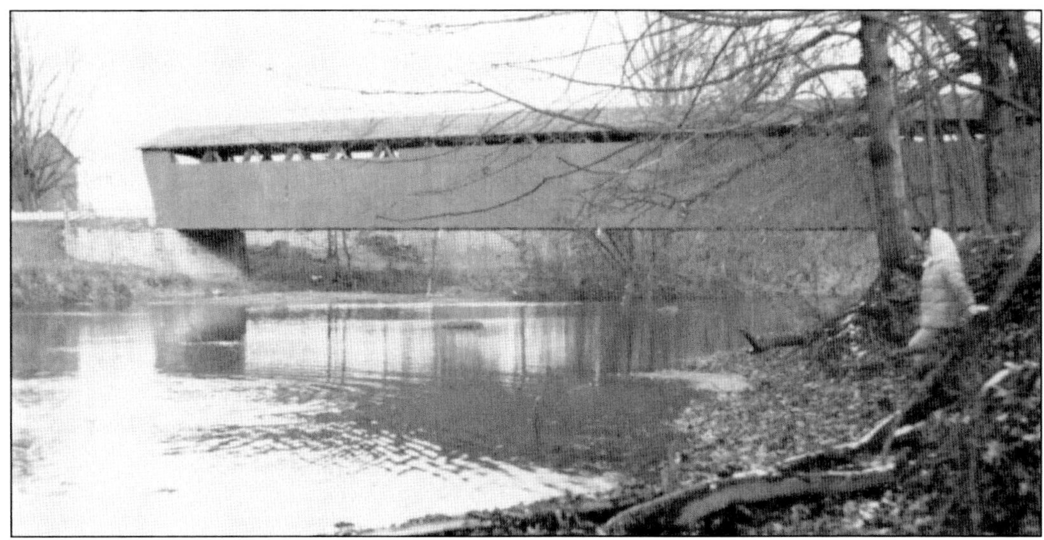

Nearly 180 feet with no center pier, Parker Covered Bridge is the second-longest covered bridge in Ohio. It was built in 1873 of oak timbers from nearby trees and is pictured stretched across the river, north of Upper Sandusky and a few miles downstream from the Indian Mill historic site. (Courtesy of Ray Grob.)

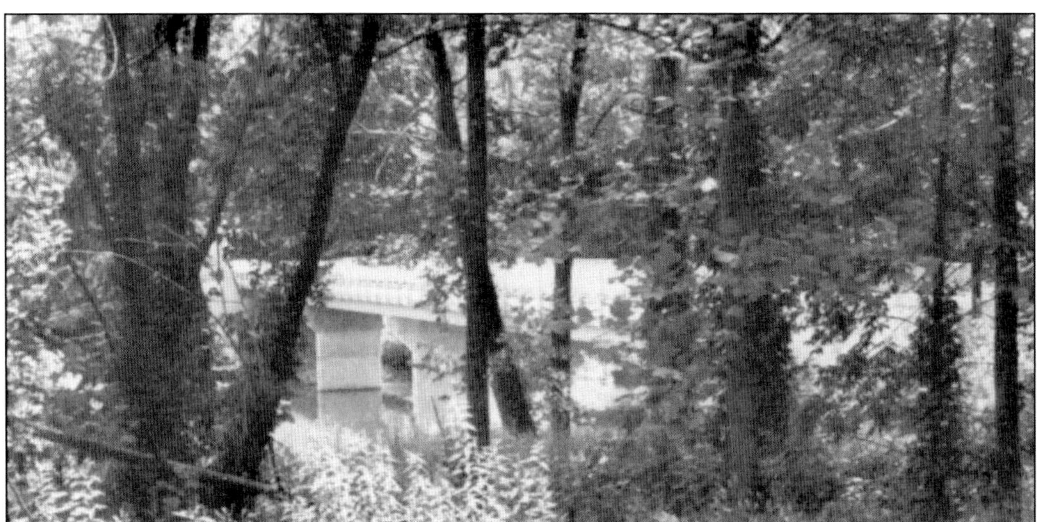

After passing below Route 103 in northern Wyandot County, the river reaches the more substantial Heck's Bridge, appearing between trees in a heavily forested stretch of the river. Over 250 acres in this area were the first to be purchased by the state as part of the Ohio Scenic Rivers Program. (Courtesy of Ray Grob.)

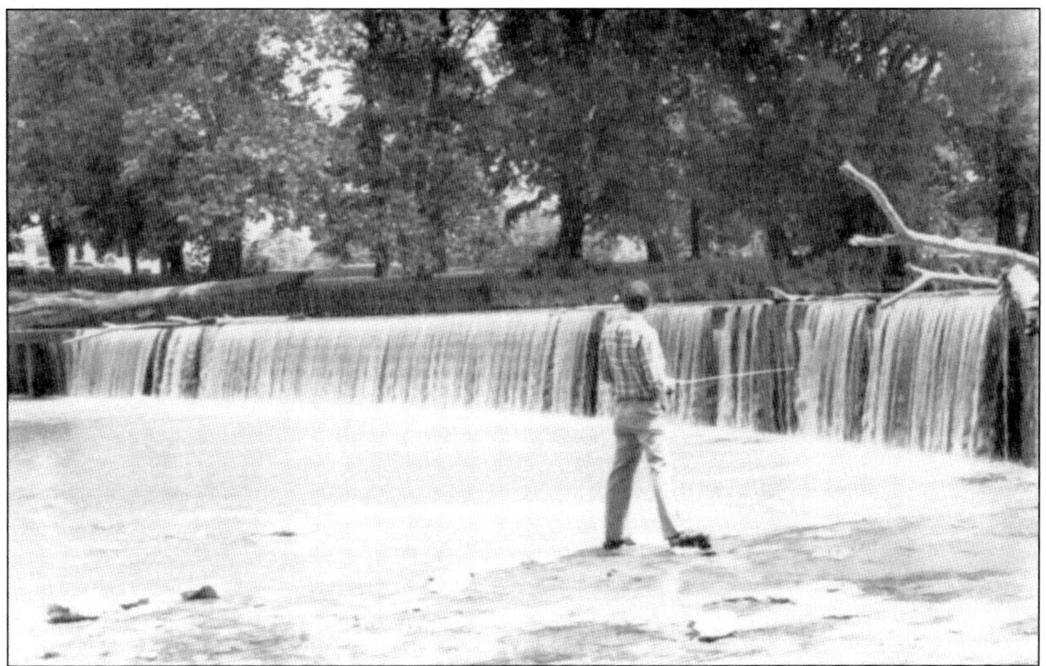

Continuing north, the river arrives at this spillway near St. John's Bridge, a longtime popular fishing site for smallmouth bass, channel catfish, and perhaps a muskellunge stocked by the Ohio Division of Wildlife. North of Seneca CR 90, the Sandusky travels through about a six-mile remote area that looks much the same today as Native American communities would have seen it centuries ago. (Courtesy of Ray Grob.)

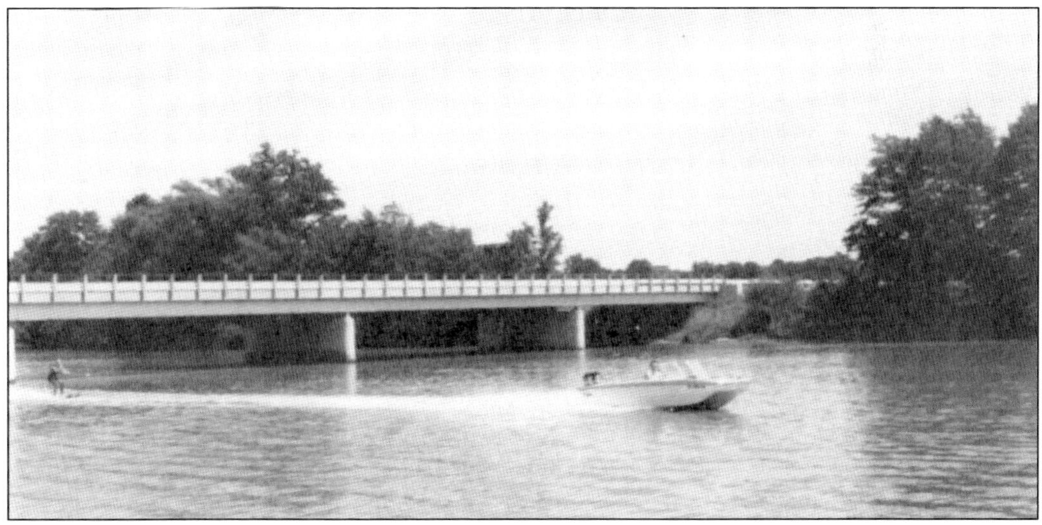

Just south of Tiffin, busy Route 224 crosses a wide section of the river on this substantial modern bridge. This photograph from about 1970 shows a popular powerboating and waterskiing area. (Courtesy of Ray Grob.)

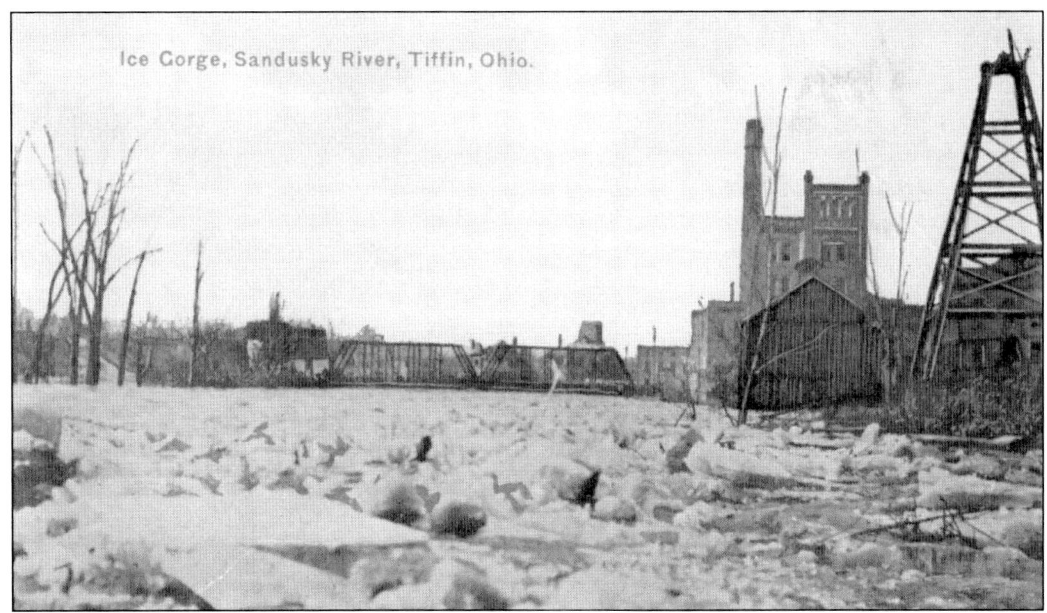

The Market Street Bridge appears in the distance as the river approaches the business district of downtown Tiffin in this early-1900s postcard photograph. Ice floes and water have risen to roadbed level, but the bridge would stand for at least another year until it was destroyed during the 1913 flood. The large building at right is the Hubach Brewery, which stood on Madison Street for approximately a century until it burned in 1966. (Courtesy of the Seneca County Museum.)

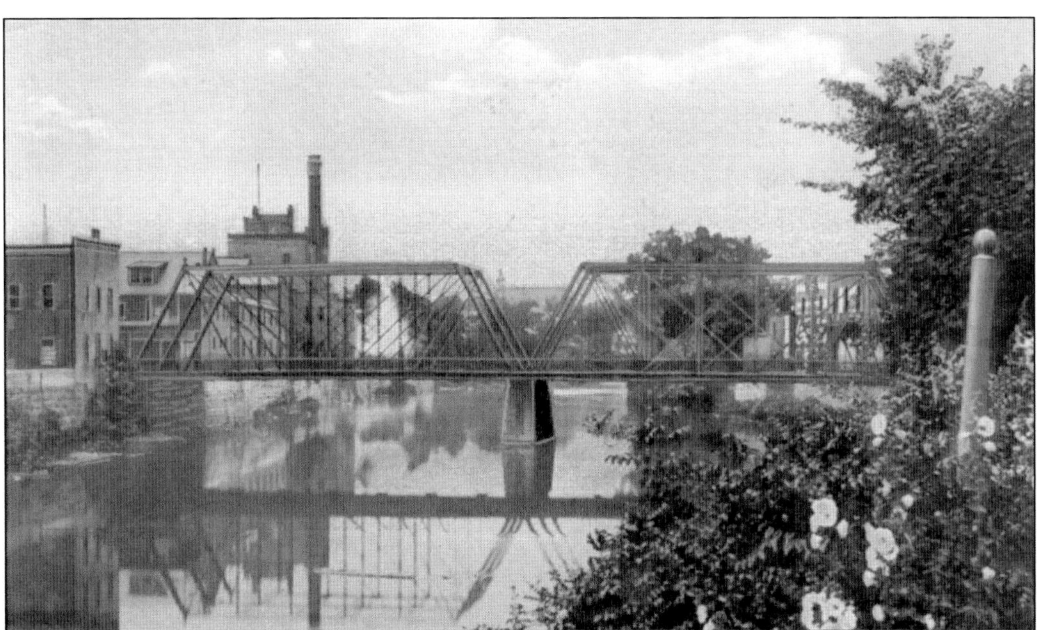

This postcard view of the pre-flood Market Street Bridge looks south from Perry Street. The Hubach Brewery can be seen again beyond the bridge. (Courtesy of the Seneca County Museum.)

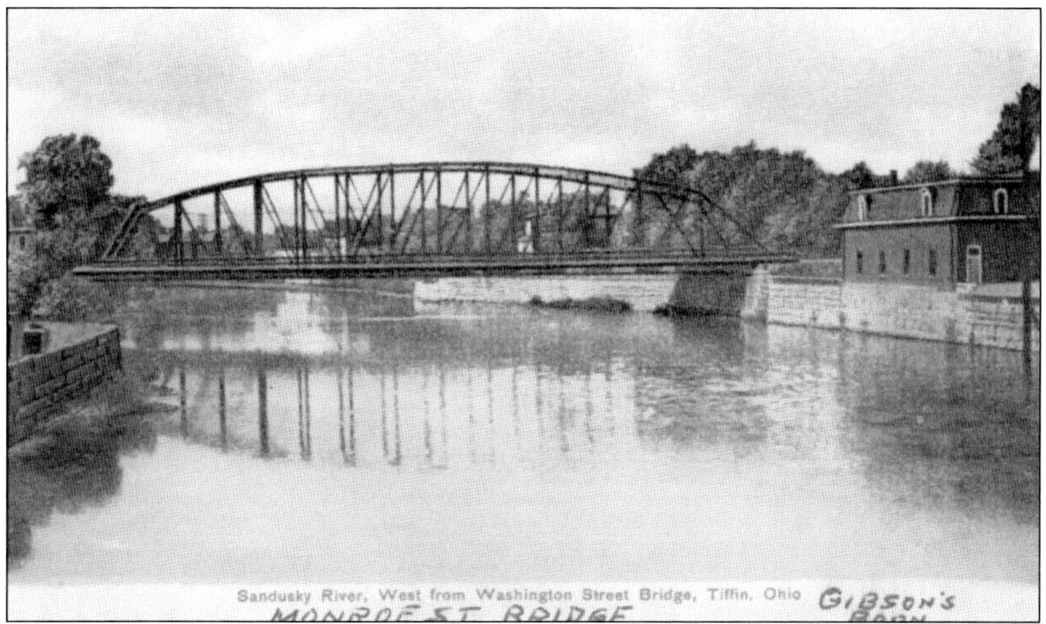

Another early postcard shows the Monroe Street Bridge with its camelback design. It was the only bridge that would not be rebuilt after the flood. As the river curves east above downtown Tiffin, the view in this photograph looks back upriver west from the Washington Street Bridge. The carriage barn of William Harvey Gibson, Civil War hero and famous orator, appears at right. (Courtesy of the Seneca County Museum.)

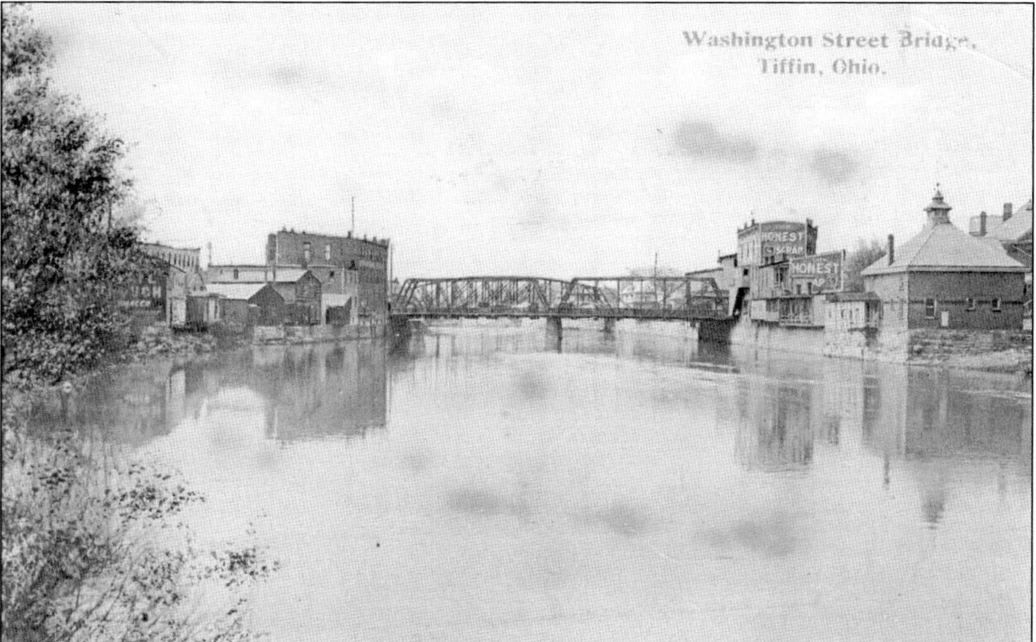

This view, looking east from the Monroe Street Bridge, shows the old Washington Street Bridge and the railroad trestle behind it. At right stand the Noble family barn and part of the house, which appear in several 1913 flood images. On the south bank at left are some of the downtown buildings on Washington Street. (Courtesy of the Seneca County Museum.)

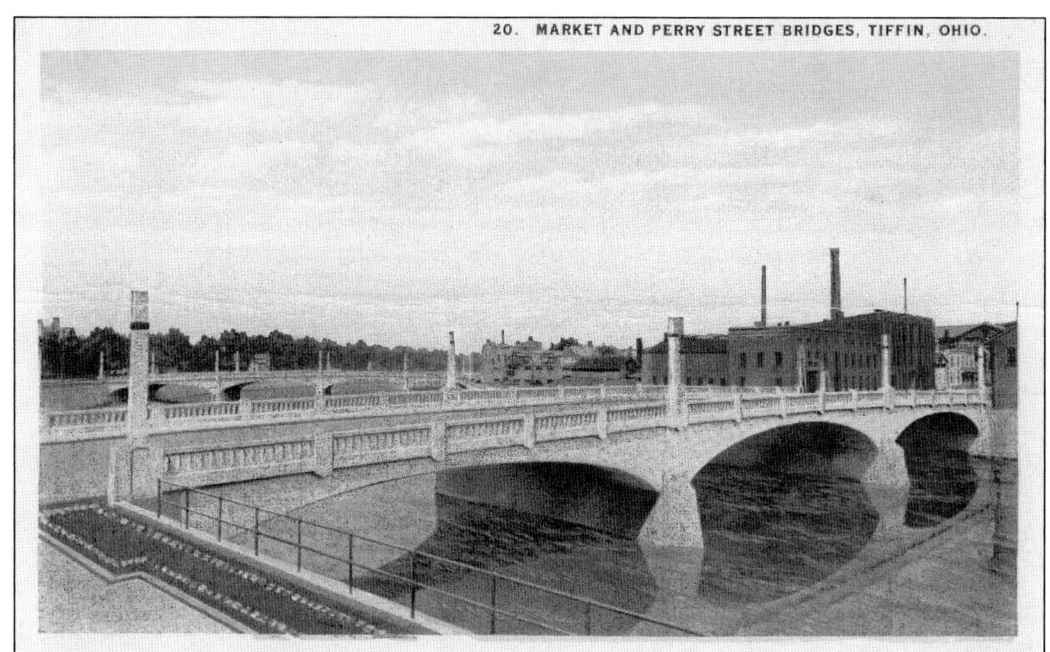

After the flood carried away all the downtown bridges, it was decided to rebuild with cast concrete. The result was the pleasing, clean lines of the Market Street Bridge, pictured with the Perry Street Bridge beyond it. They have both stood the test of time and still are heavily traveled. (Courtesy of the Seneca County Museum.)

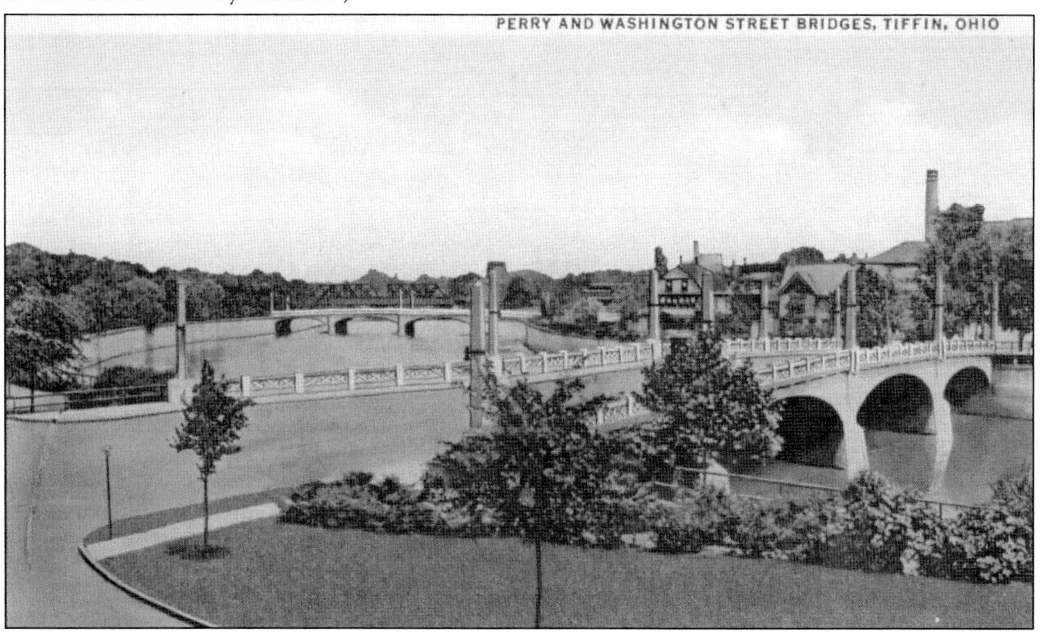

The post-flood Washington Street Bridge appears downriver from the new Perry Street Bridge in the foreground of this postcard image. The trees at left on Water Street (now Frost Parkway) replaced the houses at the edge of the river that were either moved or swept away. In the distance is the old railroad bridge, the only river crossing not destroyed in the flood. (Courtesy of the Seneca County Museum.)

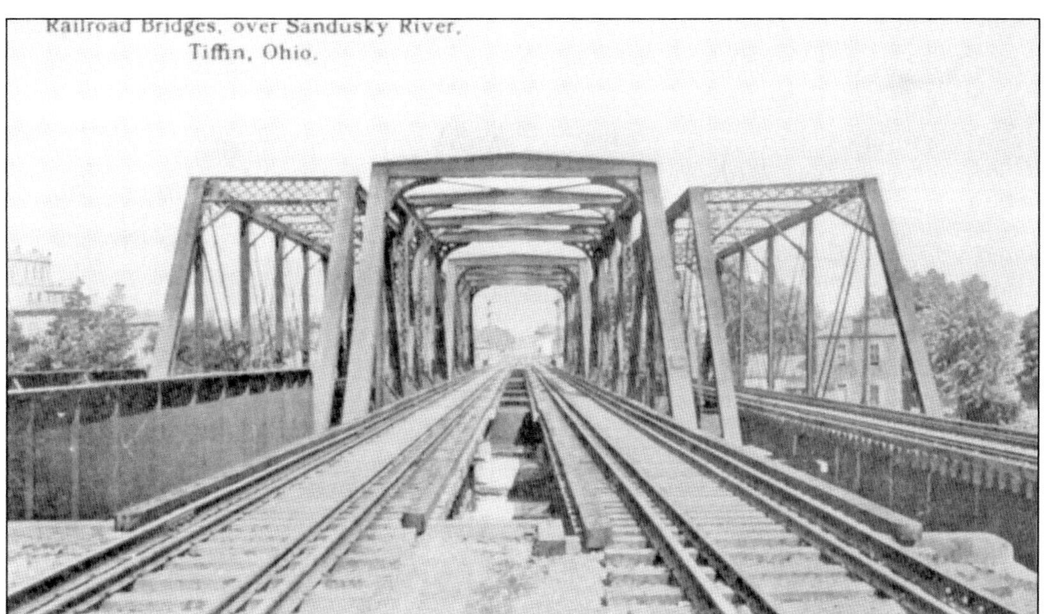

Four tracks run over the river on three parallel railroad bridges in this early-20th-century postcard photograph. Railcars were moved out on the bridges during the flood, which added to their massive weight and helped both bridges and cars survive the torrents of water. For a while after the flood, these bridges were the only means for crossing the river. (Courtesy of the Seneca County Museum.)

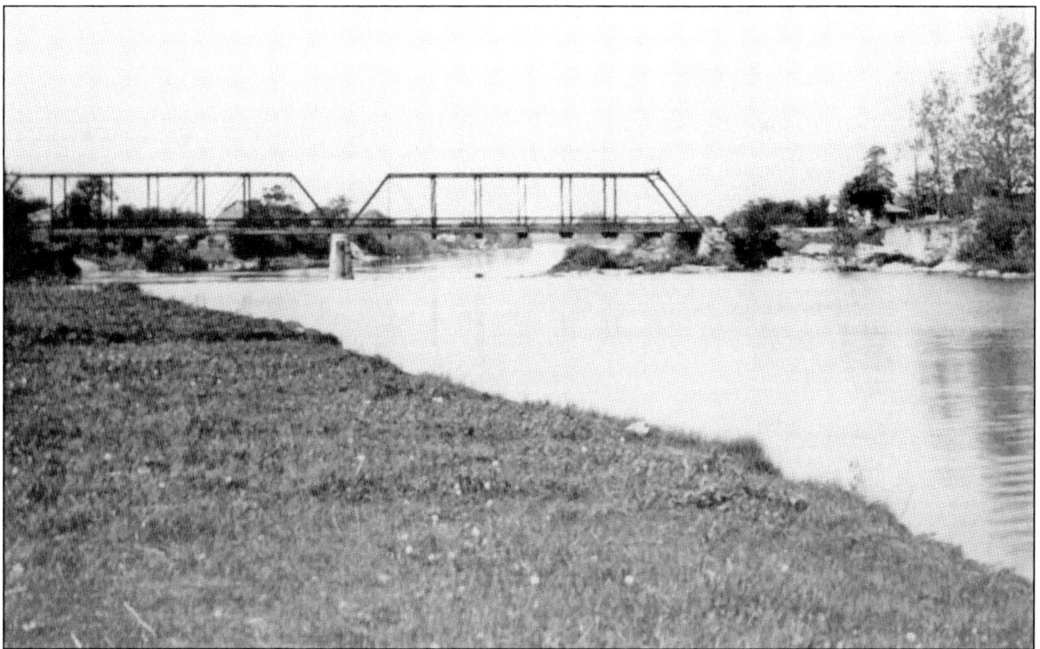

The Huss Street Bridge on the north side of Tiffin was no match for the flood. Riverside Park, pictured at the east end of the bridge off to the right, was a popular place to visit at this time in the early 1900s. (Courtesy of the Seneca County Museum.)

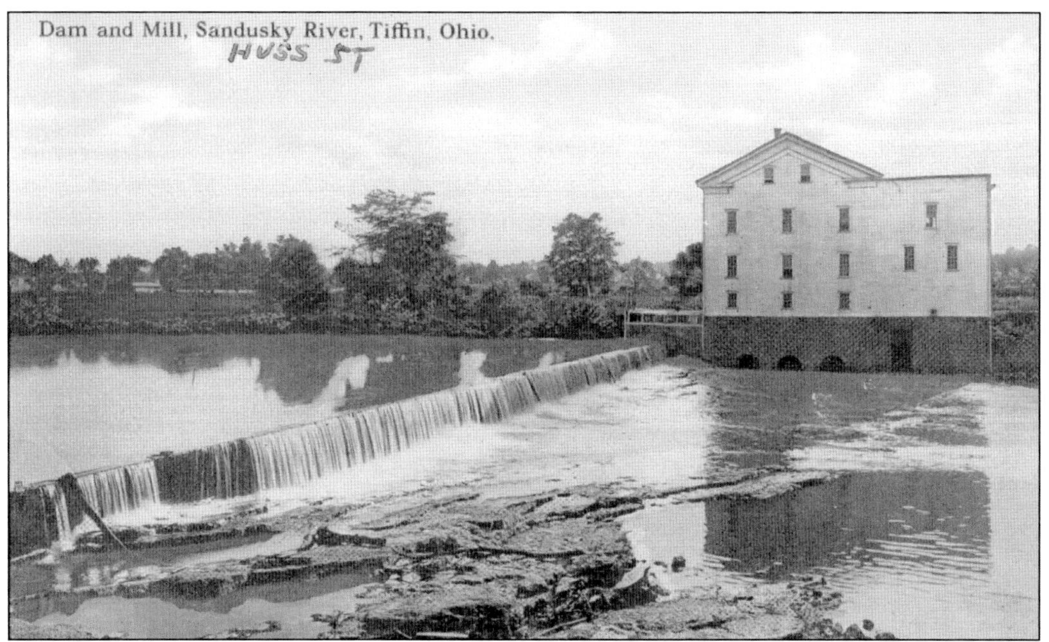

This dam near Huss Street powered the imposing Speck's gristmill pictured in this postcard. It was built in 1846 by Harry Speck, remained in operation well into the 20th century, and was razed in 1947. The mill was adorned with a triangular Greek Revival gable above its third story. The many dams along the Sandusky testify to its importance as a source of power for milling and later for electricity. (Courtesy of the Seneca County Museum.)

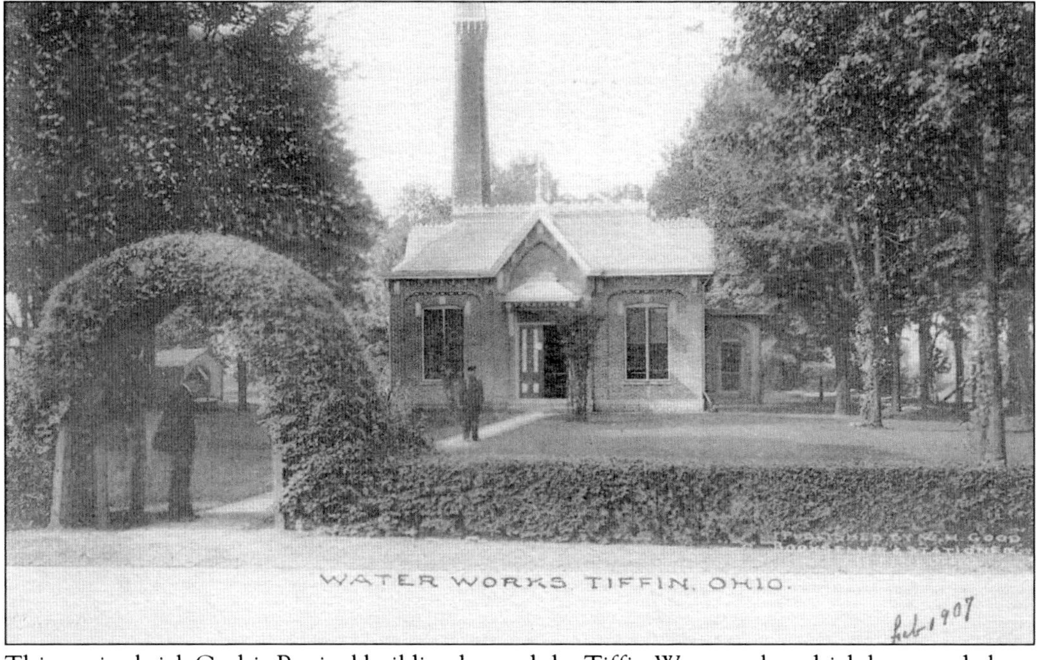

This quaint brick Gothic Revival building housed the Tiffin Waterworks, which has stood along the river since the late-19th century. A sculptured hedge was carefully shaped over the gateway arch in this photograph taken in February 1907. (Courtesy of the Seneca County Museum.)

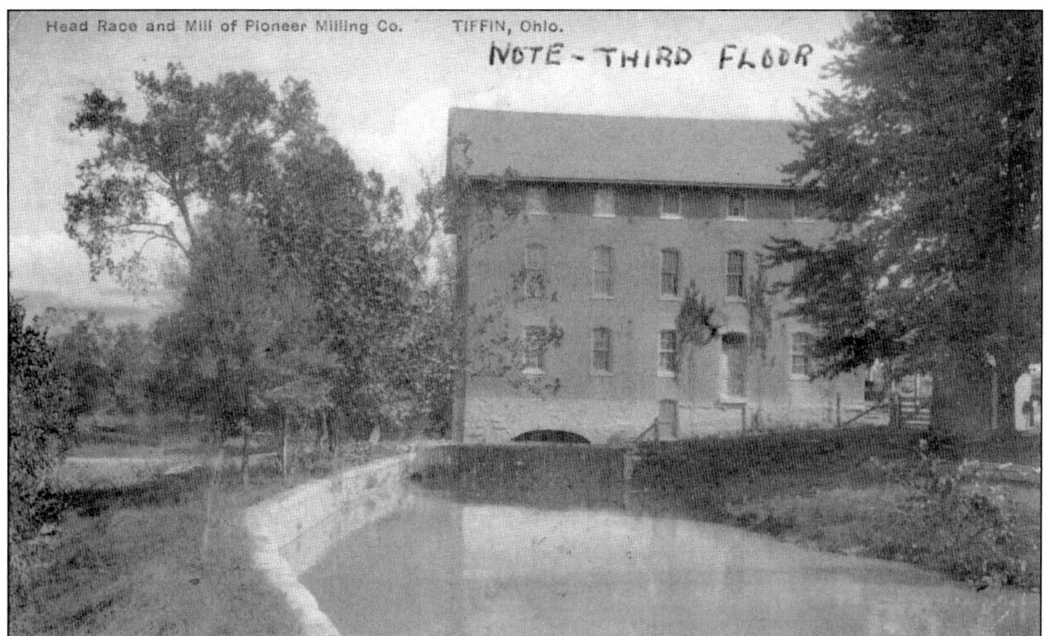

The millrace of the Pioneer Milling Company is shown in the foreground of this 1909 postcard. Still well known as a restaurant, the massive brick building pictured was reconstructed in 1875 after a fire, and survived the flood of 1913 and a second fire in 1937. (Courtesy of the Seneca County Museum.)

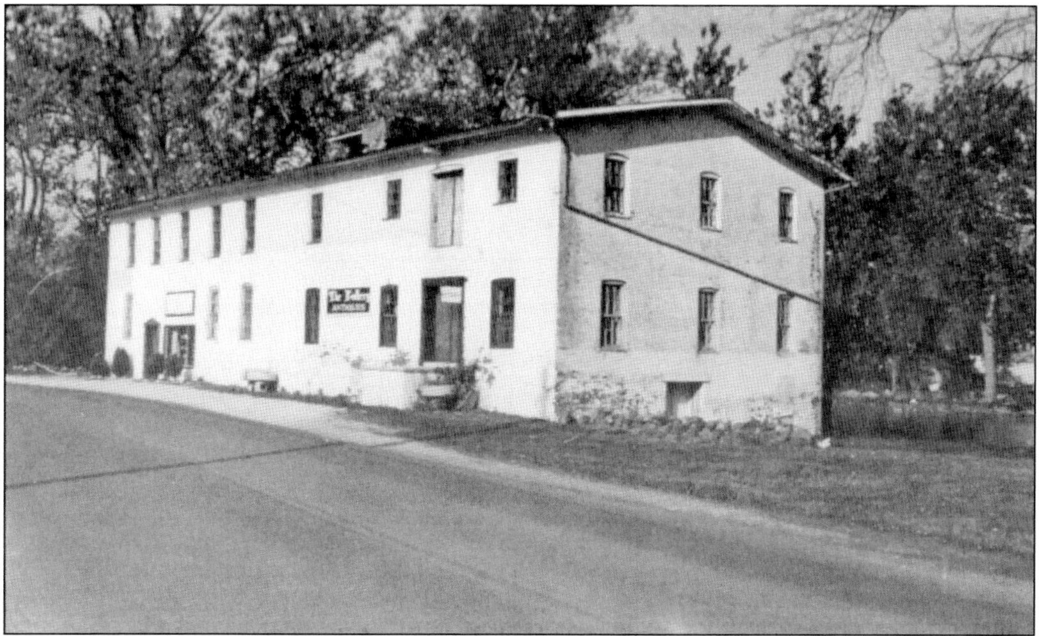

Built as the Eagle Rye Distillery in the early 1860s, this venerable old building still stands next to the Pioneer Mill on Riverside Drive. It became a soap factory in the 1890s, later was occupied by the Tiffin Robe and Tanning Company, and currently houses an antiques business. (Courtesy of the Seneca County Museum.)

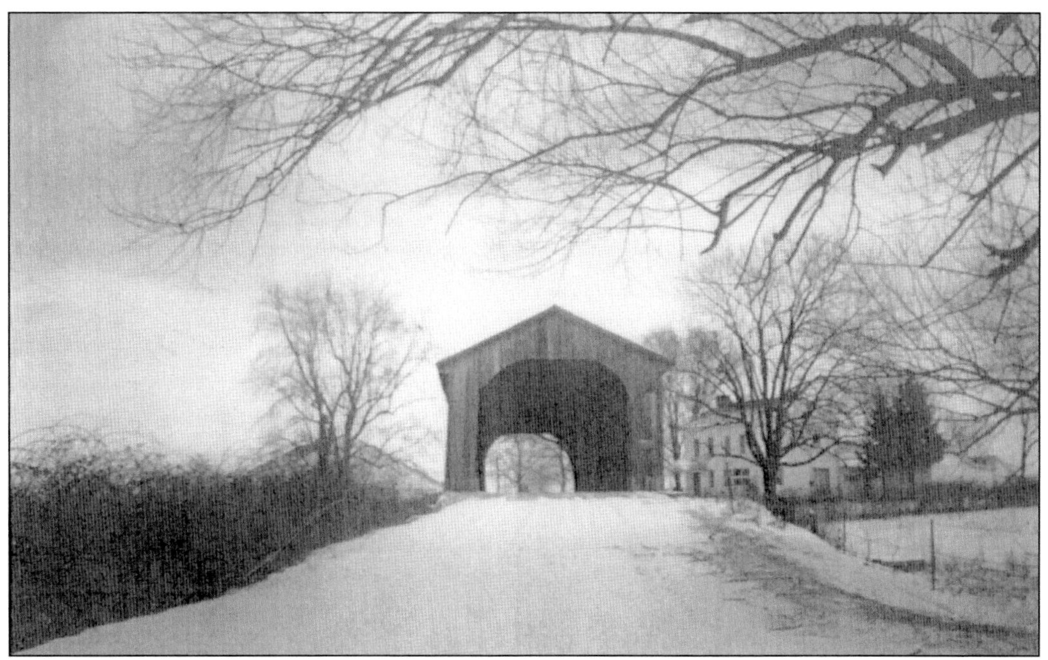

Covered bridges were built to protect wooden roadbeds from the elements, but they are now a nostalgic link to the past, as evoked by these photographs. Pictured are two views of Mull Covered Bridge, the last covered bridge in Sandusky County. It was constructed by Henry Mull near his mill seven miles south of Fremont in 1851, at a "cost not to exceed $75," and built with oak floor planks and white pine walls. Above, Mull's farmhouse stands to the right of the bridge. Mull Covered Bridge carried traffic over Wolf Creek, a tributary of the Sandusky River, until it was no longer deemed safe for automobiles in 1962. It is now preserved as a historic landmark. (Below, courtesy of Krista Michaels.)

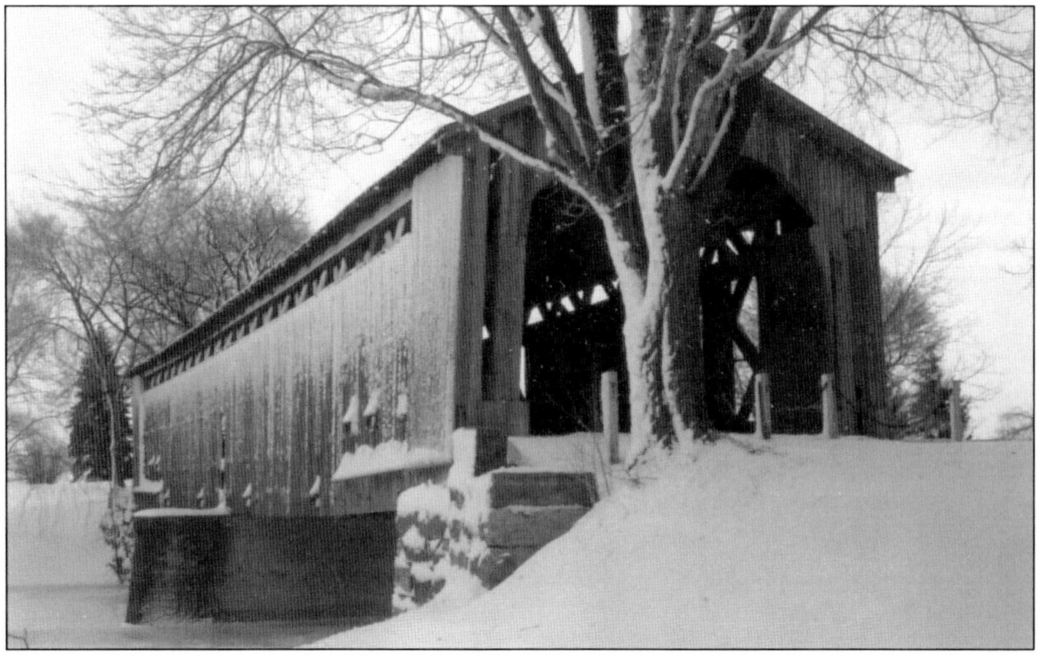

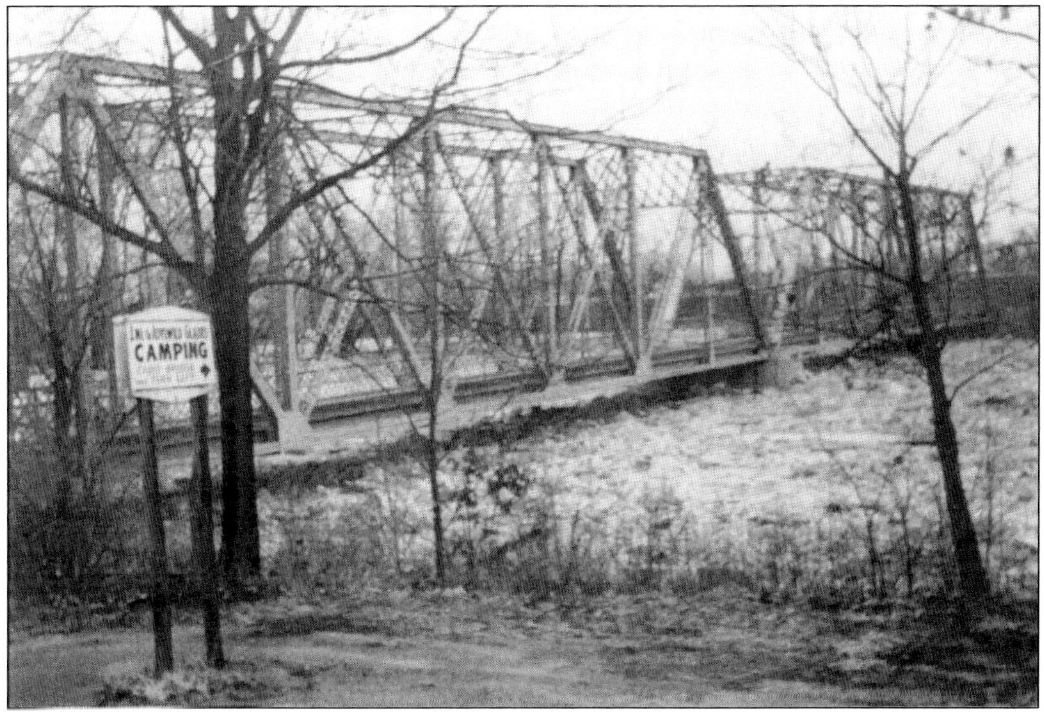

This iron Tindall Bridge replaced an earlier covered bridge in 1916 and is still in use a century later. It is pictured with late-autumn high water and ice encroaching the roadbed. The Tindall family lived across River Road at the west end of the bridge.

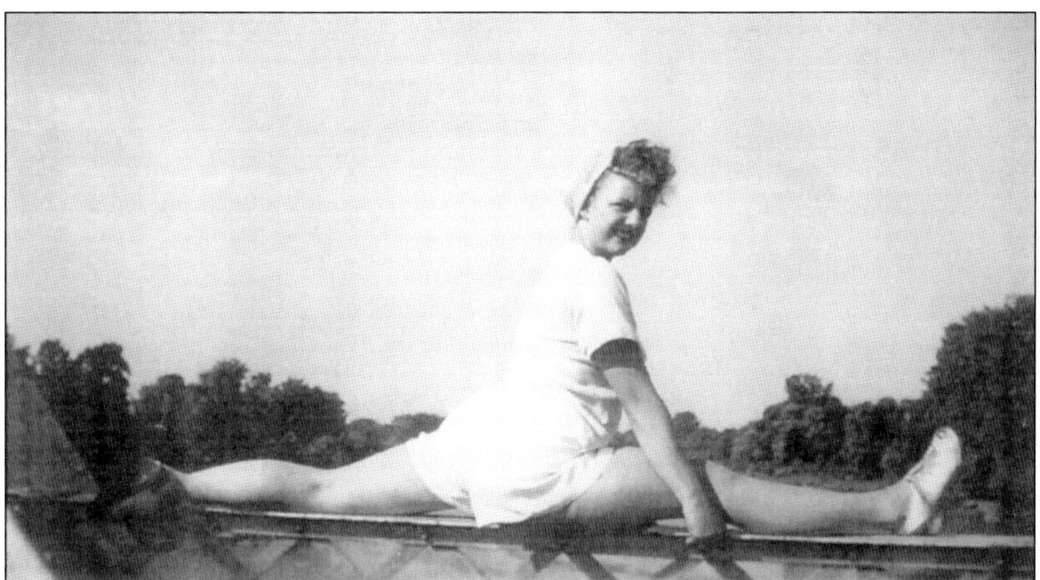

In this whimsical mid-century photograph, a fearless Jean Michaels poses on the Tindall Bridge, a recreational activity not recommended for most river sightseers.

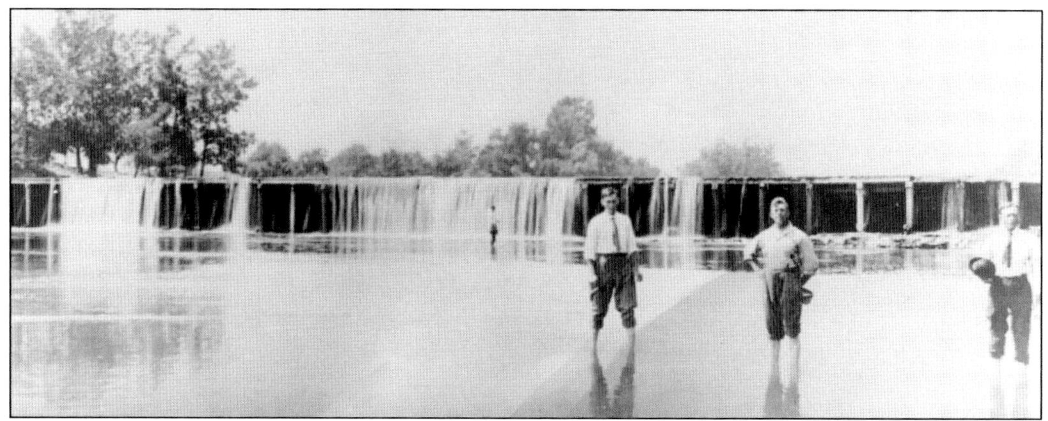

Waders pose in shallow water at the bottom of the spillway of the old Tucker Dam. Located along Buckland Avenue at the end of Tucker Road, the small dam funneled water into the race that powered the mill. Two of the gentlemen pictured are wearing neckties.

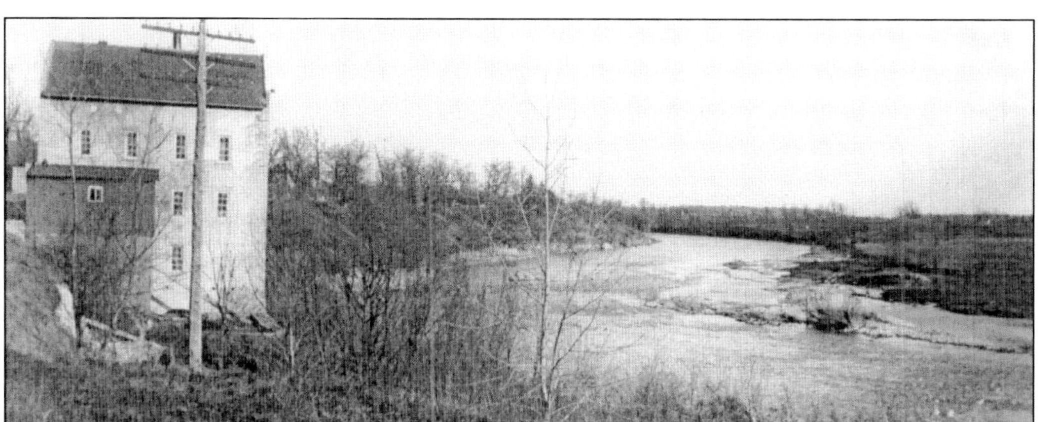

As the river neared Fremont from the southwest, it once passed the old Riverside Mill. The mills along this section of the river were gone by the 1920s, but their old foundations can still be seen. In this photograph from about 1900, the river is curving past Oakwood Cemetery (behind the mill) toward the old Ballville Dam around the bend to the left in the distance.

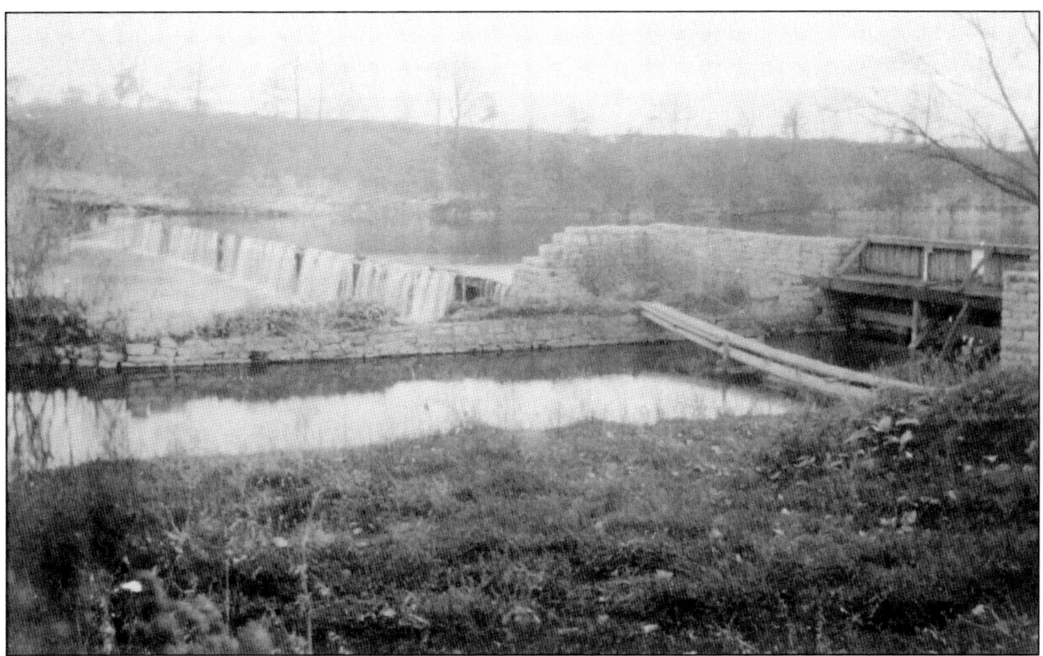

The old Ballville Dam is seen in this c. 1900 photograph, with a view looking toward the high ground on the southwest shore of the river. The high stone walls around the gateway at right are a distinguishing feature of this early dam.

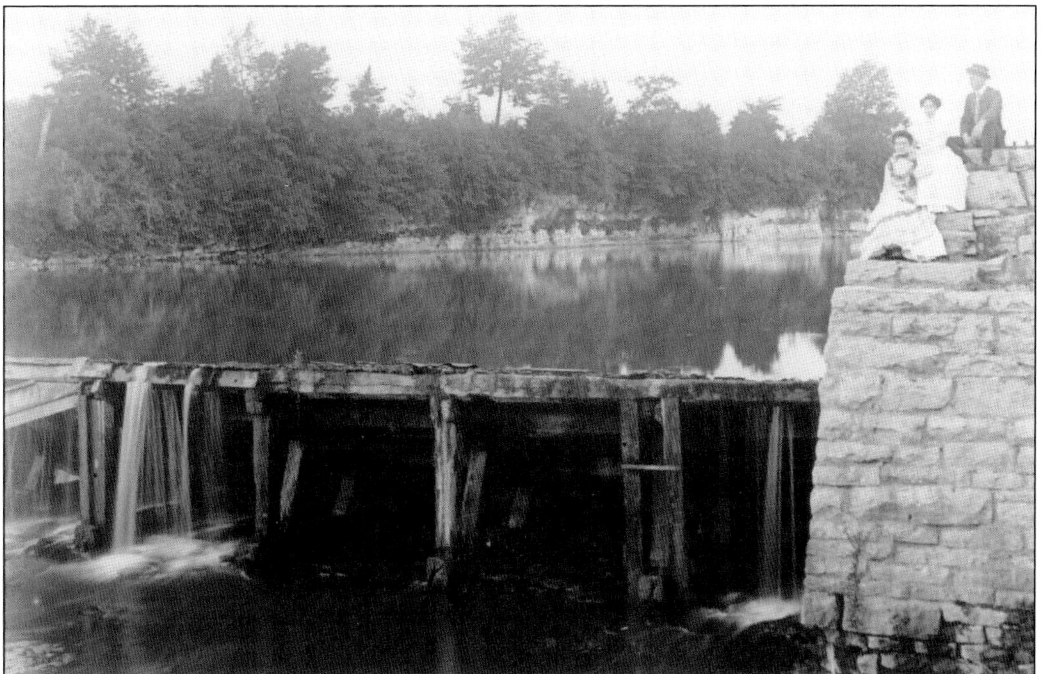

Two young ladies and a gentleman have ventured out to pose on the stone wall next to the dam, seemingly oblivious to any danger or the restrictions of their cumbersome late-Victorian clothing. This early photograph gives a close-up view of the spillway's wooden framework.

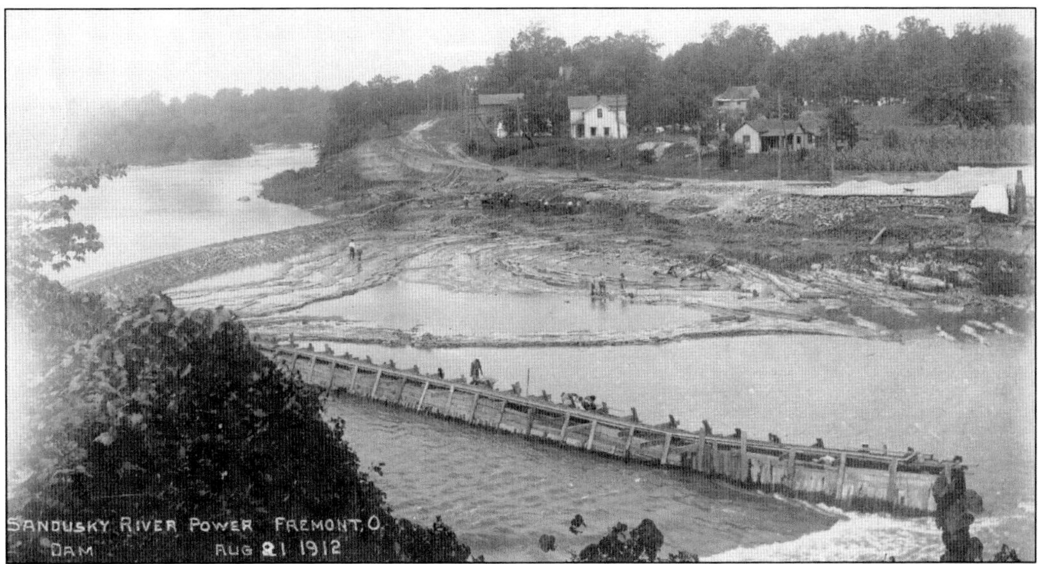

This panoramic photograph, with a view looking north, captures the early preparations in the building of the new Ballville Dam. Water has been diverted, as seen in the foreground, to allow workers to begin construction. The large house up on Cemetery Street still stands, and Oakwood Cemetery is visible at upper right. The photograph is dated August 21, 1912.

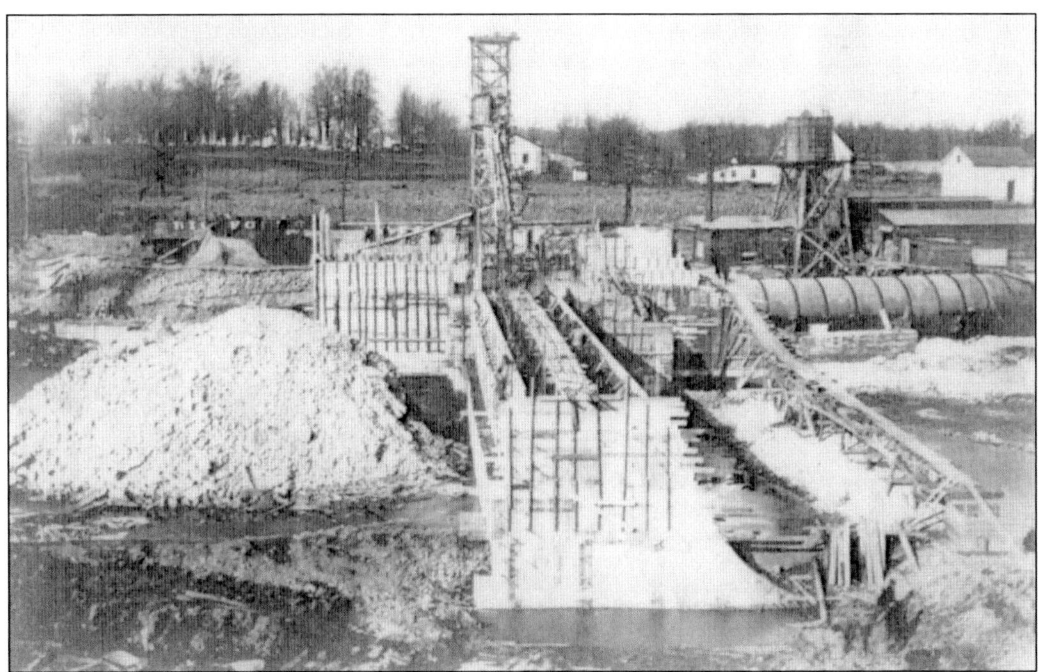

The large dam is taking shape in this detailed construction photograph. The flume extends to the right of the dam along the north shore of the river. Oakwood Cemetery is again seen on the hill at upper left. (Courtesy of the Hayes Presidential Center.)

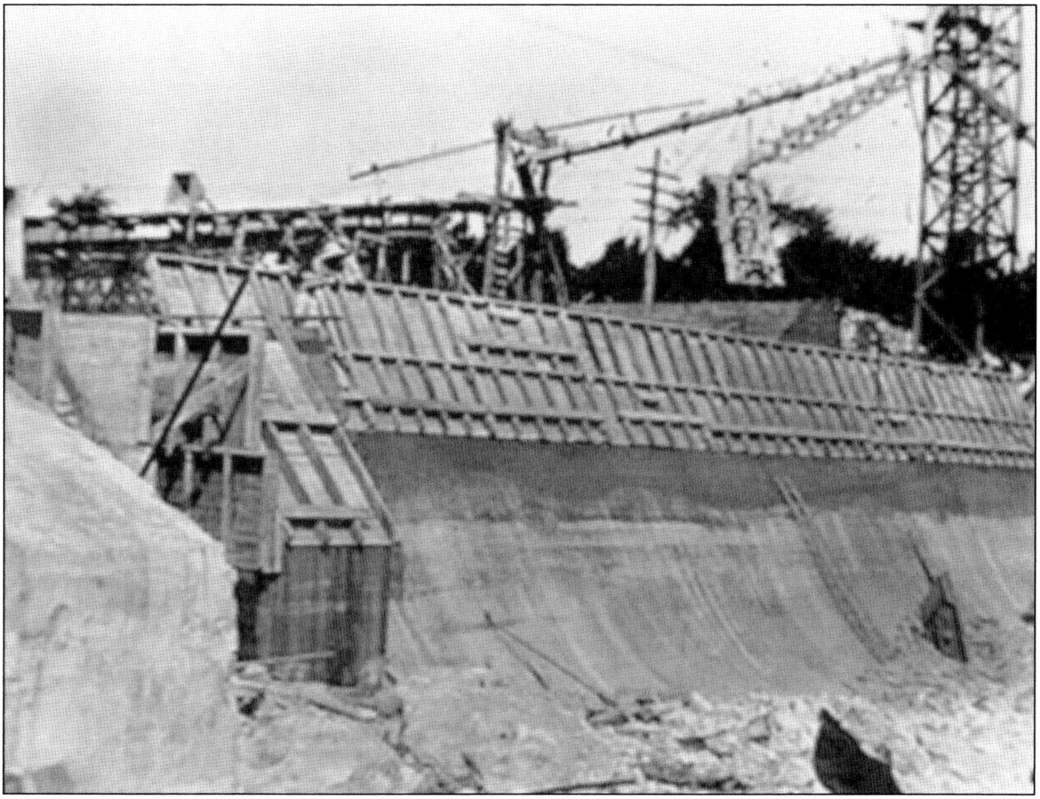

The Ballville Dam was nearing completion when this photograph was taken. Building the dam was the largest construction project on the river until the floodwall was completed in the early 1970s. (See chapter 4 for more information.)

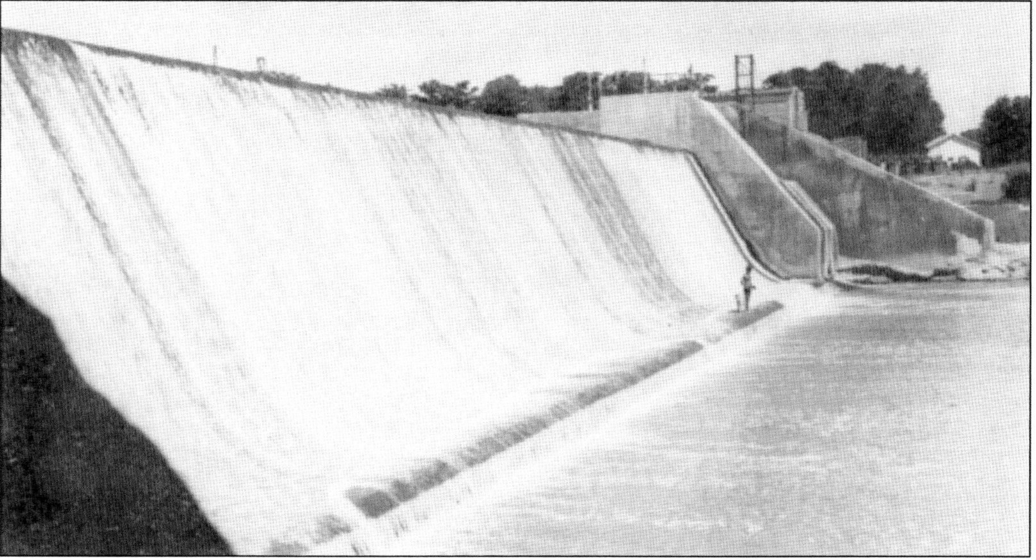

Pictured about 1970, the Ballville Dam has changed very little over the years. It has been useful for more than a century, but modern circumstances have dictated its removal to improve the natural flow of the river. There is a person standing at the foot of the dam. (Courtesy of Ray Grob.)

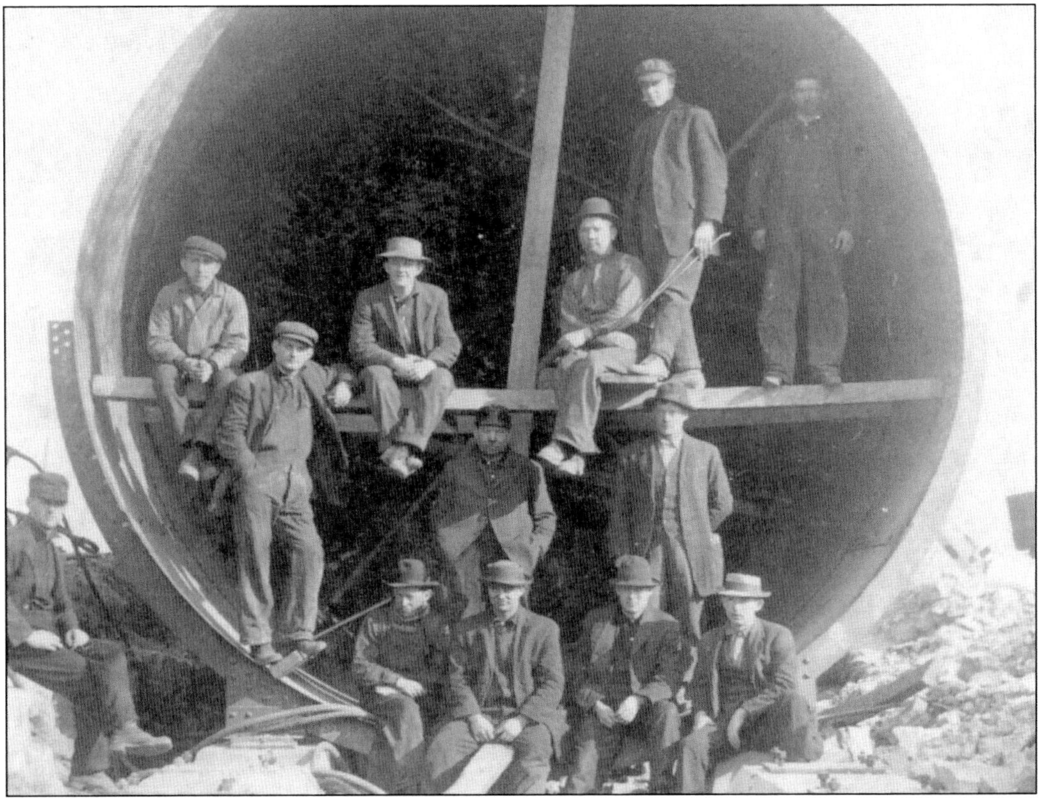

Work is being done on the huge flume pipe that ran along the north bank of the river and carried water from the dam to the hydroelectric plant. The size of the 18-foot flume is apparent in this photograph with men posing inside the pipe. The dam provided power principally for the Lake Shore Electric interurban line in Fremont.

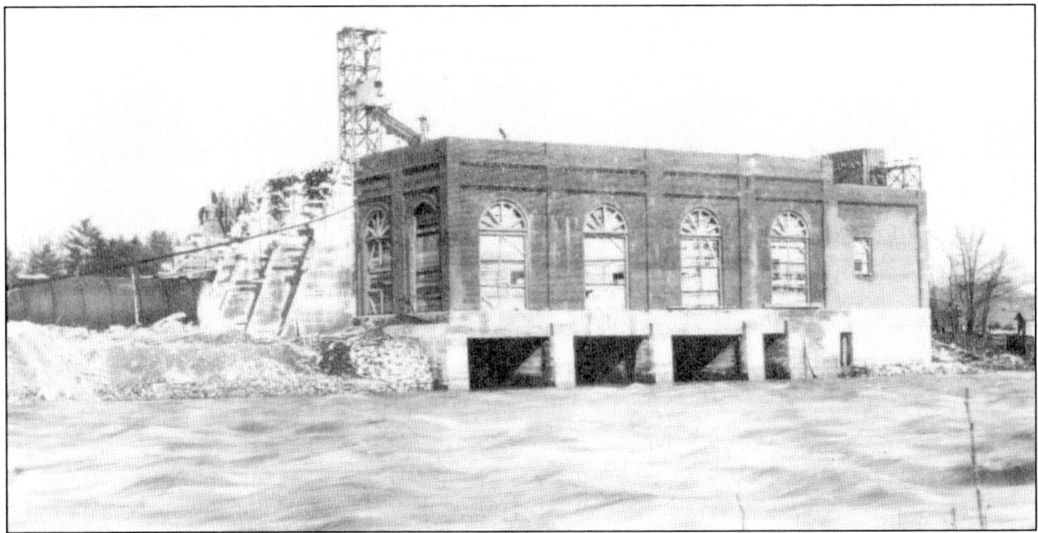

The view in this early-1900s photograph looks northeast across the river during high water, showing the flume entering the old hydro plant on Tiffin Street. The shell of the old building, which ceased operation about 1940, still exists and is open before Halloween as the Haunted Hydro.

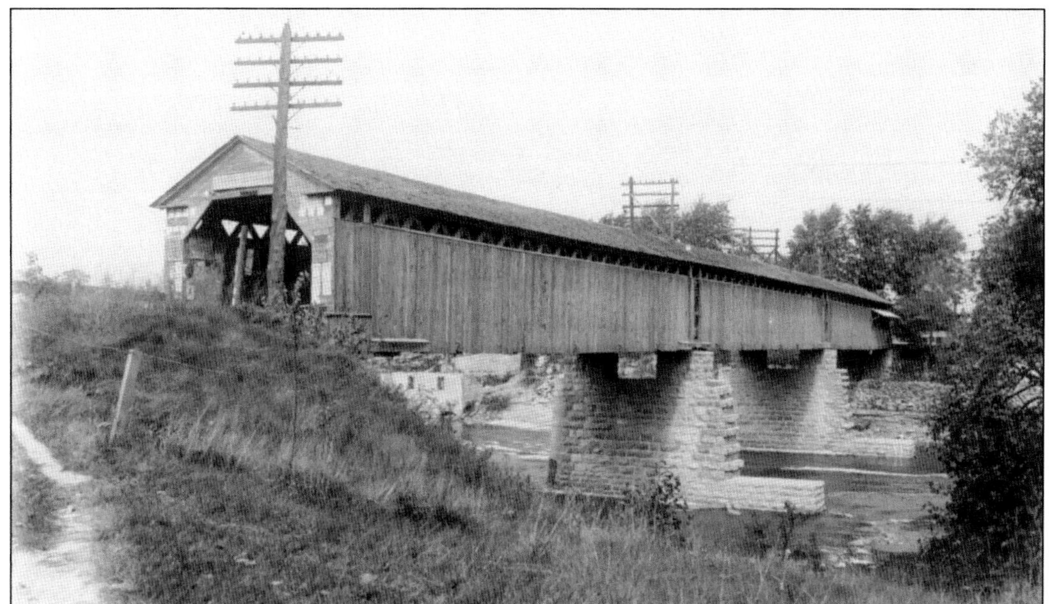

Just downstream from the dam is the Ballville Bridge, which brings Tiffin Road across the river to connect with Tiffin Street in Ballville at the southern edge of Fremont. This is one of the oldest intersections in the area, as Tiffin Street was laid out in 1850 and the first Ballville Bridge (pictured) was built in 1858. This view of the old covered bridge looks southeast from Tiffin Street.

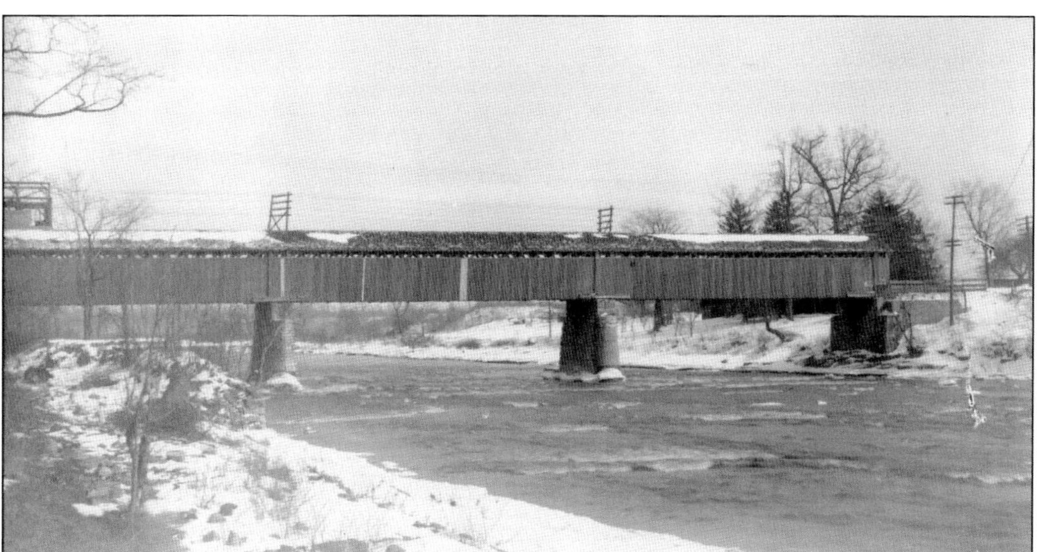

In this early photograph, the covered Ballville Bridge is seen from the east, in this view looking back upstream toward the dam. Tiffin Street is at right, and in the foreground are foundations of early mills that once were prevalent all along this section of the river. The old bridge survived the 1913 flood, but burned in 1924.

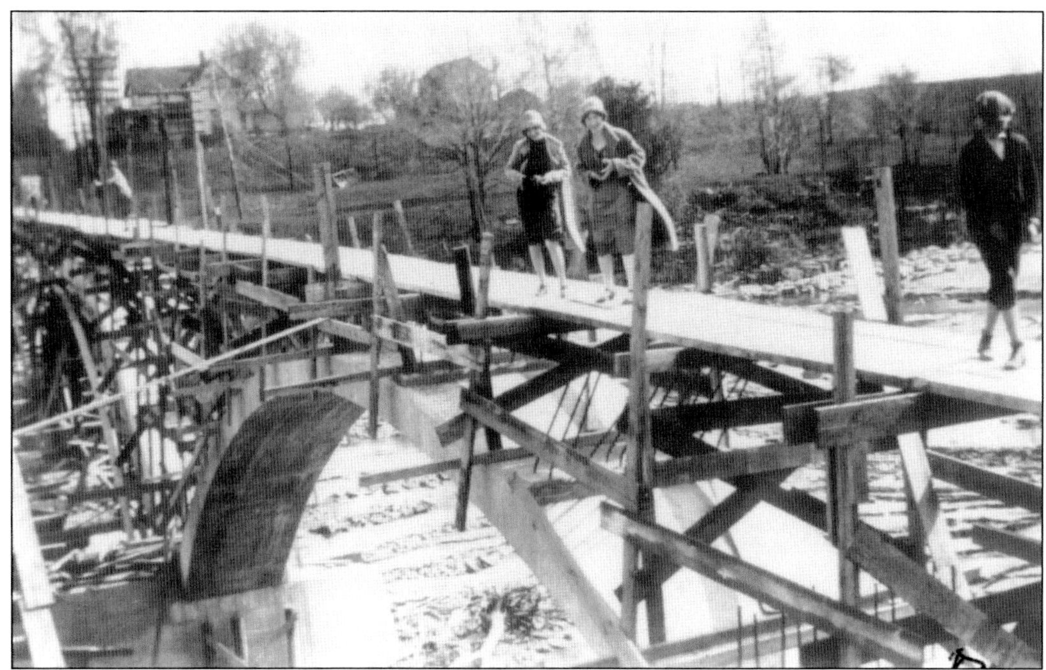

These intrepid ladies of the Roaring Twenties have ventured out on temporary planks used during the construction of the second Ballville Bridge in 1926. The view looks southwest from Tiffin Street.

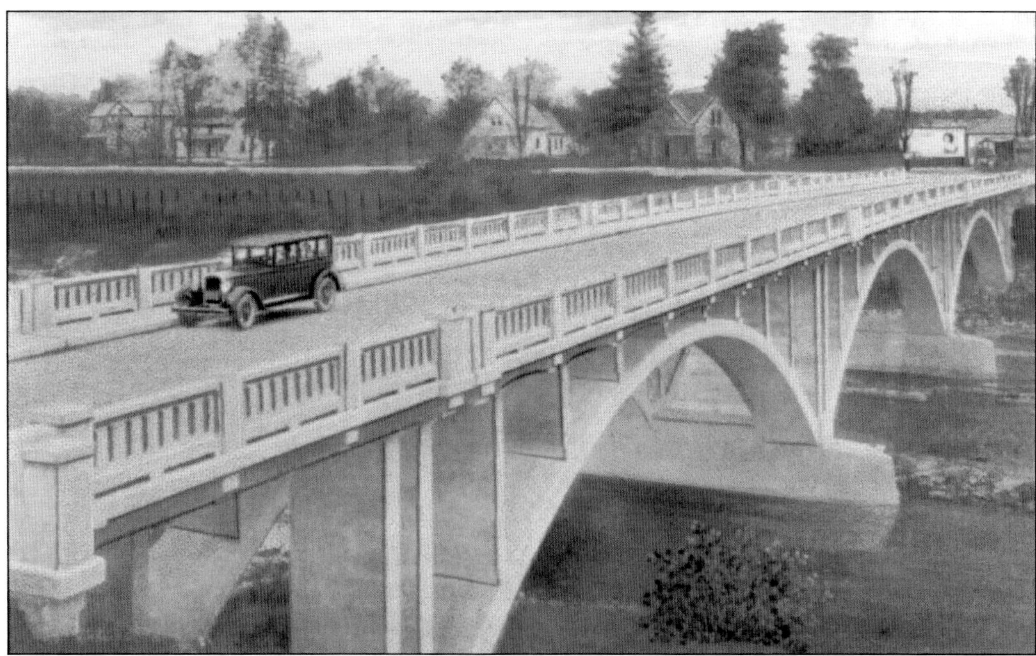

Taken shortly after the bridge was completed, this photograph has a view looking northwest toward Tiffin Street, showing the modern design of the sturdier concrete structure. Many were upset when it was replaced in 1973 with the current flat streamlined bridge, even though this bridge was still in good condition. The houses on Tiffin Street in the background still stand.

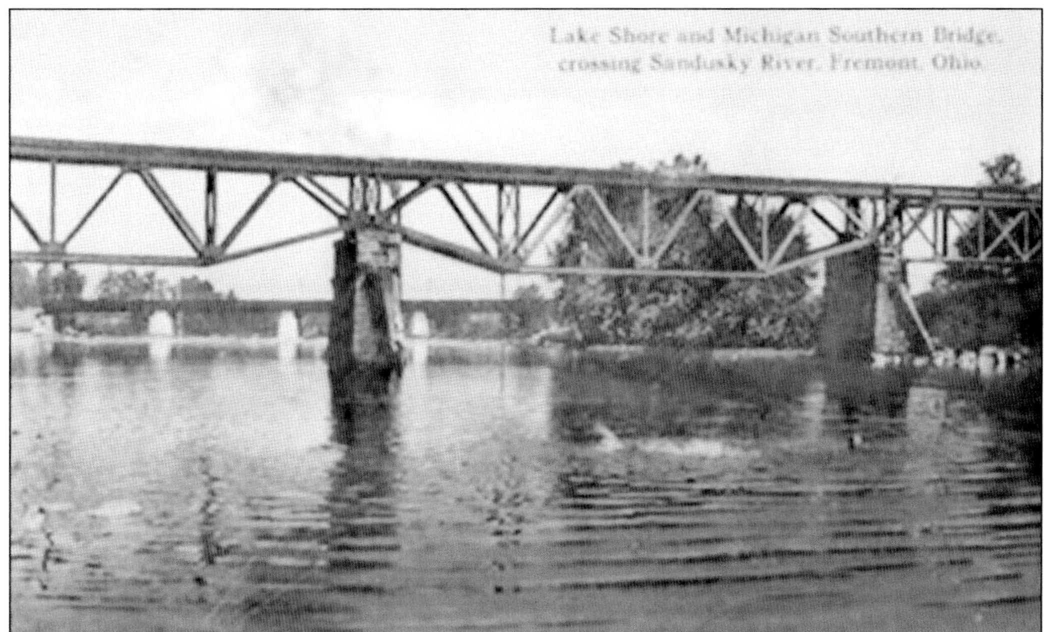

An early-1900s postcard shows the Lake Shore & Michigan Southern Railroad Bridge crossing the Sandusky south of Fremont. The bridge now carries the North Coast Inland Trail across the river, offering a scenic view well-traveled by cyclists and enjoyed by walkers. The bridge further north in the distance is still used by the Norfolk Southern Railroad.

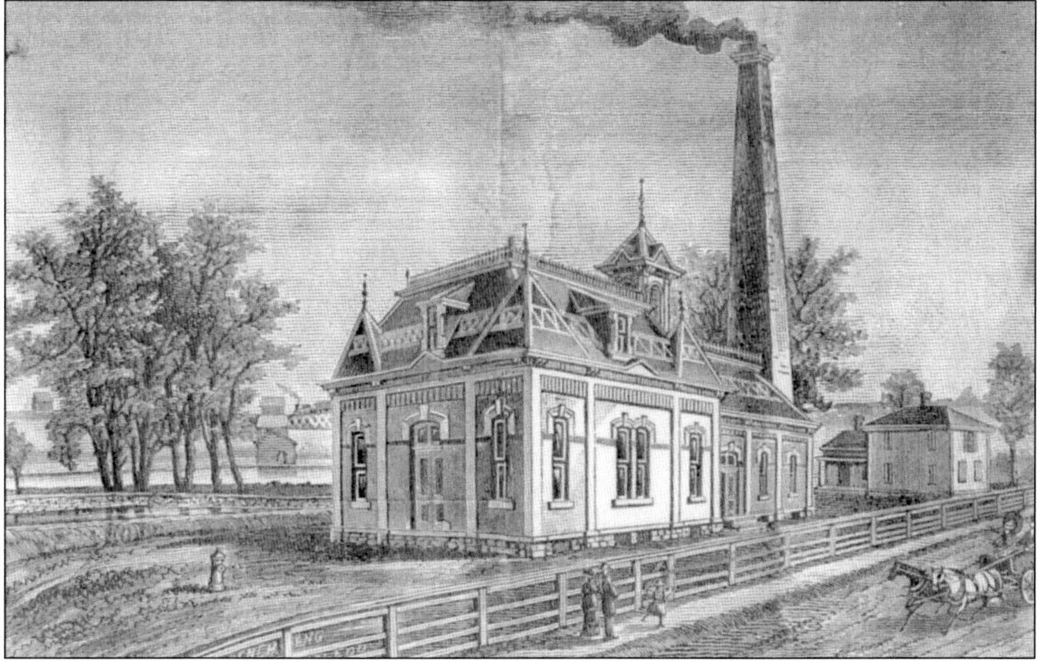

Depicted in the 1874 *Historical Atlas of Sandusky County*, the old Fremont Waterworks stands along the river in all its Second Empire glory, even if its decorative tower is dwarfed by the tall smokestack. In this artistic interpretation, a train crosses the bridge to the left of the building.

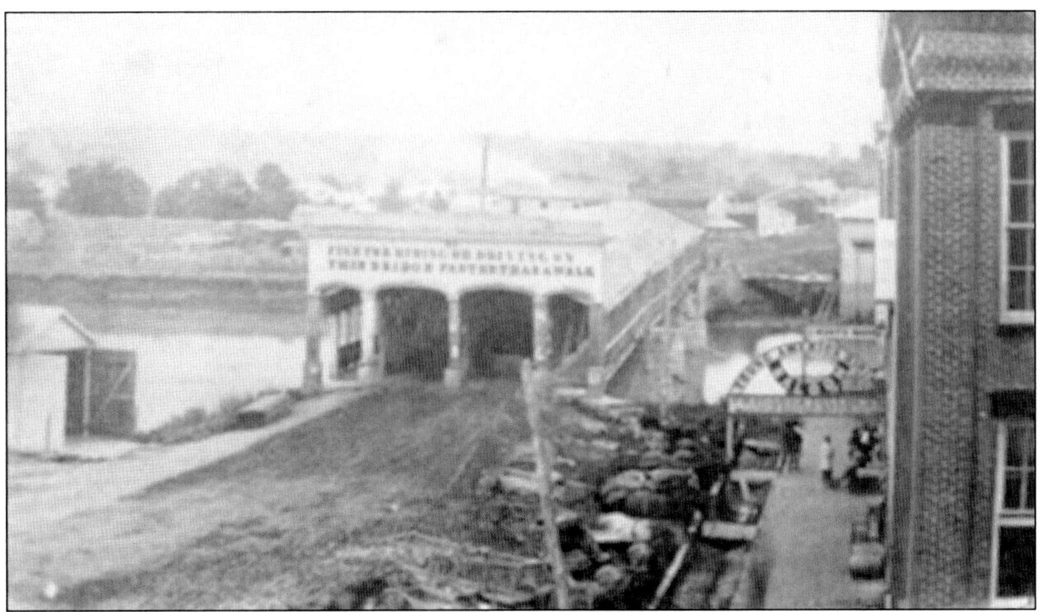

This wide covered bridge, which dates back to the early 1840s, was the second to cross the river at State Street (then called the Maumee & Western Reserve Turnpike), the only road through the Great Black Swamp. A fragile, earlier 1828 bridge was washed away by a flood in 1833. Though fines were levied for traveling faster than a walk, this covered bridge lasted through nearly 35 harsh winters, and it is pictured here in 1862.

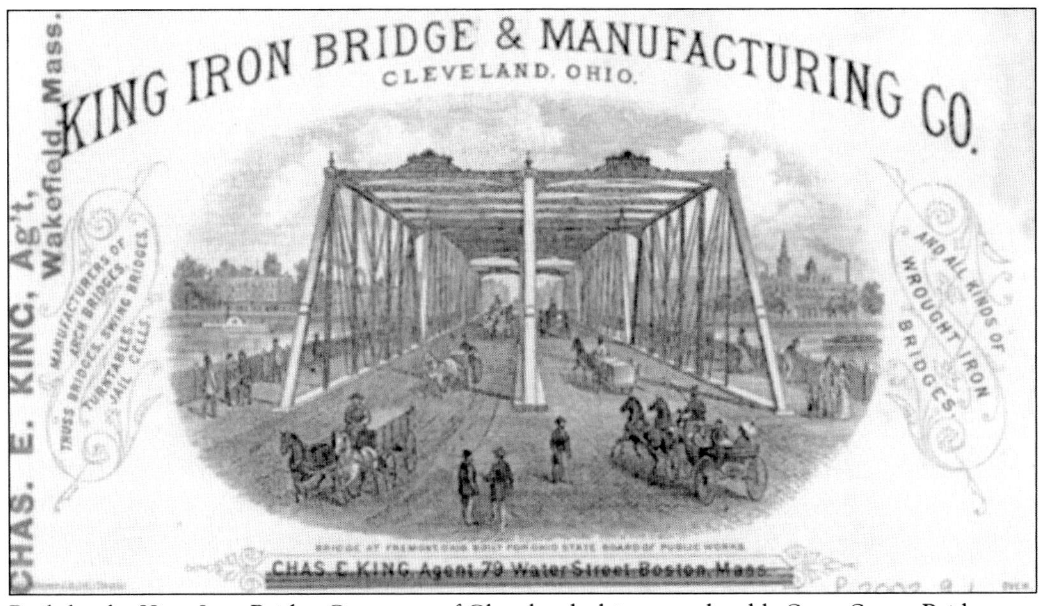

Built by the King Iron Bridge Company of Cleveland, this more durable State Street Bridge was completed in 1877. The advertisement was true to its word, and the bridge lasted until 1926.

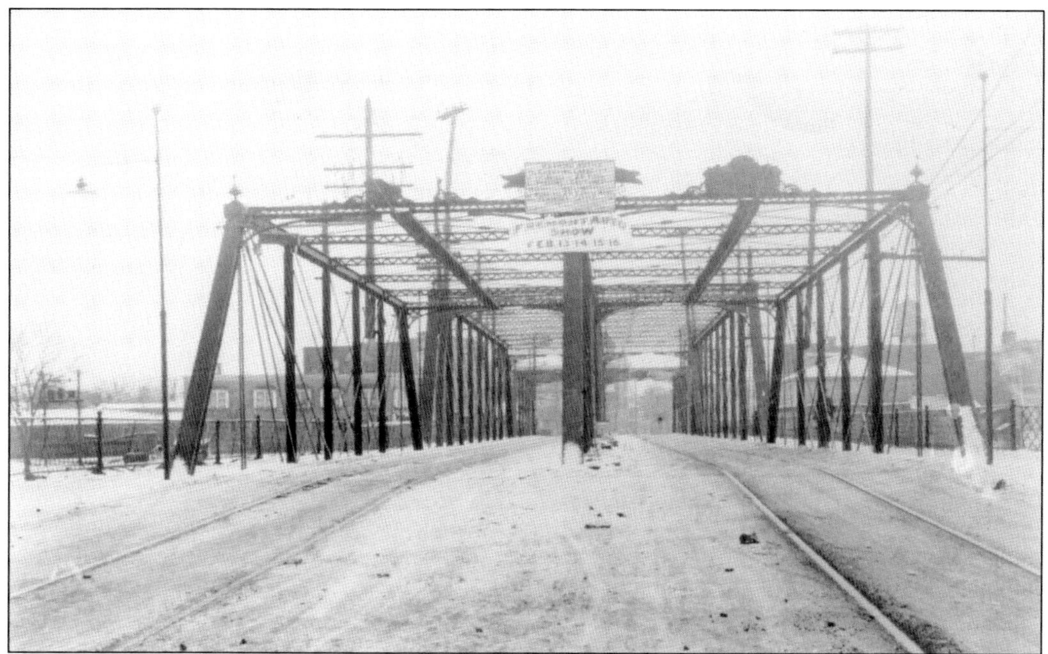

This view of the iron bridge from the early 1900s looks east, showing the interurban tracks that crossed the river in both directions. The capacity of the bridge was 20 tons, and the sign warns that no more than 20 horses or cattle were allowed on the bridge at one time. Another sign advertises an early automobile show.

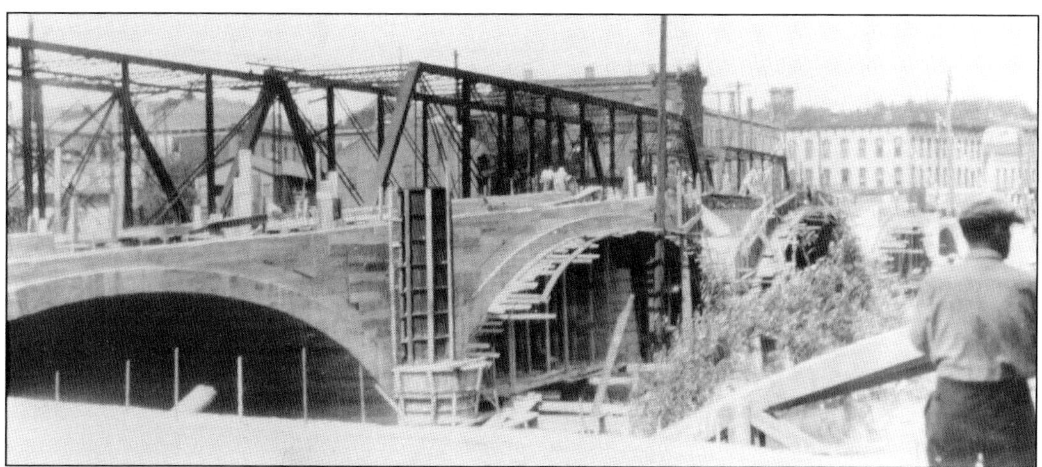

A man stands in the foreground of construction on the State Street Bridge in 1926. The concrete arches are taking shape from their wooden framing, even as the superstructure of the old iron bridge can be seen in the background. The view looks west toward the busy intersection of Front and West State Streets in downtown Fremont.

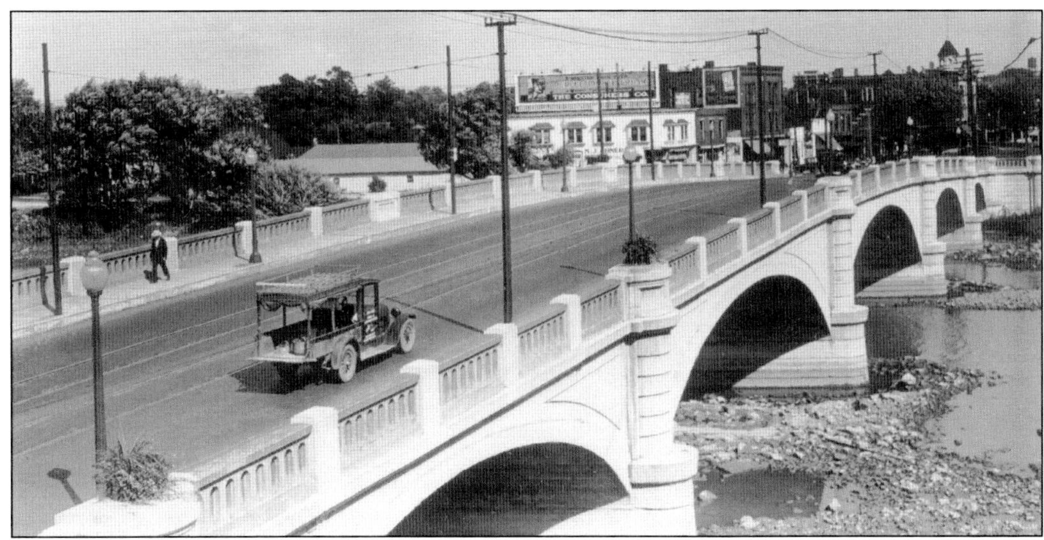

An old truck crosses the State Street Bridge to the east side in this photograph taken not long after it was completed. It is similar in design to the bridges built in Tiffin after the flood and is still in use today. There is no center line, but the bridge had interurban tracks until the late 1930s.

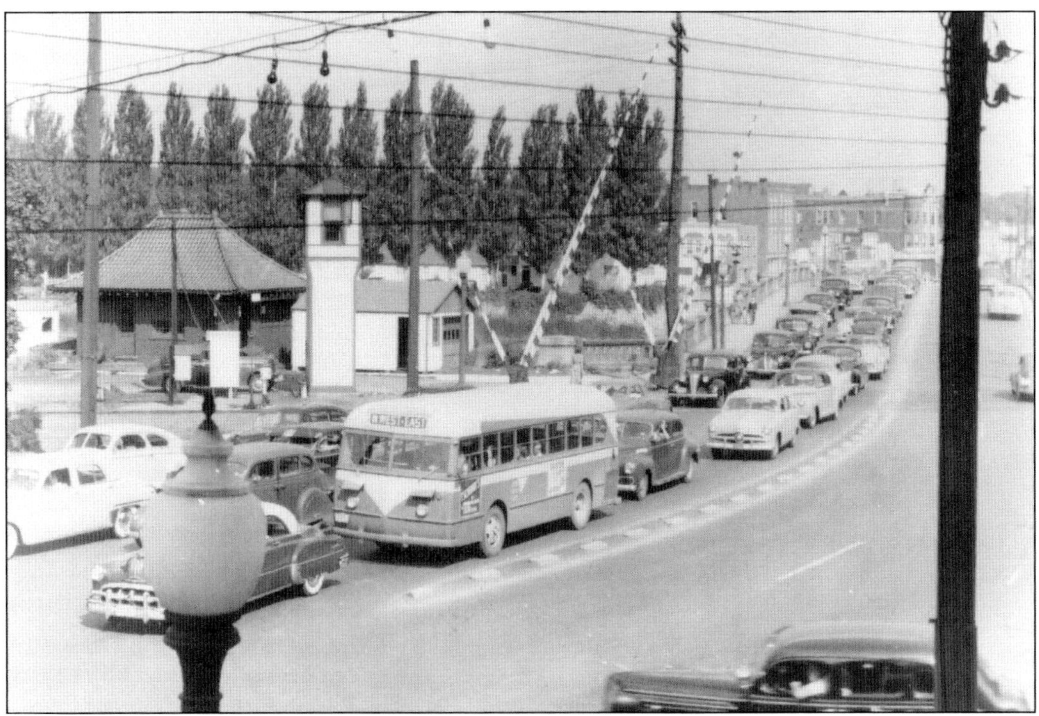

More cars are traveling west than east in this mid-century view of the State Street Bridge. The tracks are gone, but the buses that replaced them (pictured) did not last very long. A crossing gate tower is visible, as is as a row of trees lining the far side of the river before the floodwall was built.

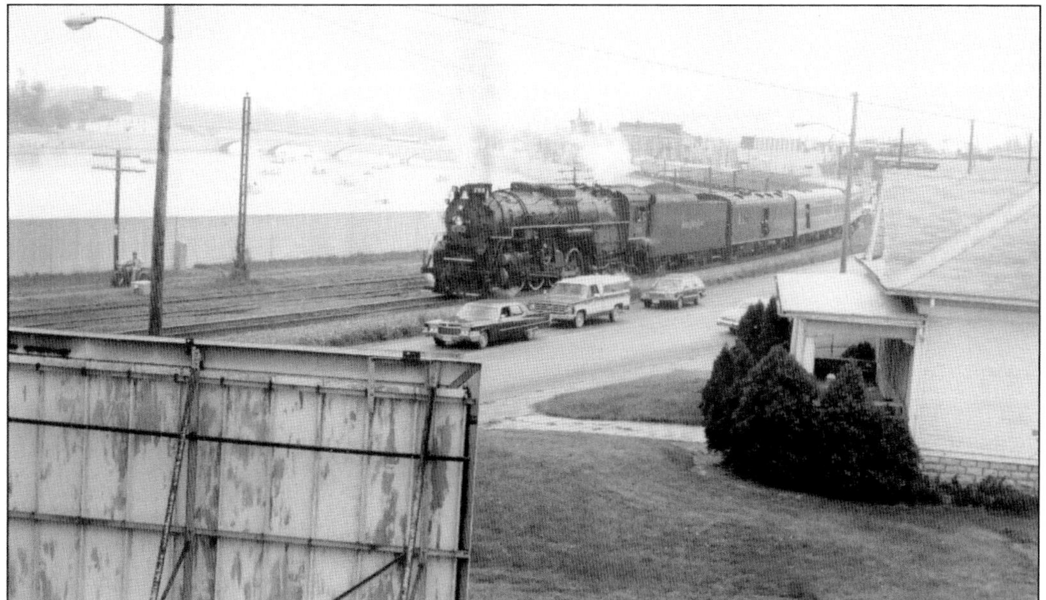

A steam train heads north along Front Street, as seen from the trestle bridge in this view looking back toward downtown Fremont. The State Street Bridge appears in the distance beyond the train, and there are a number of small boats in the river.

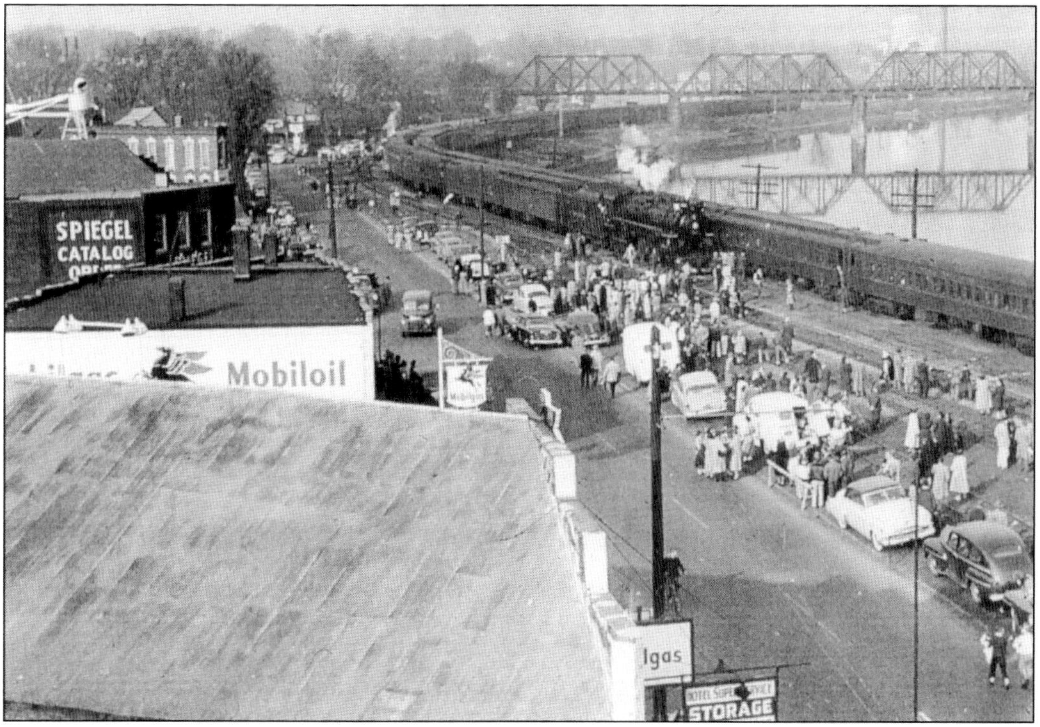

It is a busy day on North Front Street, with many cars and people waiting to meet the trains. This photograph was taken from the Hotel Fremont on the corner of Front and West State Streets. The view looks north toward the trestle bridge, which carried a railroad spur across the river and Brady's Island to the Heinz plant and other industries on the east side.

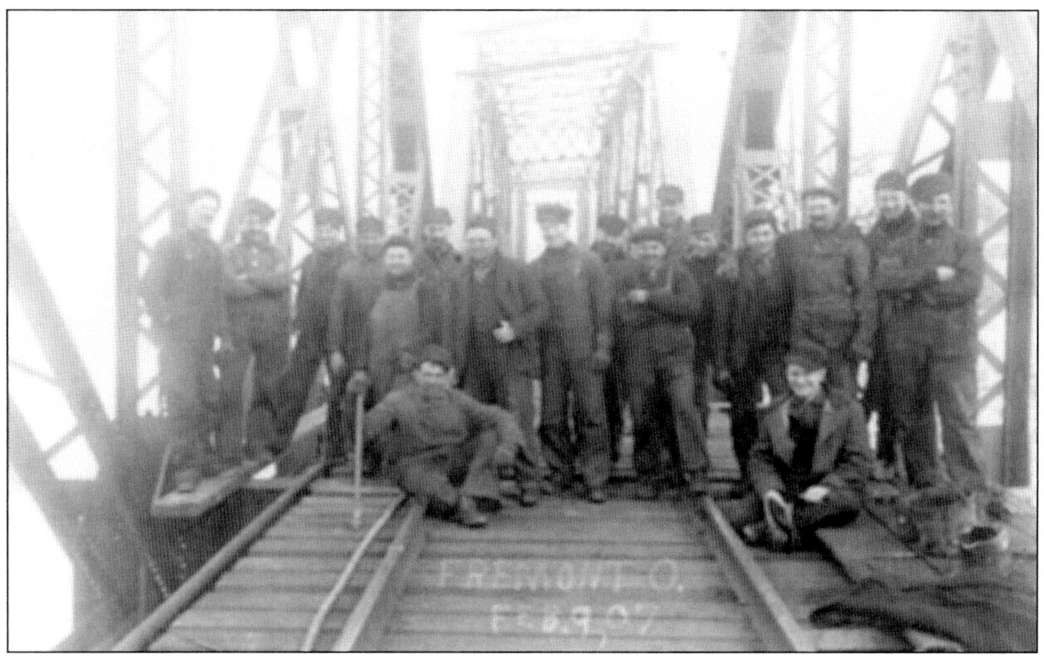

A work crew poses on the trestle bridge in 1907. Young people have been killed while crossing the single-track span when a train would approach suddenly.

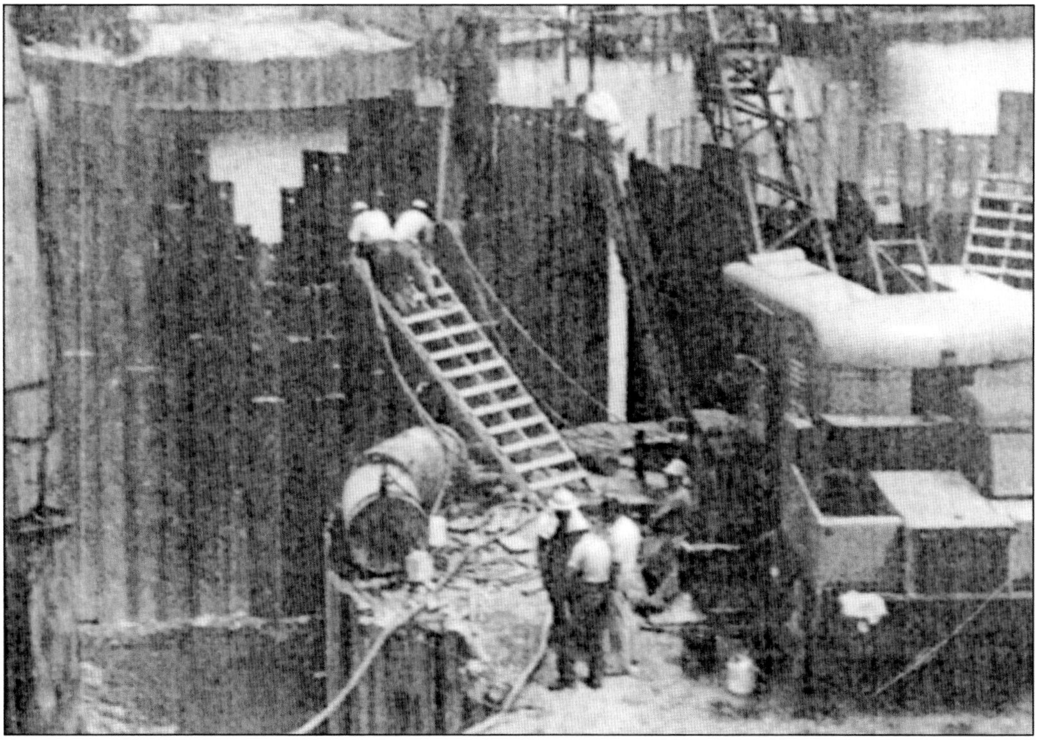

The northernmost bridge over the Sandusky River is on the US Route 20 bypass, completed in 1958, which circles around the north side of Fremont. Work on the piers is progressing in this photograph taken during the construction of the bridge. (Courtesy of the Hayes Presidential Center.)

Four

Floods on a Dangerous River

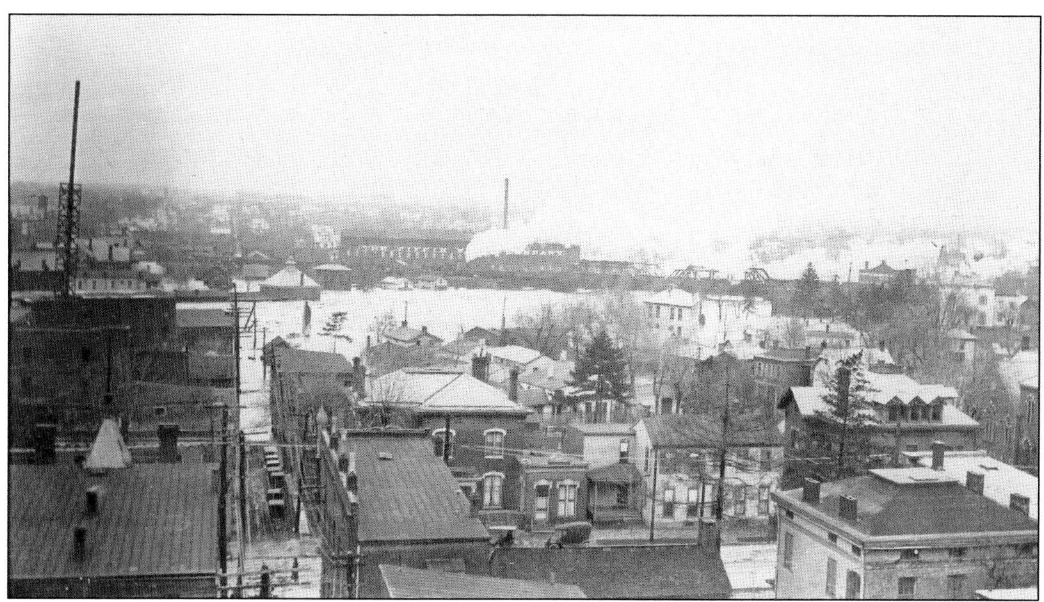

The devastation of the 1913 flood does not appear as bad in this view looking north from high up in the 1883 courthouse tower. However, 19 lives were lost in Tiffin during those dark late-March days of incessant rain when the Sandusky River reached its highest level ever recorded. Water floods the houses across the river in front of the large Tiffin Wagon Company, and railcars can be seen anchoring the railroad bridge beyond the Van Nette apartments. (Courtesy of the Seneca County Museum.)

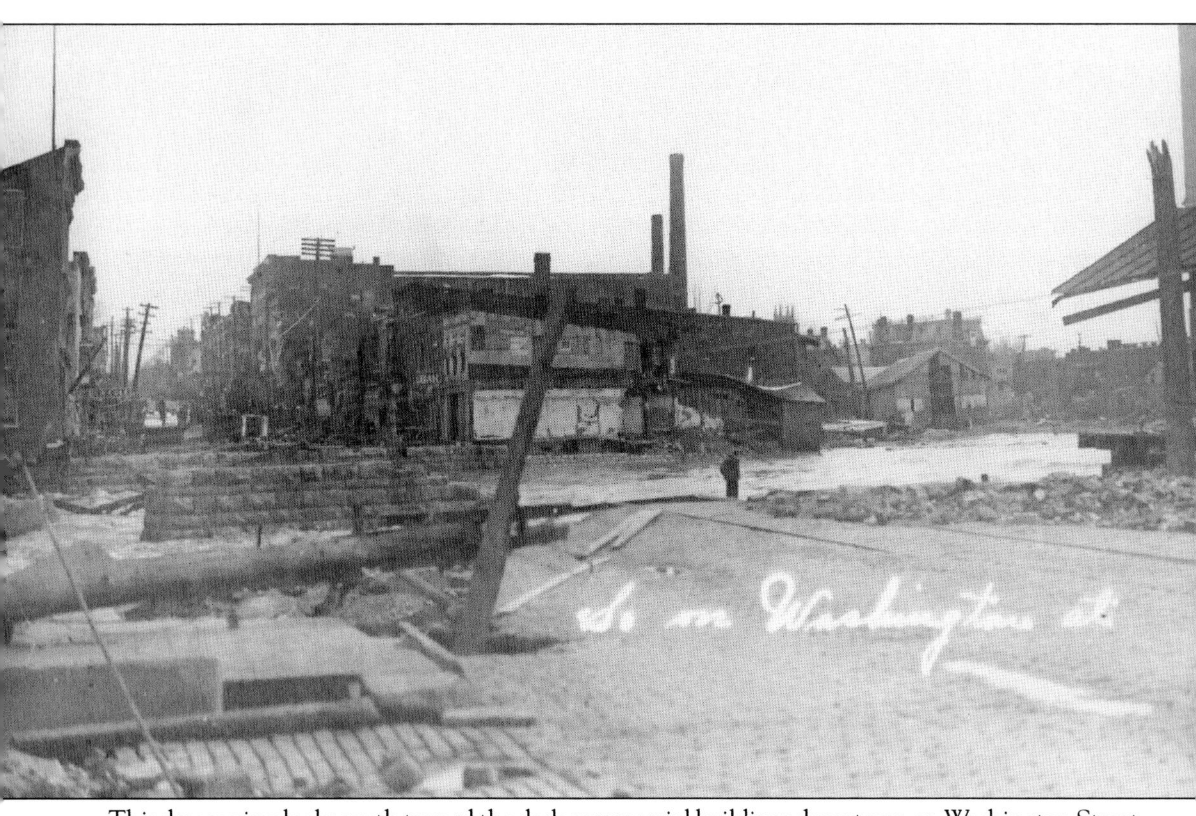

This dreary view looks south toward the dark commercial buildings downtown on Washington Street across the swollen river that destroyed the bridge. (Courtesy of the Seneca County Museum.)

The extent of the flooding is outlined on this map, which also gives the names of some of the victims who perished when their houses were swept off their foundations on Water and East Davis Streets. The low-lying Mechanicsburg neighborhood was hit particularly hard by the floodwaters.

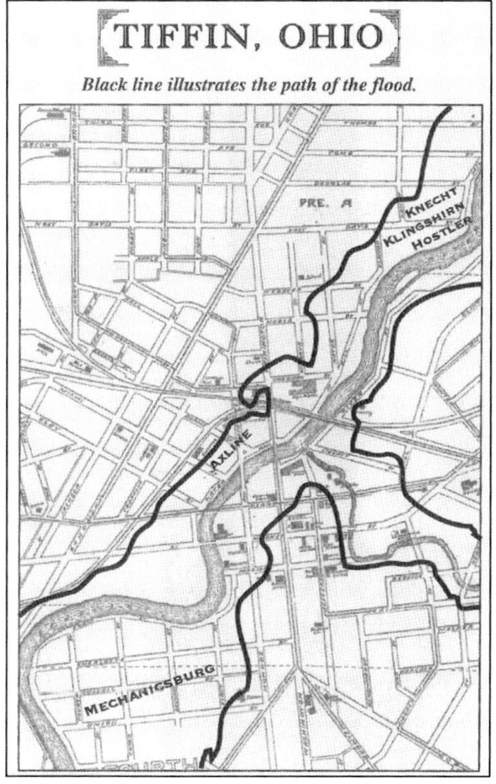

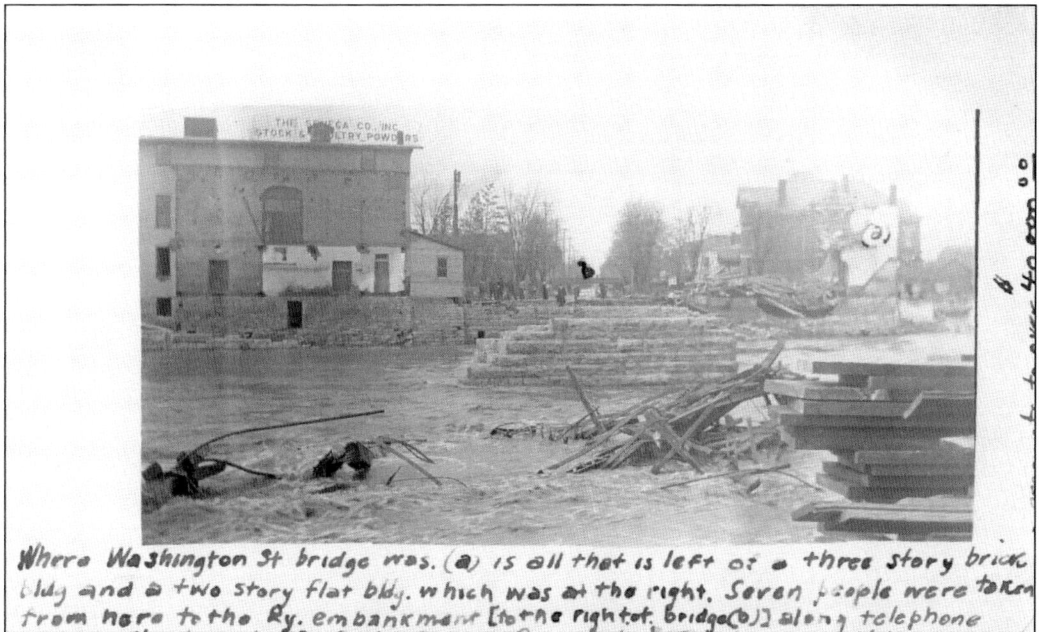

The flood left bridges in twisted ruins, as seen in this view looking north on Washington Street where the bridge once stood. Only the stone support beams remain as the water rushes past. The railroad viaduct over North Washington Street is visible in the distance. (Courtesy of the Seneca County Museum.)

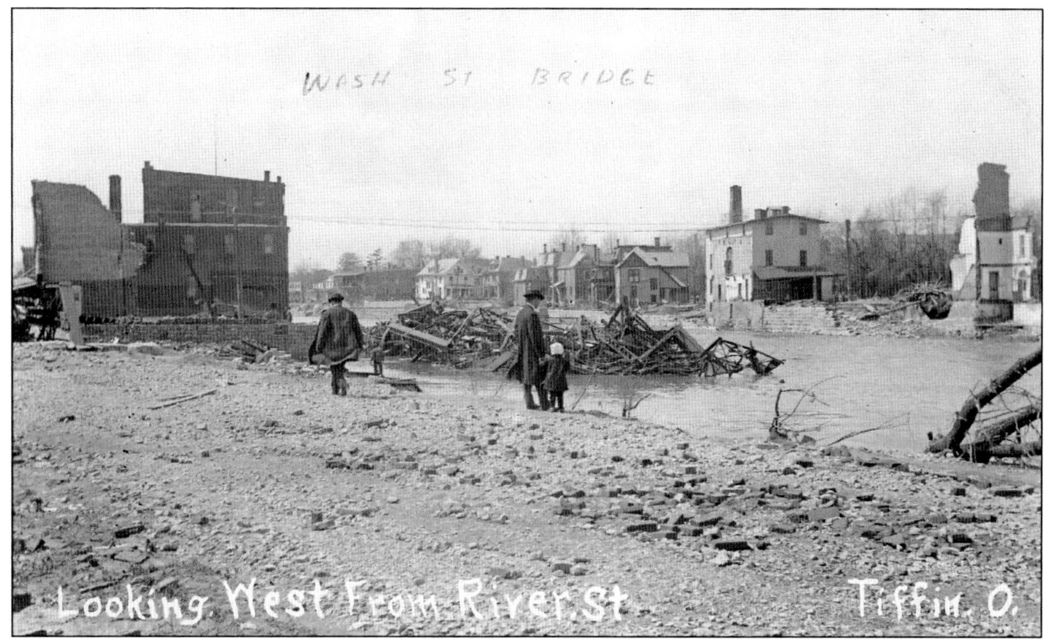

When the water receded, people came to view the destruction, as seen here near River Street. Wreckage of the Washington Street Bridge is piled behind the man with the child. Only a fragment of the three-story structure at far right remains. The sturdy Seneca Stock Company building and some of the houses further west on Water Street still stand beyond the bridge debris. (Courtesy of the Seneca County Museum.)

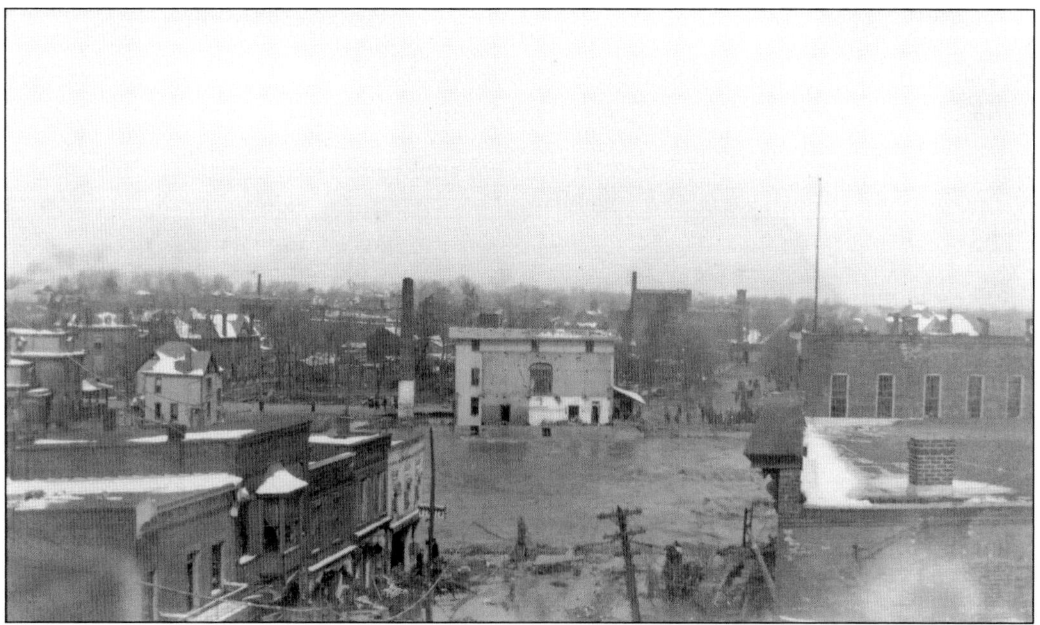

Even the supports of the swept-away Washington Street Bridge are submerged in this view, which looks north during the height of the flood. The Seneca Stock Company, with water all around it, appears again in the center of this photograph. (Courtesy of the Seneca County Museum.)

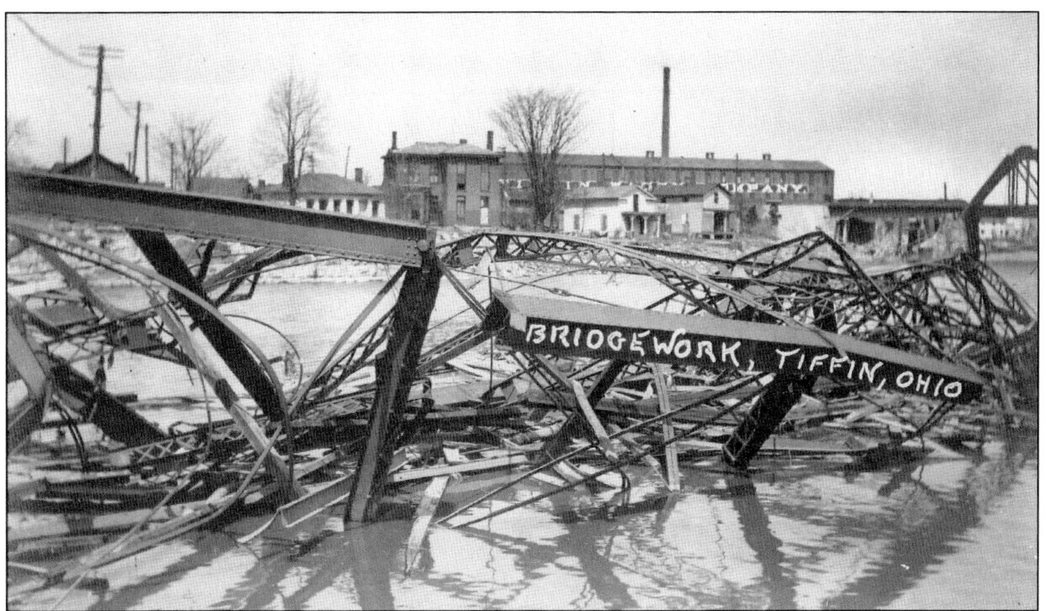

The sheer power of the rushing water is clearly demonstrated by the way it could bend even iron bridges into such twisted shapes (pictured) as the water was receding. This photograph was taken east of Washington Street; the view is looking north toward the Tiffin Wagon Company and the railroad bridge at far right. (Courtesy of the Seneca County Museum.)

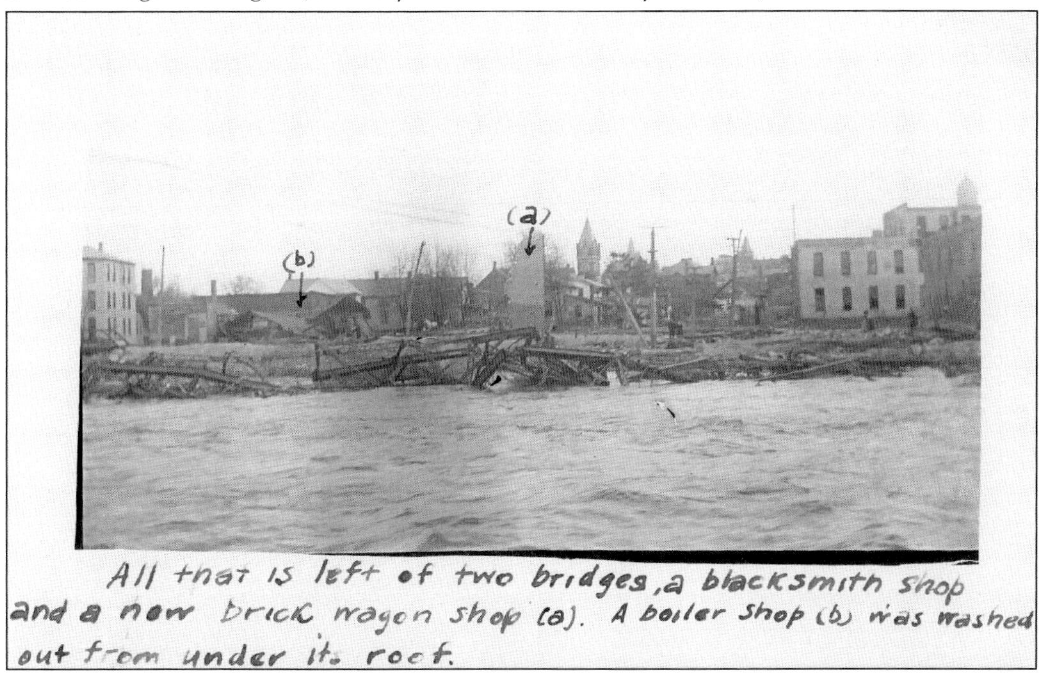

The water is running high in this photograph, which was probably taken from the Wagon Company building, with a view looking south toward downtown Tiffin. The ruins of a brick wagon shop (a) and a boiler shop (b) are marked. The Van Nette apartment building, formerly a shoe factory, stands at far left, the tower of Columbian High School appears in the center, and the top of the courthouse peeks over buildings at far right. (Courtesy of the Seneca County Museum.)

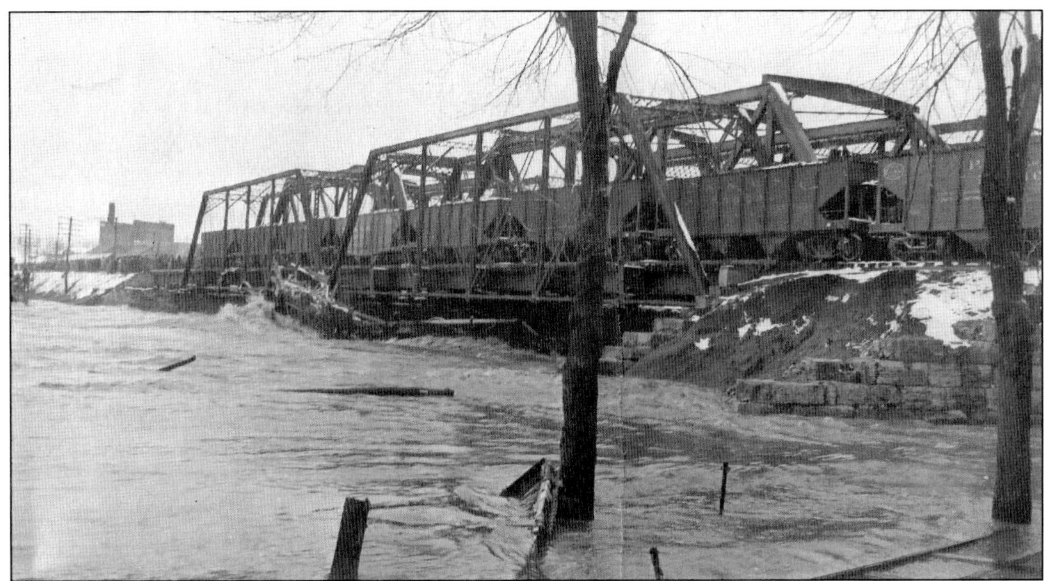

The railroad bridge northeast of the Washington Street Bridge was the only river crossing to survive the flood, despite all the debris being pushed against it. (Courtesy of the Seneca County Museum.)

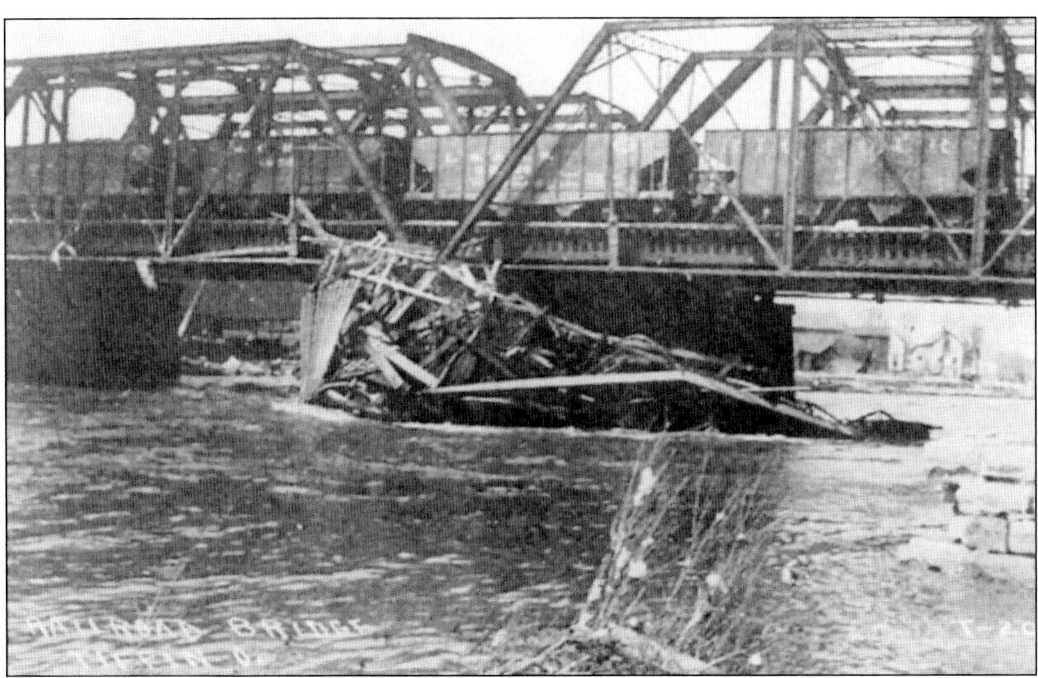

Train cars were moved onto the bridge by quick-thinking railroad workers, which was instrumental in keeping it from being washed downriver like all the other bridges. More flood remains are pictured pressed against the bridge pier as the water subsides. (Courtesy of the Seneca County Museum.)

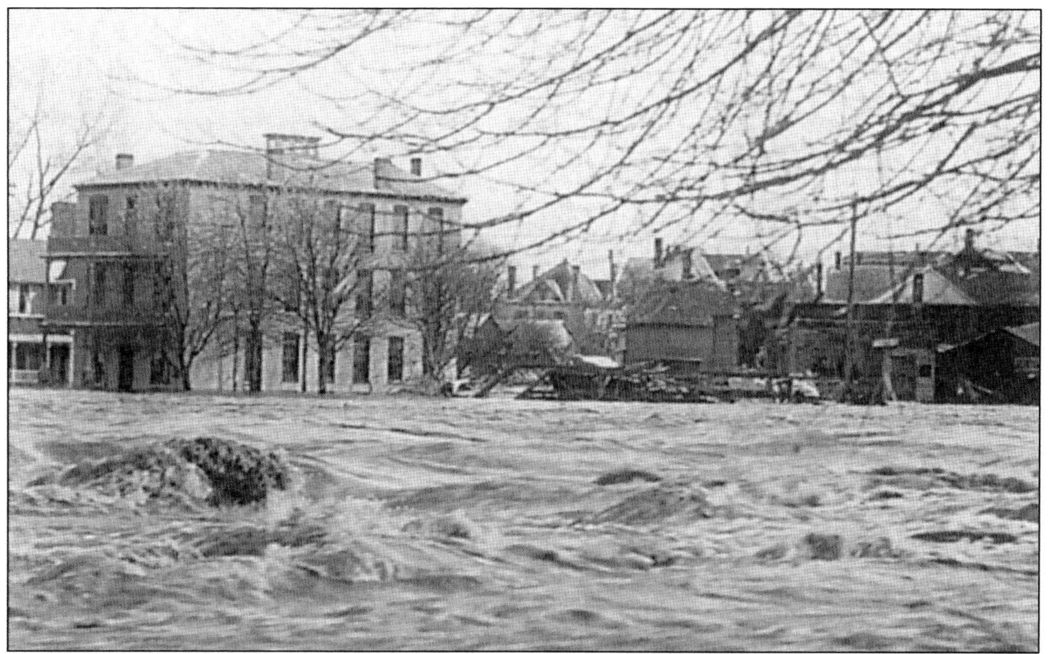

One of the worst areas of flooding was where Rock Creek flowed into the Sandusky River just east of Washington Street. In this photograph, the water surges past the Van Nette apartment complex (a landmark that appears in many of the pictures), which survived the flood and still exists today. (Courtesy of the Seneca County Museum.)

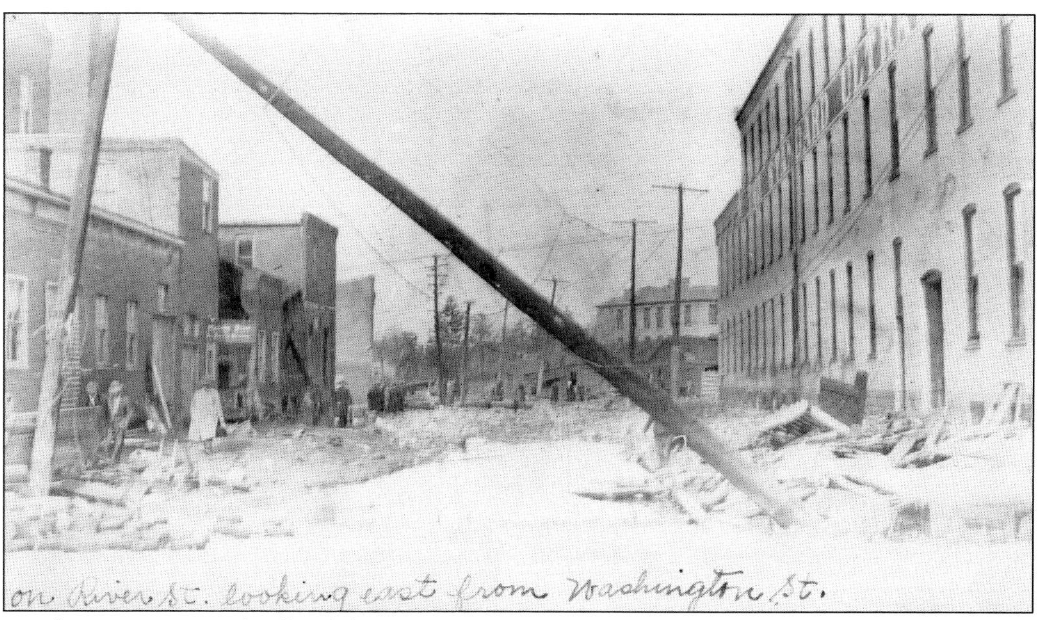

People are surveying the flood damage on River Street in this photograph with a view looking east from Washington Street. The Van Nette building is in the distance beyond the commercial blocks at right. (Courtesy of the Seneca County Museum.)

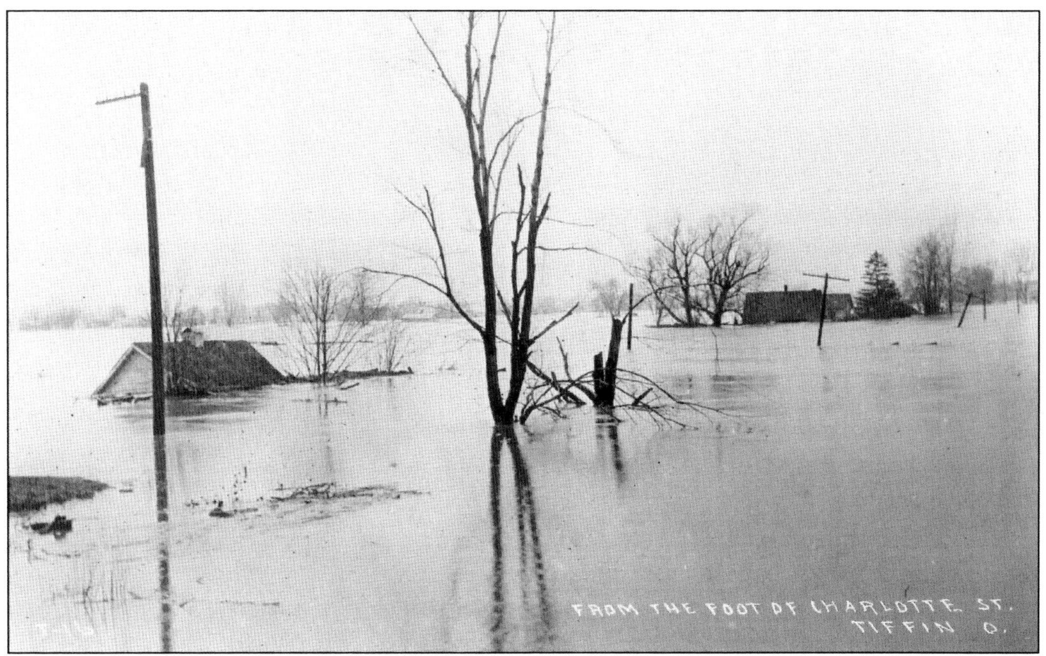

Mechanicsburg, southwest of downtown near the river, was one of the most devastated areas in the city. Only rooftops of houses appear along the river in this photograph taken by a dauntless shutterbug. The depth of the water is apparent by its height compared to the utility poles along Charlotte Street. (Courtesy of the Seneca County Museum.)

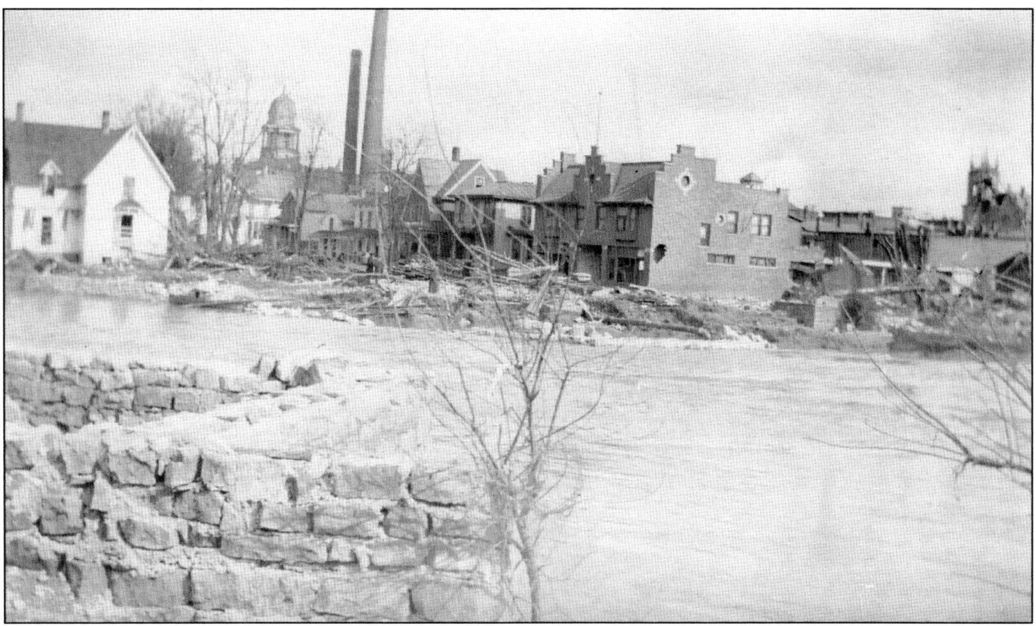

Another landmark in the flood was the Standard Garage on West Perry Street at the east bank of the river. Its distinctive shape and crenulated roofline appear in the center of the photograph, along with the courthouse dome toward the left and the tower of St. Paul's Methodist Episcopal Church on Madison Street at far right. The Perry Street Bridge had already washed away when this photograph was captured. (Courtesy of the Seneca County Museum.)

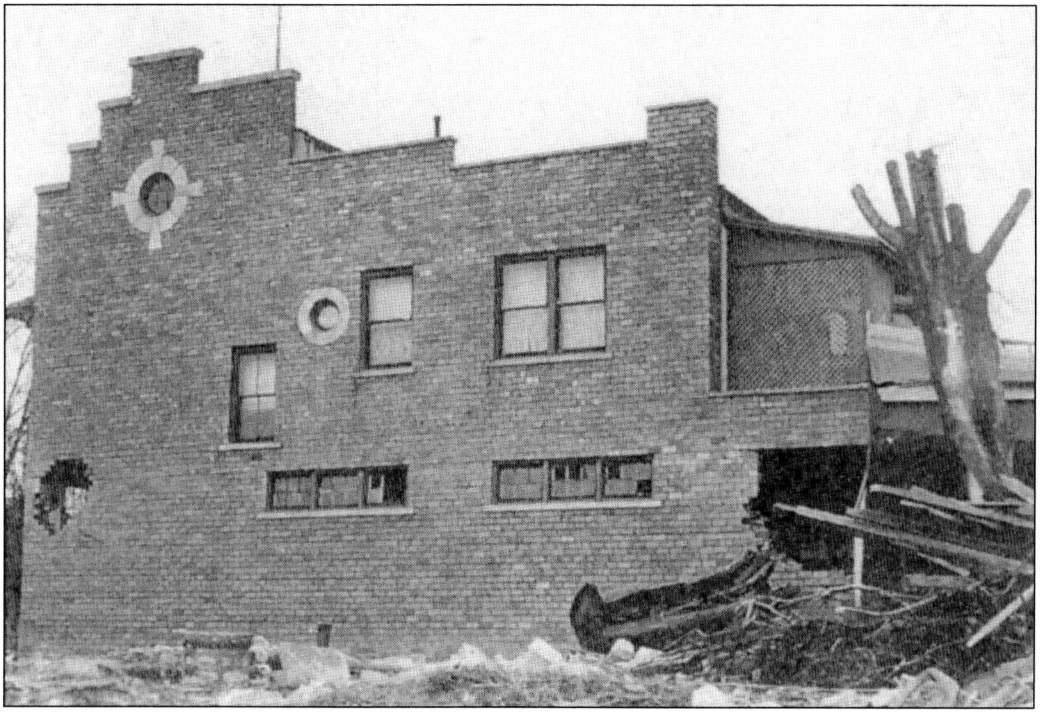

This close-up view is of the Standard Garage after the flood. Damage to the brickwork was caused by debris rushing downriver. (Courtesy of the Seneca County Museum.)

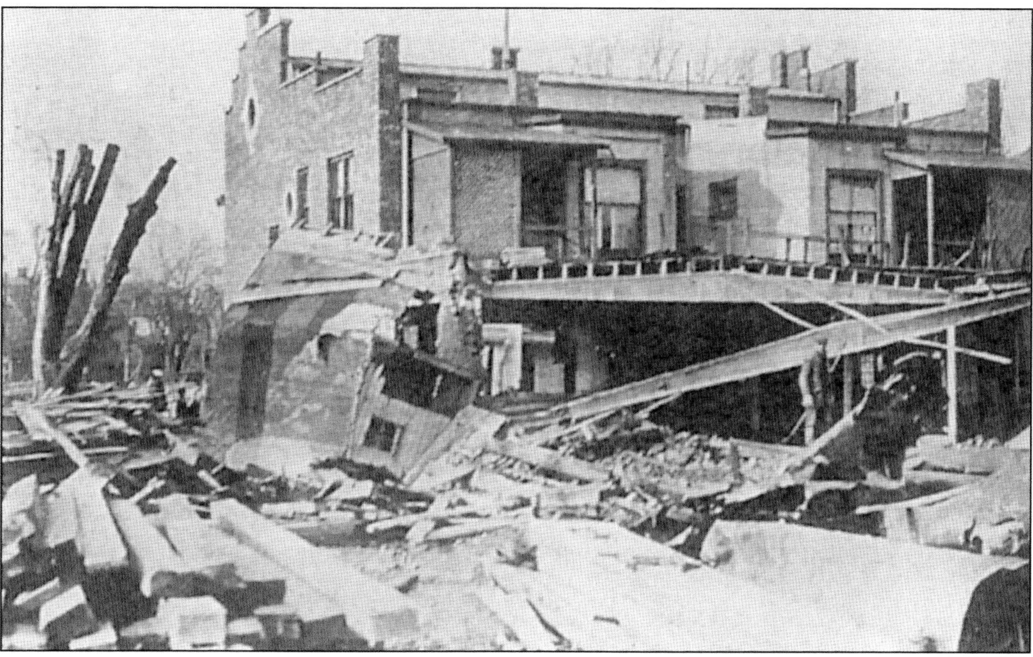

Another photograph of the Standard Garage shows how much wreckage was pushed against the back of the building. However, the sturdy old garage still anchors the east end of the Perry Street Bridge today. It had a large addition in the back, where a man is seen standing among the rubble. (Courtesy of the Seneca County Museum.)

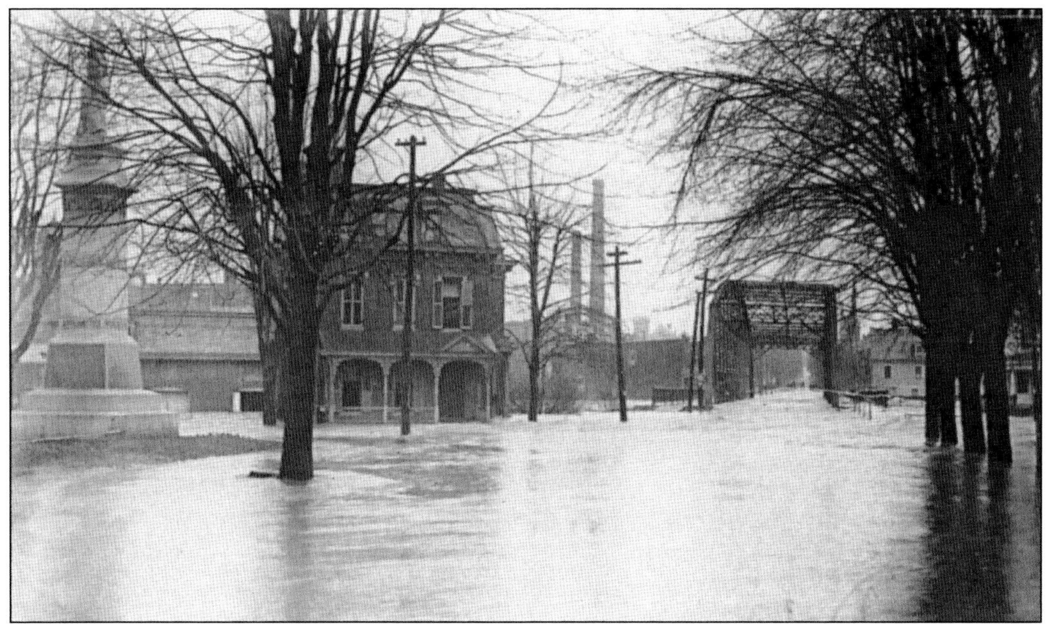

Water rose around the Soldiers and Sailors Monument at left on Monroe Street in this view looking south toward the bridge. It would not long outlast this photograph, and the Monroe Street Bridge was the only bridge not replaced after the flood. The Second Empire house in this photograph belonged to William Harvey Gibson, a famous Civil War general and orator, whose statue still graces the empty courthouse square on the northeast corner of Washington and Market Streets. (Courtesy of the Seneca County Museum.)

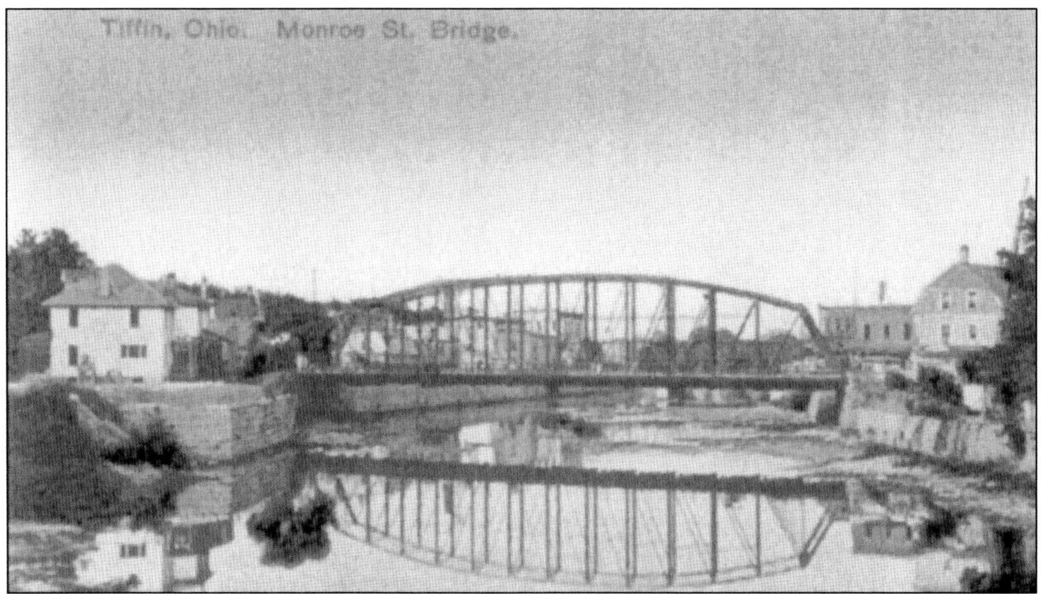

This photograph of the still-tranquil river was taken in 1908 and shows the Monroe Street Bridge with the Washington Street Bridge behind it. Pictured during shallow water, the low stone walls along the banks offered little protection against the surging floodwaters of 1913. The house at left was the home of the Axline family, whose members lost their lives when it was torn from its foundations by the flood.

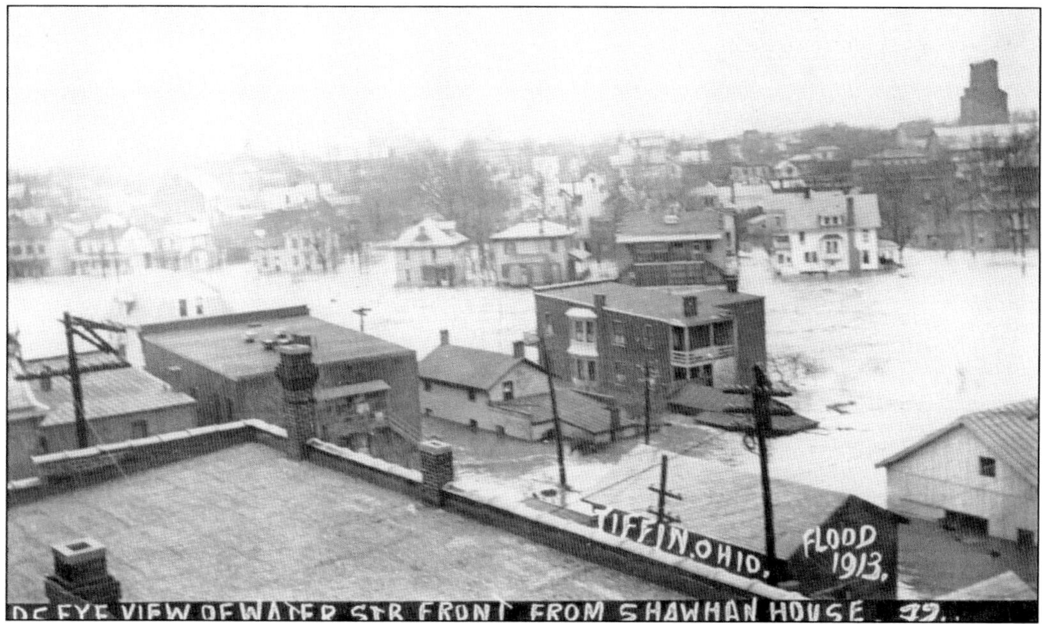

This view looks northwest across the rising river from the roof of the downtown Shawhan Hotel on the corner of Washington and Perry Streets. The Axline home was at left of the houses in the foreground across the river. The husband and wife were warned to leave. The Calhouns next door did evacuate, but Addline Axline refused—a decision that would prove fatal. (Courtesy of the Seneca County Museum.)

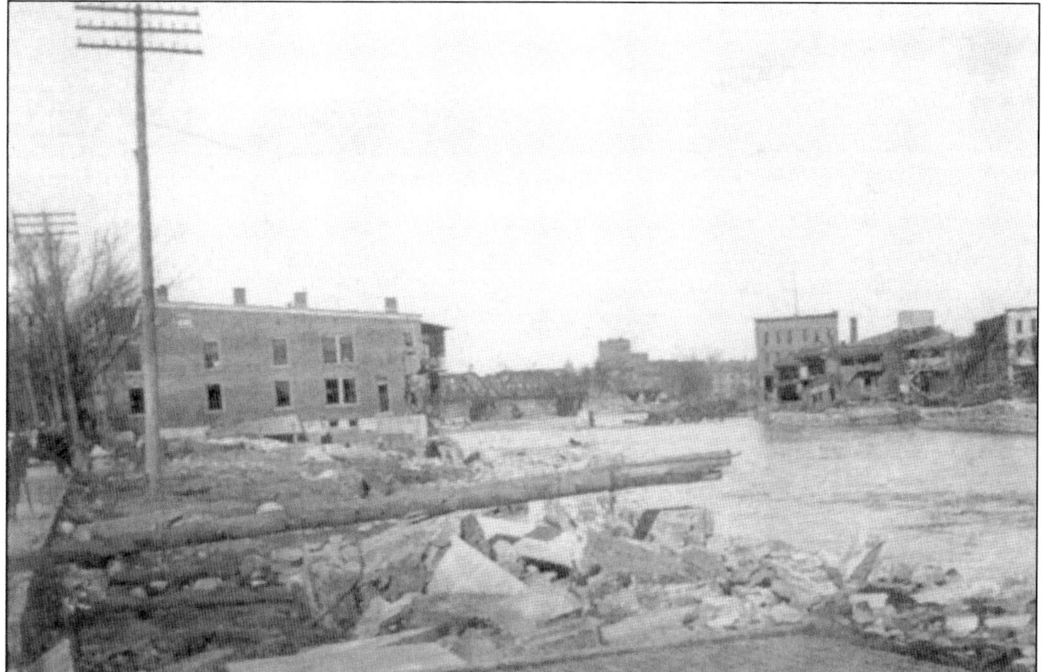

The foundations of the Axline and Calhoun homes appear in the foreground of this photograph during the aftermath of the flood. At left, people walk on Water Street (now Frost Parkway), and the surviving railroad bridge is visible in the distance. (Courtesy of the Seneca County Museum.)

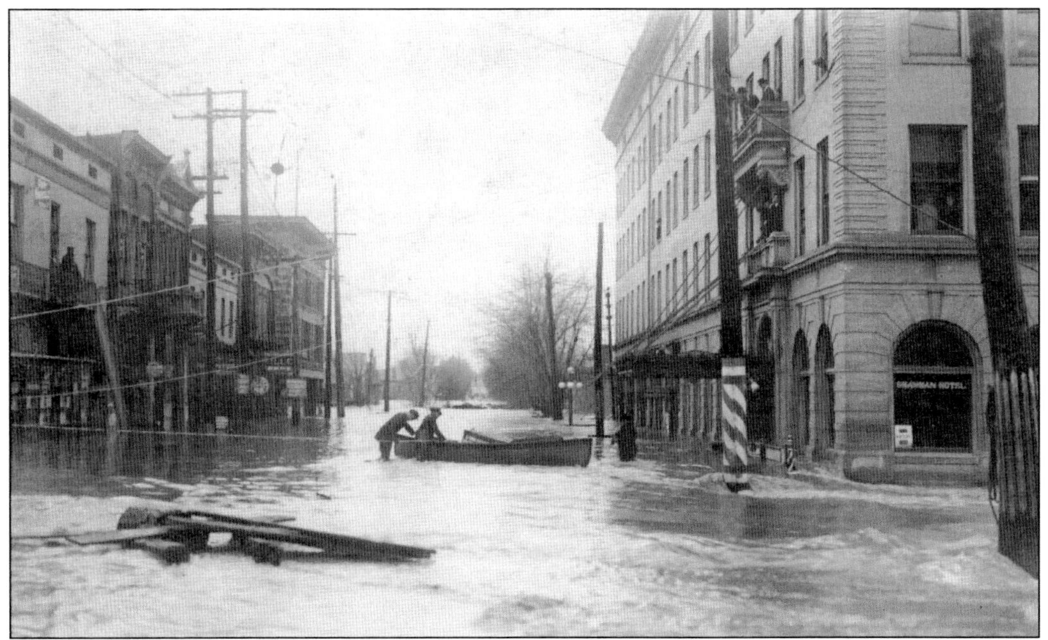

A rescue boat floats in front of the Shawhan Hotel in this view looking west across Washington Street from Perry Street. The water is nearly waist-high on the man standing in front of the boat. Many brave people risked their own lives to save others during these terrifying days. (Courtesy of the Seneca County Museum.)

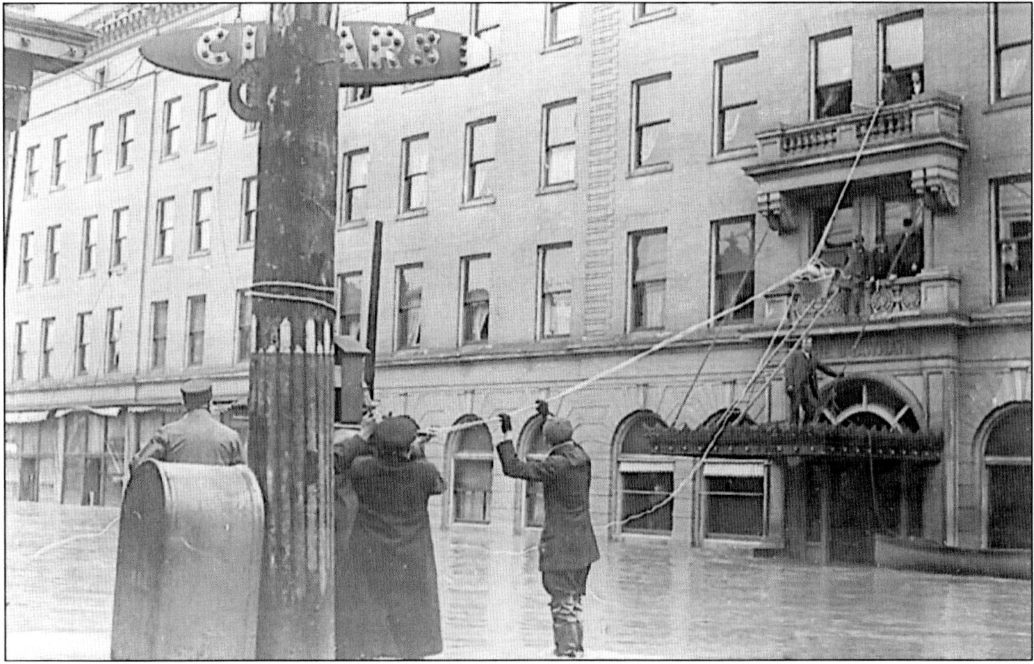

Another rescue operation at the Shawhan Hotel is seen here, as a pulley rope is stretched across Perry Street. A man stands on the roof over the door, with a ladder propped up to the second-floor balcony. The hotel was actually one of the safest places to be during the flood. (Courtesy of the Seneca County Museum.)

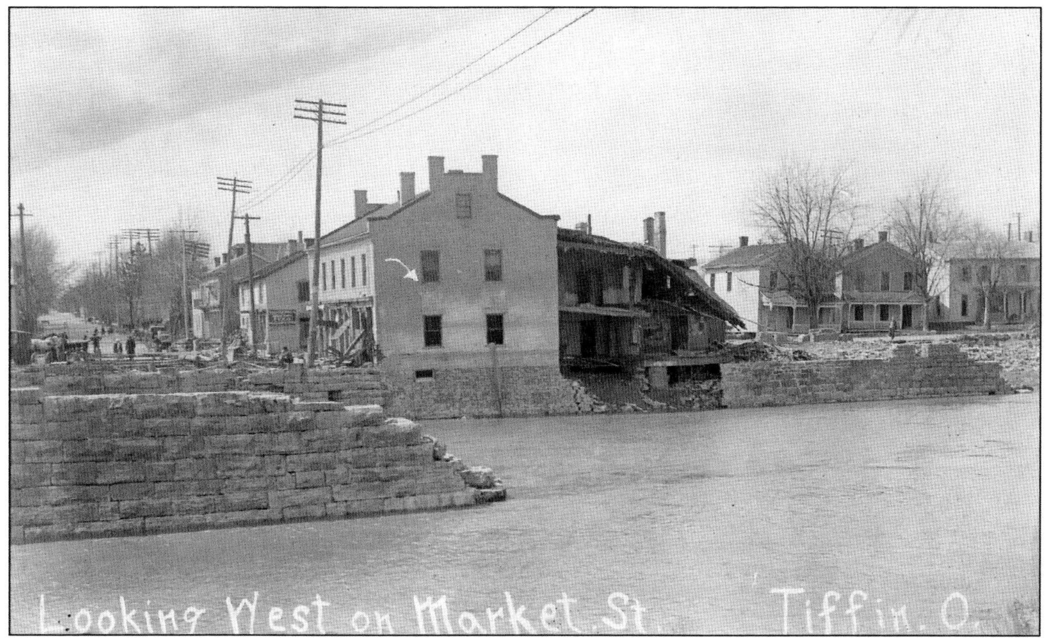

The Market Street Bridge is long gone in this view looking west across the river, as people venture out on Market Street after the water has subsided. The tree in front of a house across the river helped a family escape from the second floor during the height of the flood. (Courtesy of the Seneca County Museum.)

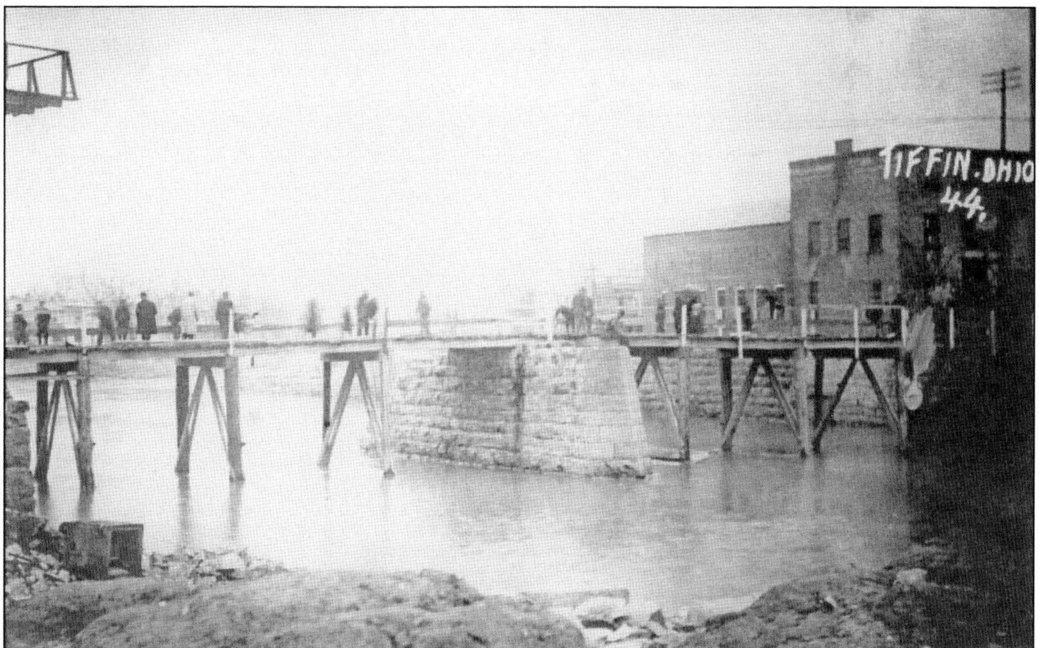

Using the stone pier, spared in the center of the river, a temporary Market Street footbridge was built with private local donations, which provided a sign of hope for the devastated city. Though it appears to still be raining, many people are out on the bridge. (Courtesy of the Seneca County Museum.)

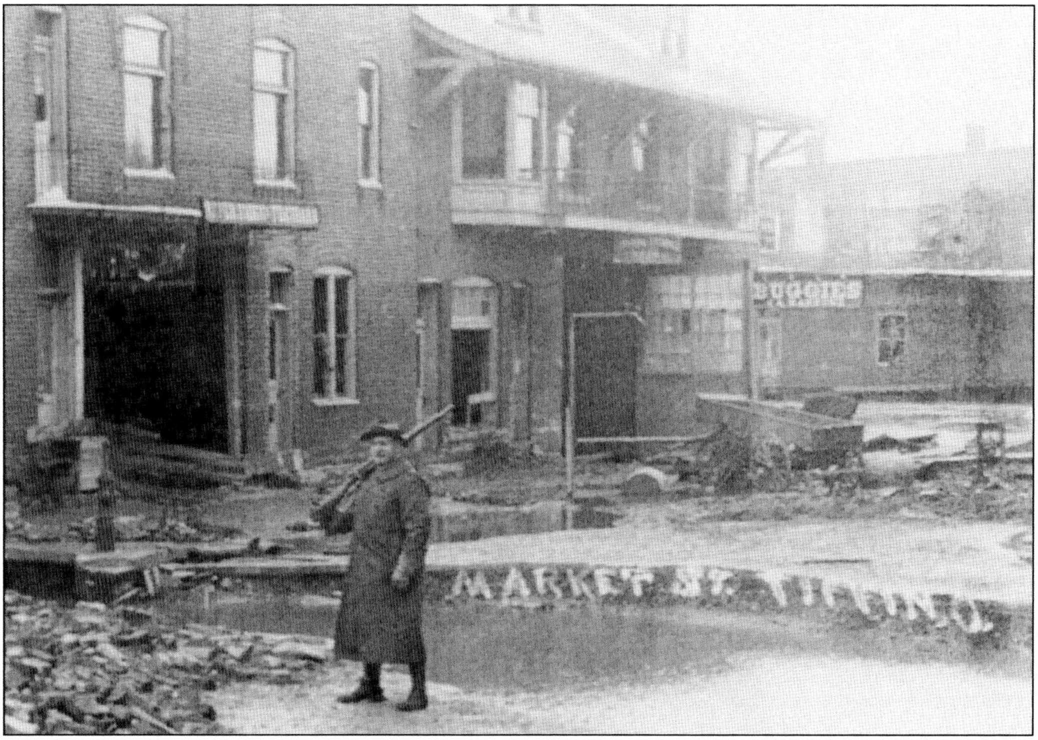

The city found it necessary to post guards to protect property owners from looters. This armed man stands on Market Street near the bridge. (Courtesy of Blair and Nellie Alsip.)

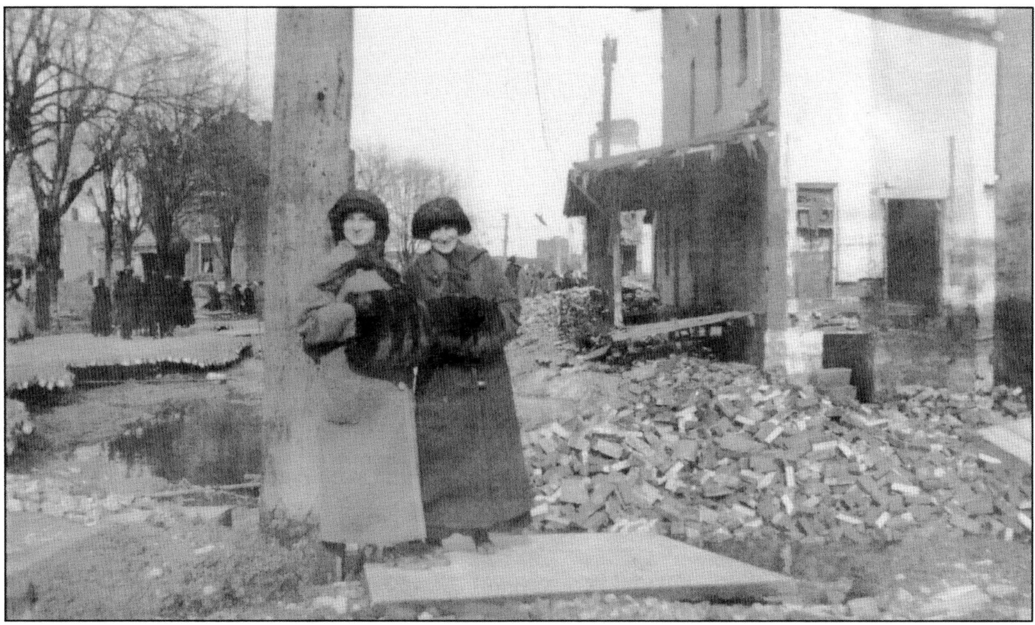

People were thankful just to be alive after the flood, and they can be seen congregating all around town amid the rubble, such as these two ladies with their muffs, who pose for the camera on Water Street. The Bacon Mill is to the right, and the Noble house is behind the pole at left. (Courtesy of the Seneca County Museum.)

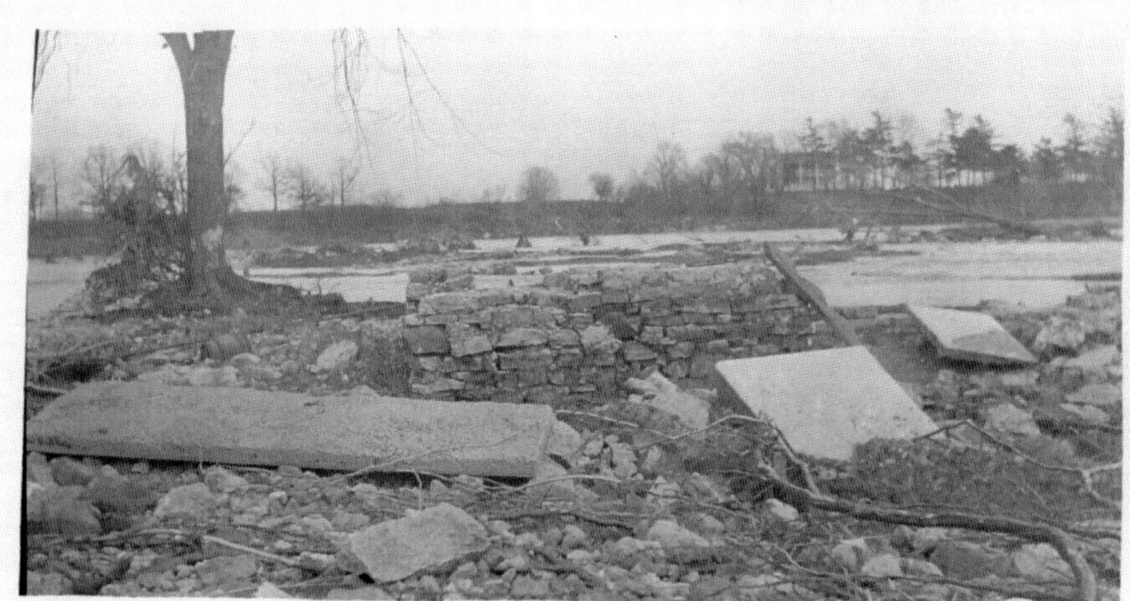

Pictured are the foundations of the Klingshirn and Knecht houses near the river at the end of East Davis Street. Eleven members of those two families were carried to their deaths by the torrents of water. (Courtesy of the Seneca County Museum.)

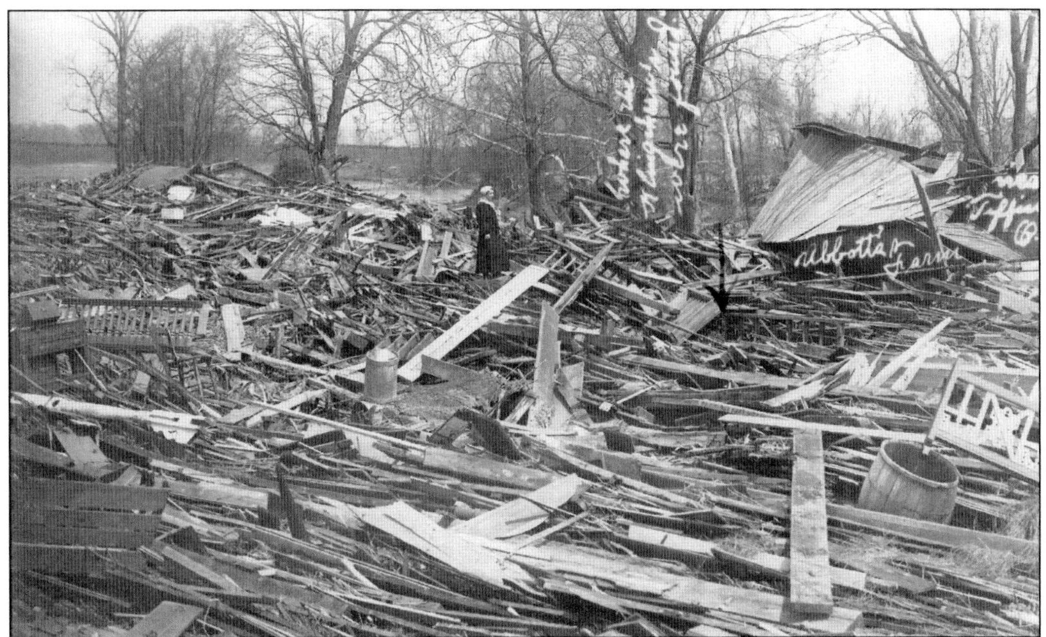

Bodies of many of the flood victims were found amid this wreckage, which was carried about six miles downstream to Abbott's Island in the middle of the Sandusky River. This sad photograph shows a searcher standing among the debris. Railings, a barrel, and a dresser can be seen among the wreckage. (Courtesy of the Seneca County Museum.)

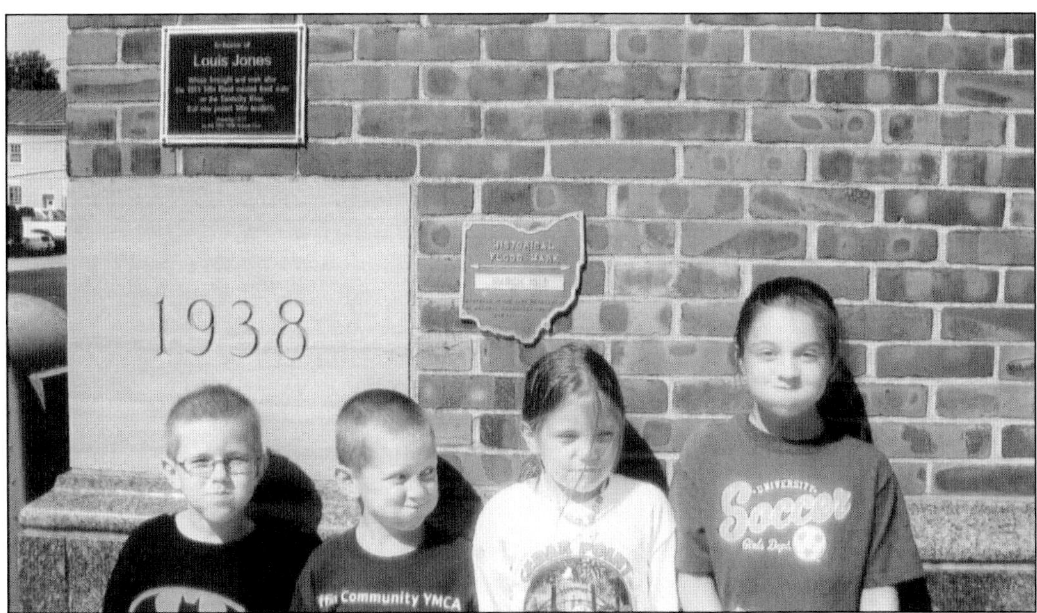

On a historical walking tour over 100 years after the flood, these children pose holding their breath by the high-water marker on the municipal building. Even several blocks from the river, the water would have been over the children's heads. The plaque honors Louis Jones, who performed remarkably erecting the flood barriers that still protect the city of Tiffin.

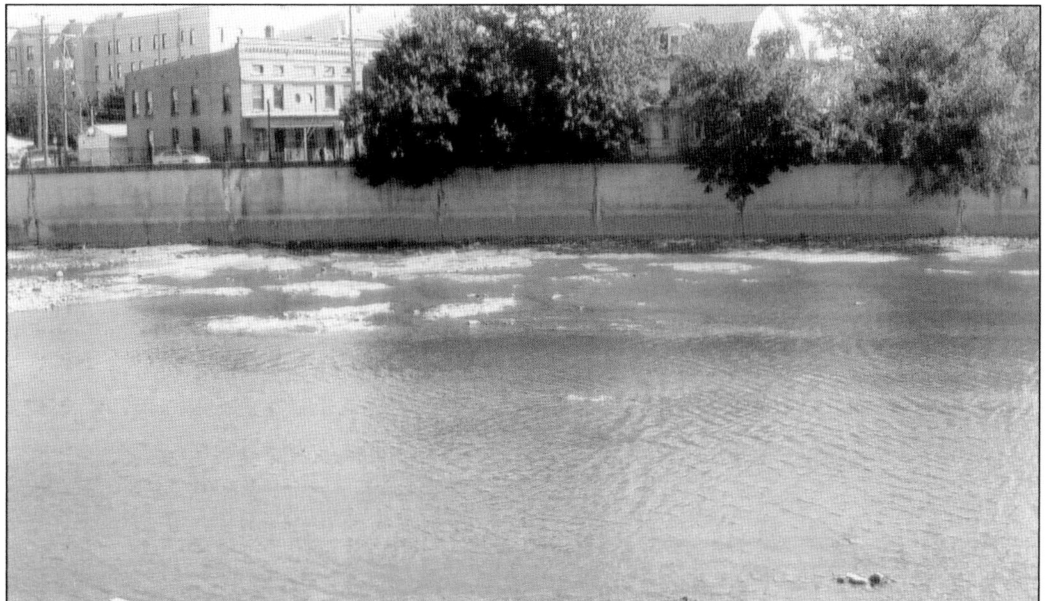

At low tide, the foundations of the Axline house can still be seen in this more recent photograph, a chilling reminder of the 1913 flood. The Shawhan Hotel, now an assisted living facility, still appears in the upper left corner of the photograph.

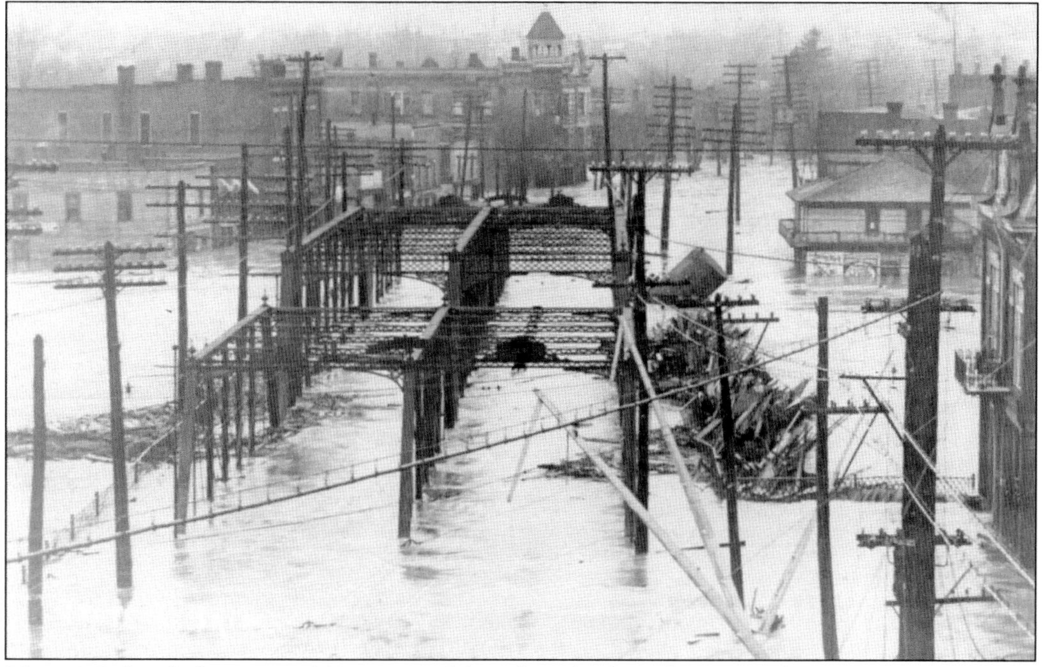

The 1913 flood also ravaged Fremont, although only three lives were lost in the devastation. This view looks east across the river and shows water above the roadbed of the iron State Street Bridge. Debris is piled against the south side of the bridge. In the distance, above the bridge, is the cupola of the Kline Block on East State Street and Sandusky Avenue, a familiar sight in other flood photographs. This bridge withstood the flood and lasted until the current concrete bridge replaced it in 1926. (Courtesy of Frank Finch.)

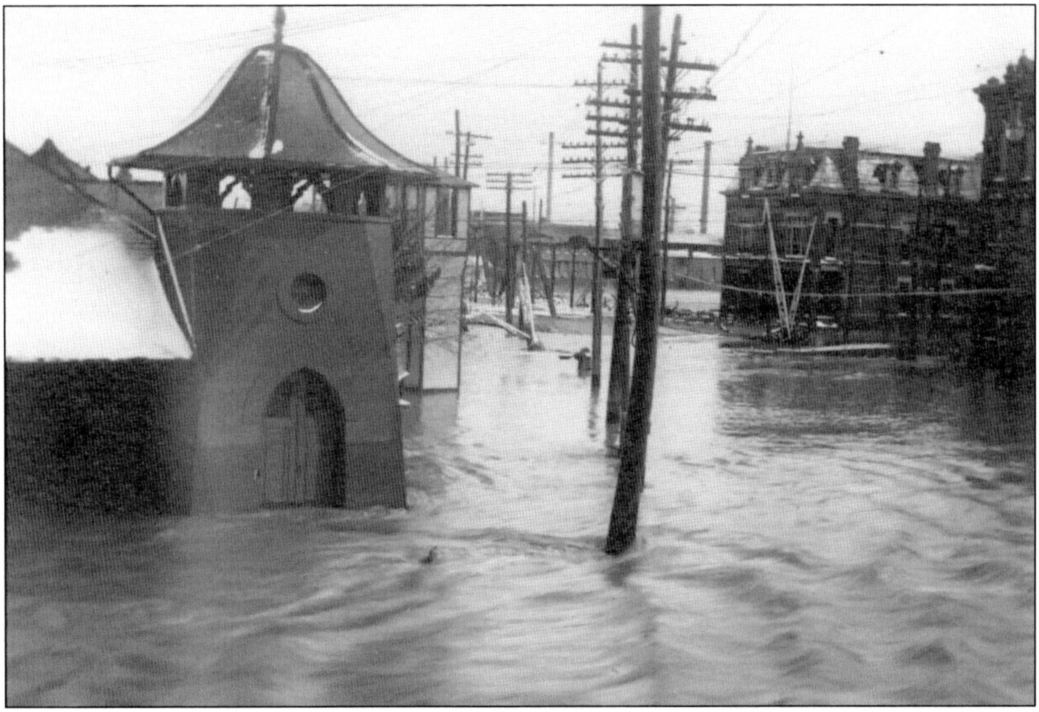

In this dramatic photograph, water has surged high above the riverbank and surrounded the pagoda-style train station on West State Street. The wooden crossing tower can be seen beyond the station; both structures survived the flood. The view is looking east toward the bridge. (Courtesy of the Seneca County Museum.)

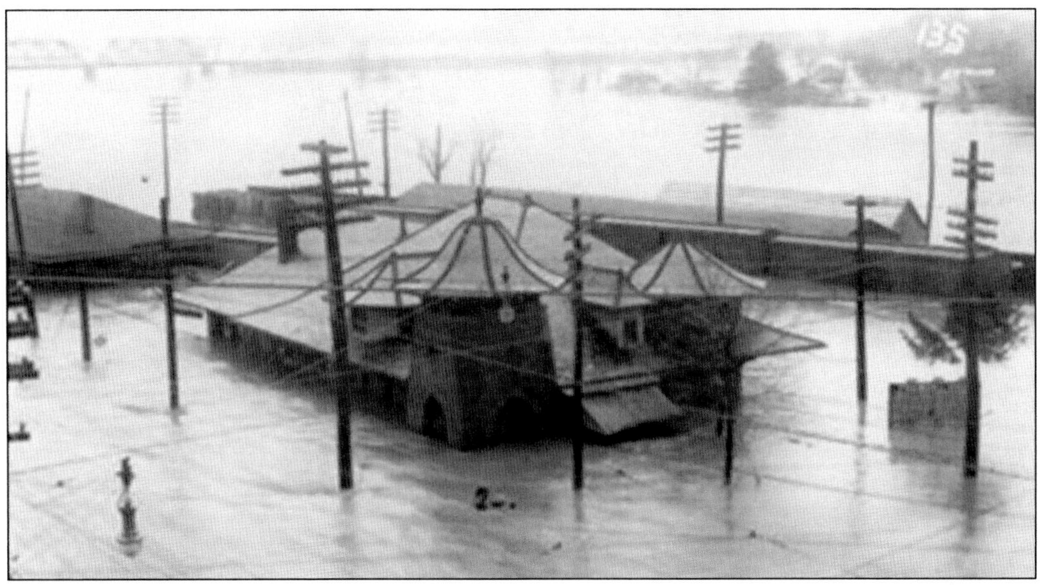

The distinctive train station is completely surrounded by water, high up on its walls in this view looking northeast toward the river. At the top of the photograph are the trestle bridge and the railroad spur across a flooded Brady's Island.

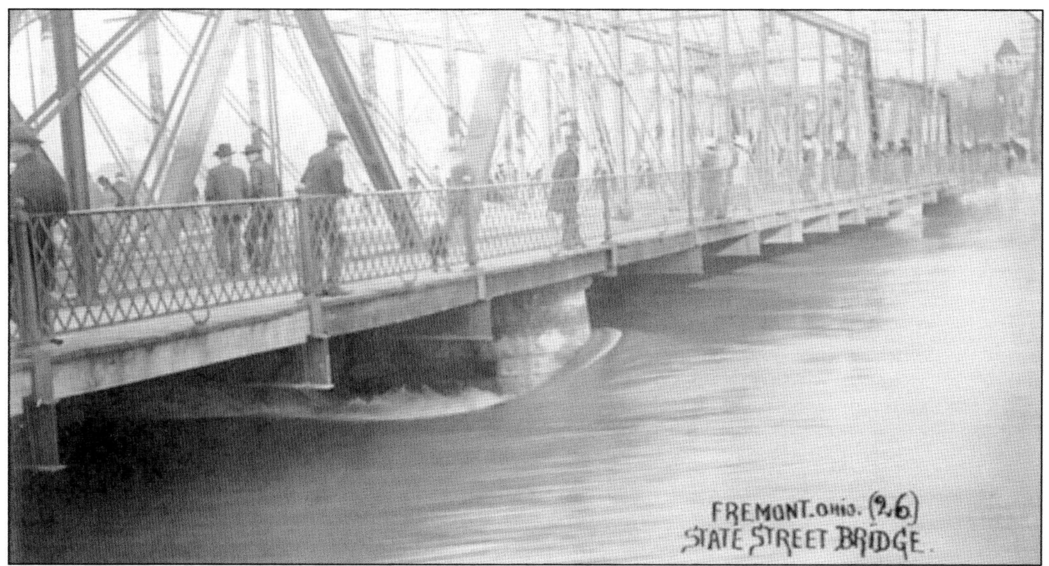

Spectators have ventured out onto the bridge in this photograph, as the water is still rising and flowing freely with no debris yet accumulated against the sides of the span. The view looks east, and the Kline Block again appears in the upper right corner. (Courtesy of Ernst Niebergall.)

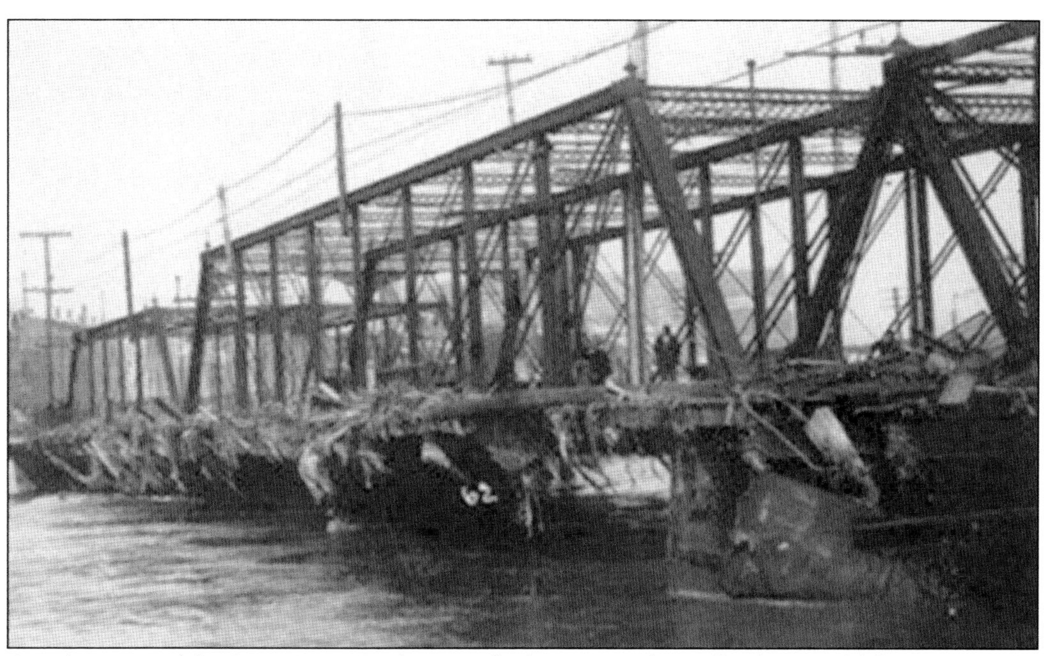

Another view of the State Street Bridge, now looking west, shows flood-carried debris against the south side of the bridge, with fewer curious people on it. (Courtesy of Frank Finch.)

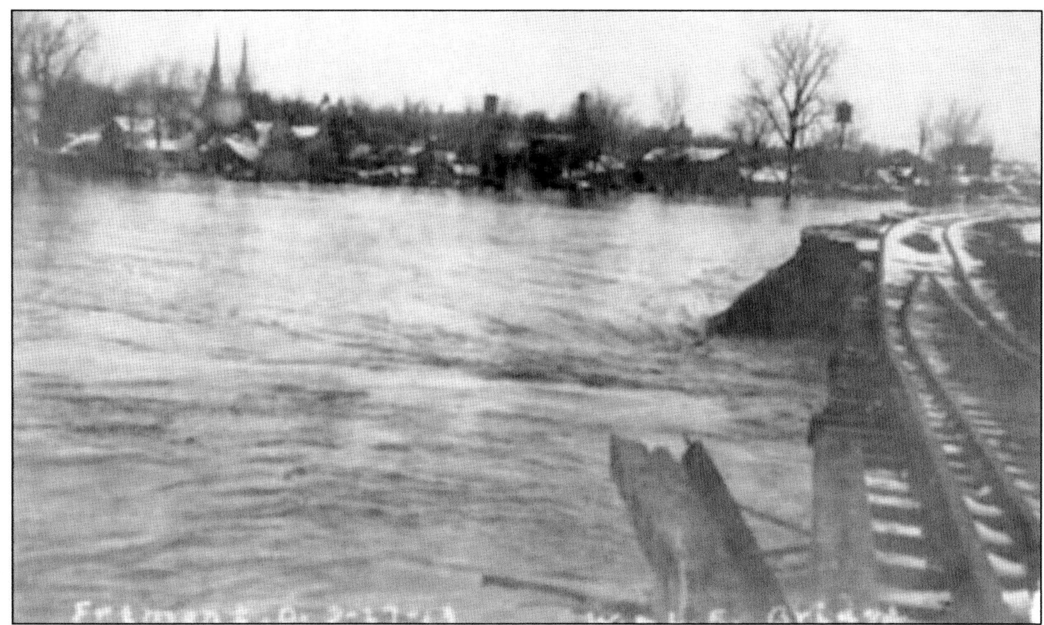

A courageous photographer ventured out to take this picture of floodwaters that have surged over damaged railroad tracks in the foreground. The tracks ran along the west bank of the river, and the water seen here has flooded over them. Downtown Fremont is marked by the two church steeples in the distance. Much destruction occurred in this area on the west bank south of downtown. (Courtesy of Frank Finch.)

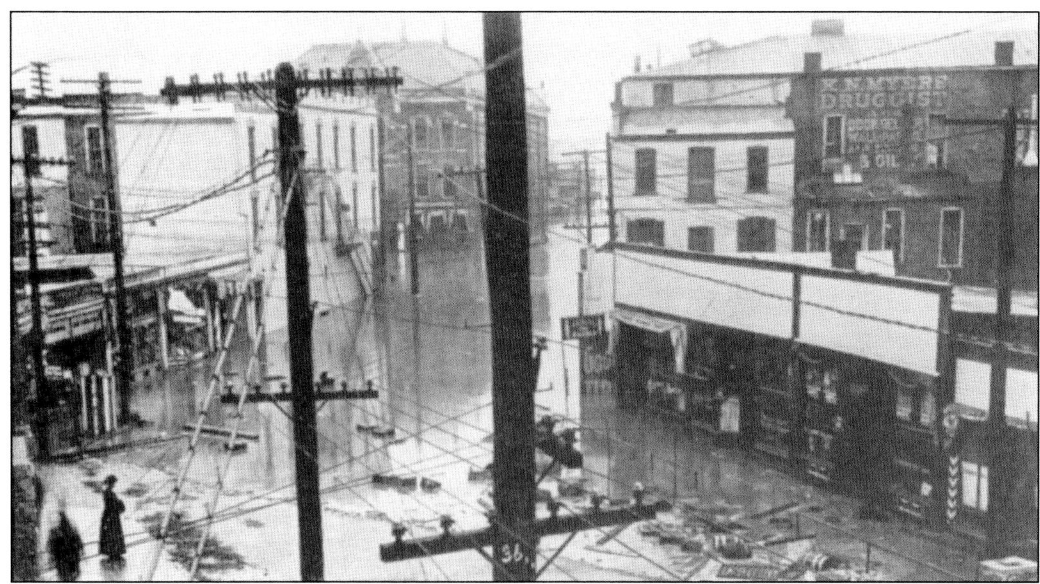

Flooding and destruction moved up the west side of the river. The view in this photograph looks north on Arch Street from Croghan Street toward West State Street after the water had receded. The Fremont Opera House stands across State Street in the center. (Courtesy of Frank Finch.)

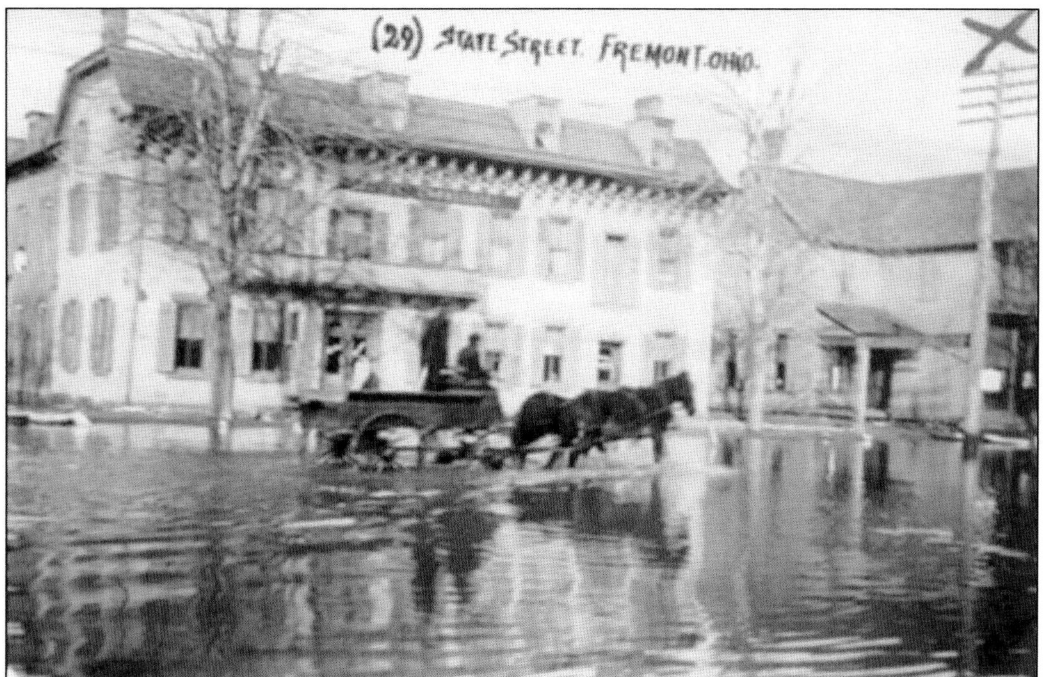

A horse-drawn wagon heads for higher ground in this photograph taken in front of the old Colonial Hotel on East State Street—one of the oldest buildings in Fremont—that probably dated back to the 1840s. The hotel survived the flood, lasting to the 1970s, and the building at right is now the Golden Dragon Chinese restaurant. (Courtesy of Ernst Niebergall.)

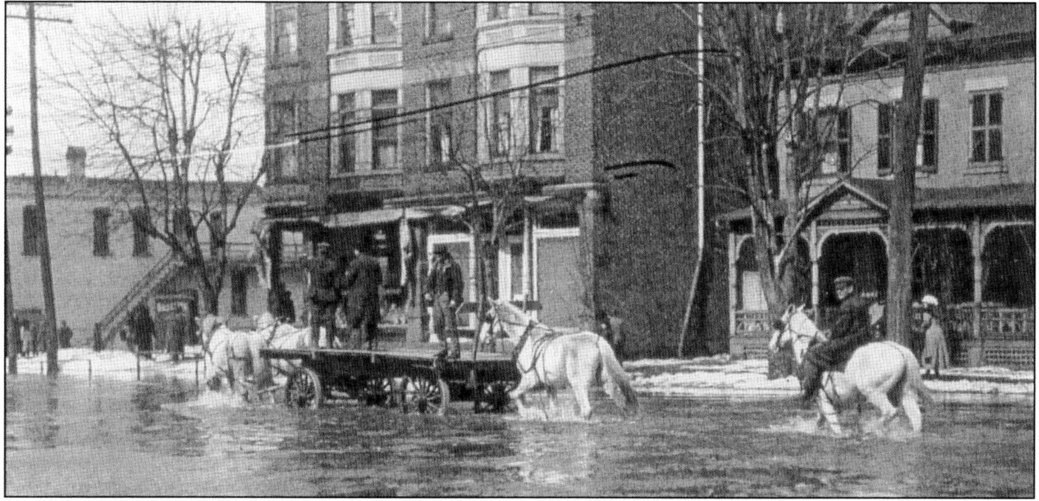

Floodwaters have traveled far up East State Street in this photograph, which captures the action of people and horses dealing with the catastrophe. Henry Kline built his commercial block on the northeast corner of East State and Sandusky Avenues in the 1890s, and his late-Victorian house is next door at right. The house is now gone, but the Kline Block remains an East State Street landmark.

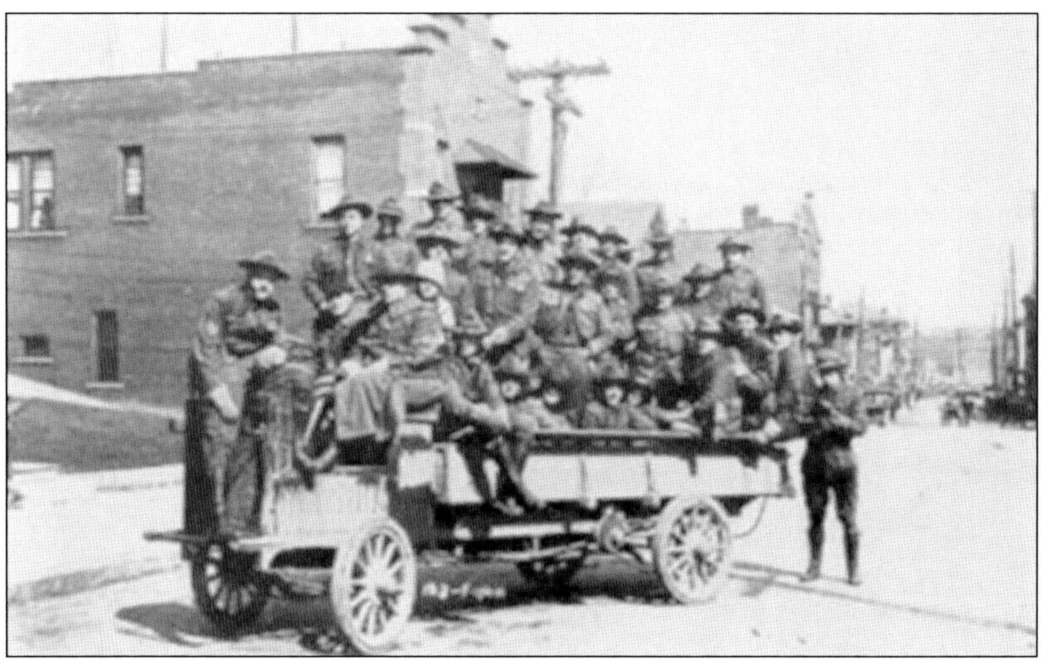

Men of Ohio Company A are crowded high on a relief truck as they pose on Croghan Street in this flood photograph. Relief troops not only helped with rescue efforts but also kept order on the streets after the flood. Frank Finch took many pictures during the worst days of the 1913 flood, and his studio was in the building behind the truck in this photograph. (Courtesy of Frank Finch.)

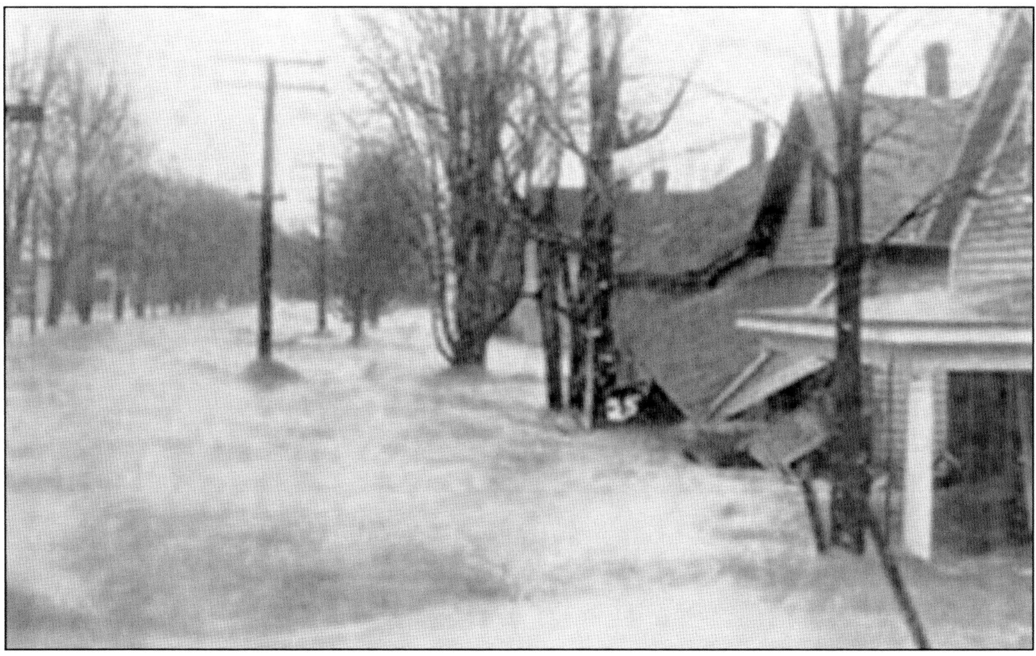

The railroad overpass at South Front and Tiffin Streets, called the dry bridge, withstood the flood but also served as a funnel that dramatically increased the flow of water through it. These three houses on South Front Street were carried away soon after this photograph was taken, and in the third house, John Homan, one of the three Fremont flood victims, lost his life.

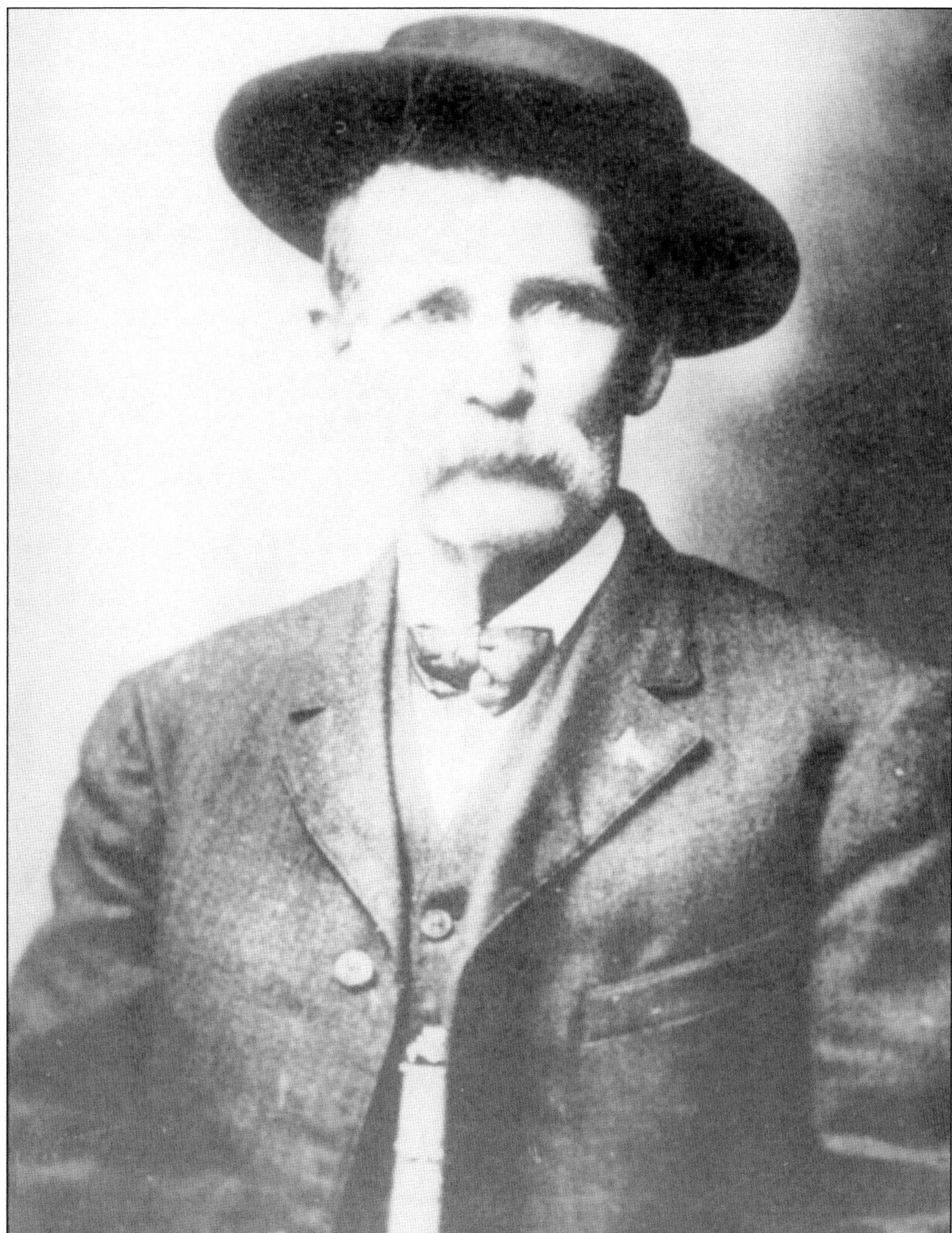

Capt. Isaac Floro came to Fremont to help with rescue operations. Tragically, he drowned on March 26, when his boat became tangled in a tree near the corner of Ohio Avenue and Howland Street. Many lives were saved by the brave volunteers who rescued people by boat or pulled them from houses that were later swept away.

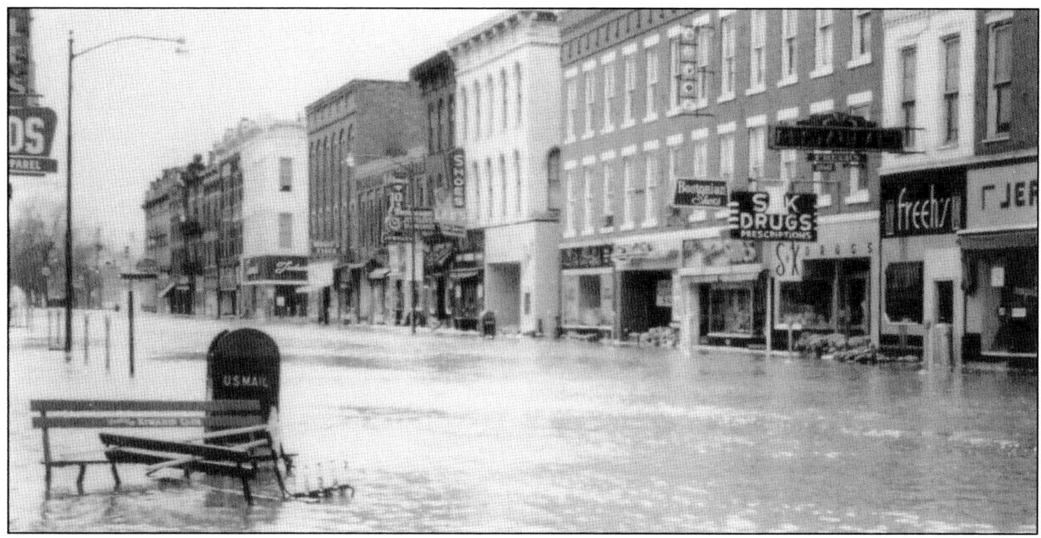

Though never as severe as the flood of 1913, many other floods occurred over the years, including an especially destructive one as early as 1883. But 1959 was the year two floods struck Fremont in one winter, which led the city to build a floodwall. The businesses on the west side of Front Street are seen in this photograph, with a view that looks south from near Croghan Street and shows sandbags piled in front of many of the stores.

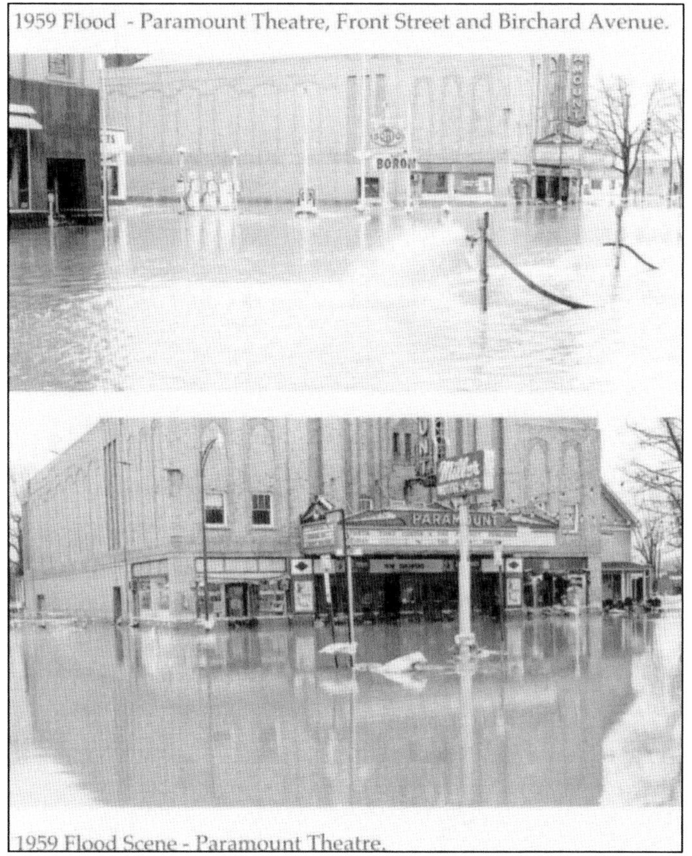

1959 Flood - Paramount Theatre, Front Street and Birchard Avenue.

1959 Flood Scene - Paramount Theatre.

The Paramount Theatre appears in both of these 1959 flood pictures but with no customers waiting to see the Tony Curtis movie. The theater, on the southeast corner of South Front Street and Birchard Avenue, was built in the early 1930s and is a fine example of Art Deco architecture. Parking meters and business signs are the only ways to tell where the curbs are. The 1959 floods were not nearly as dangerous or life-threatening as the terrible flood of 1913, but they did come at an economic cost and caused a great deal of damage for downtown merchants.

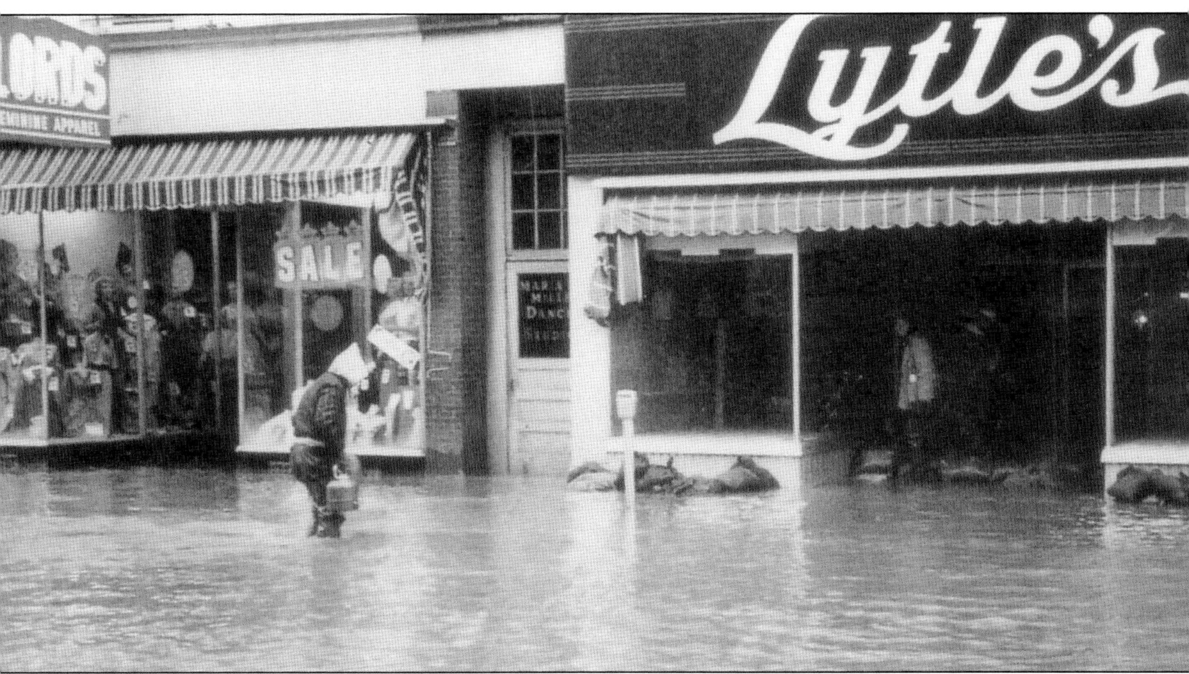

Lytle's and Lord's clothing stores in the 100 block of South Front Street also suffered much damage in 1959. Sandbags are stacked in front of Lytle's, a business on Front Street for over 100 years, while Lord's seems to only be offering items on sale.

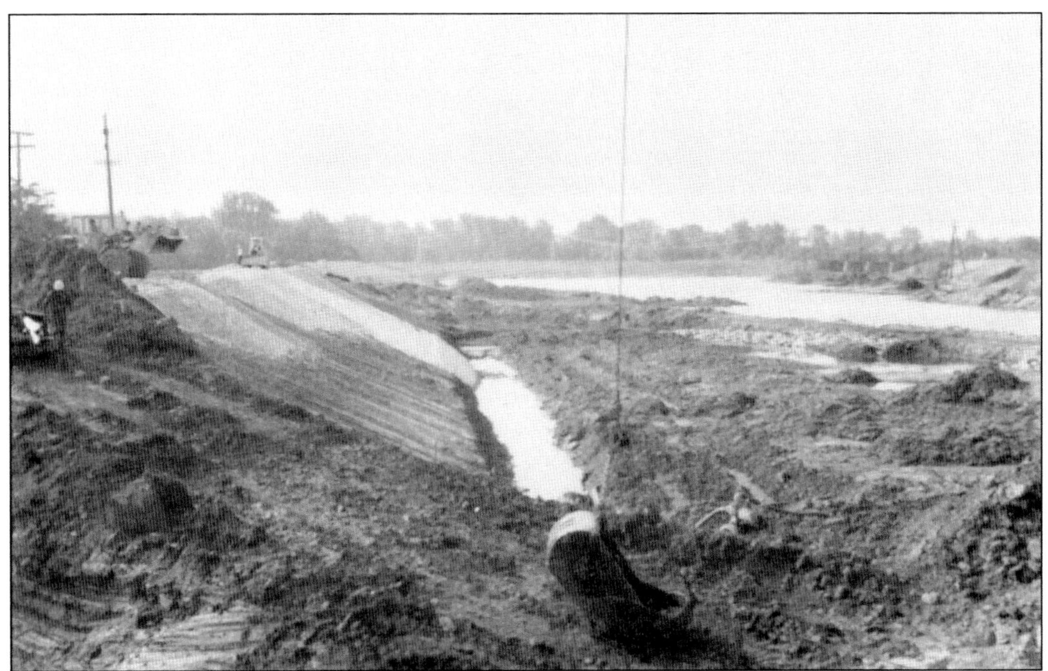

In this photograph, preparations along the riverbank are underway for the construction of the floodwall. The project was opposed by some because of the cost, but the back-to-back floods in January and February 1959 finally convinced civic leaders to begin plans for its construction. (Courtesy of Ray Grob.)

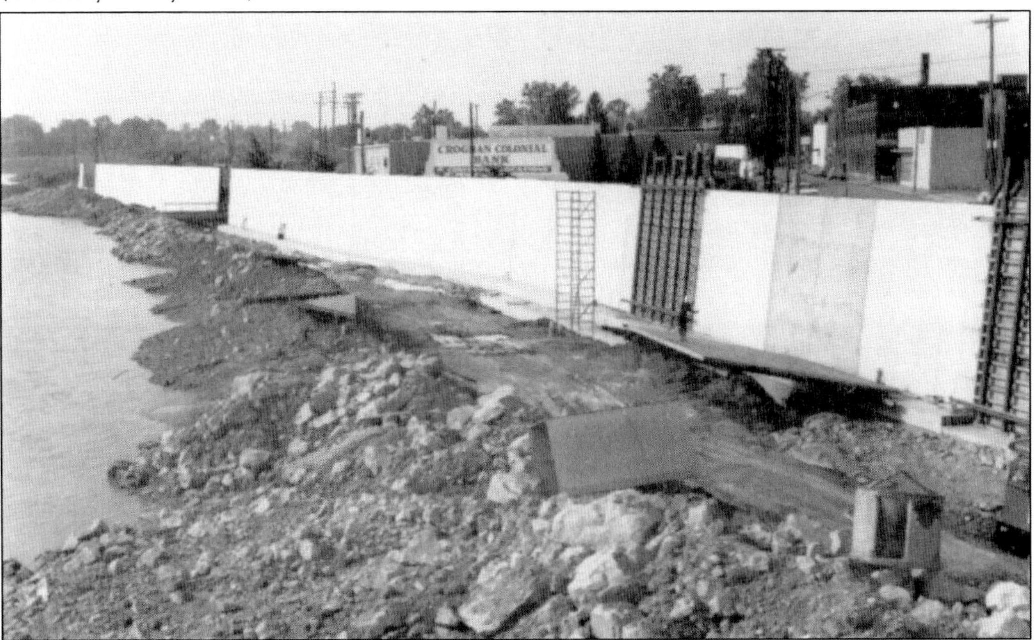

Taken about 1970, this photograph shows work on the floodwall progressing. When completed, over three miles of earthen levee had been constructed and about 3,500 feet of concrete had been laid. It has served the city well over the past 45 years, preventing much destruction that other unprotected towns have suffered. (Courtesy of Ray Grob.)

Five

History along the Shores

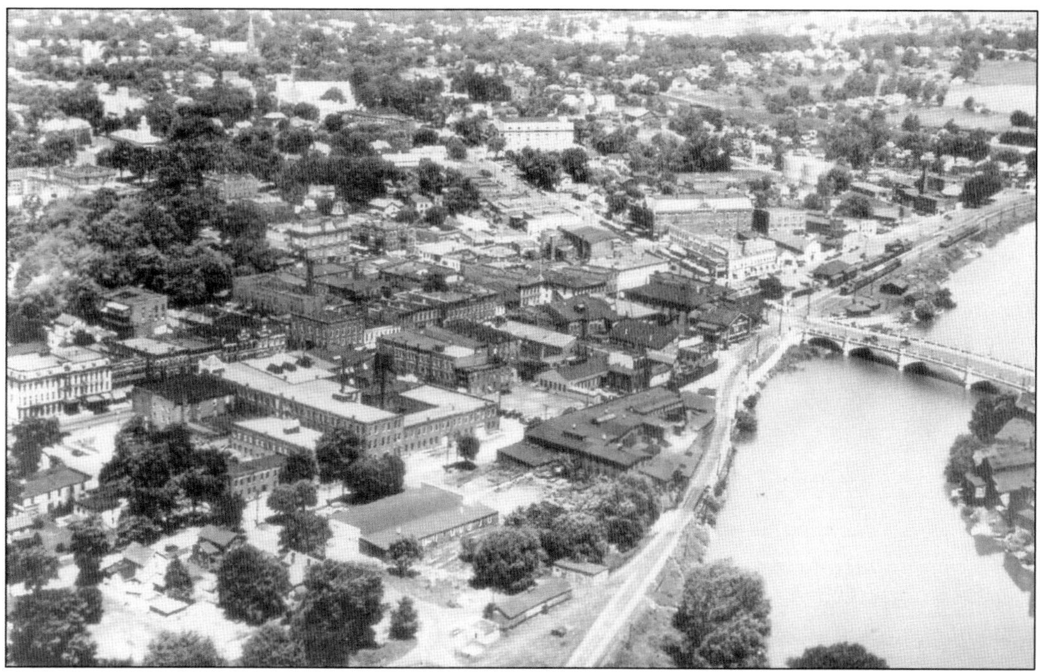

Downtown Fremont hugs the west side of the Sandusky River in this late-1920s aerial photograph, showing the importance of the river to the town's commercial development. At far left on the northeast corner of Front Street and Birchard Avenue is the Jackson Hotel, and the cluster of trees above it marks the location of Fort Stephenson.

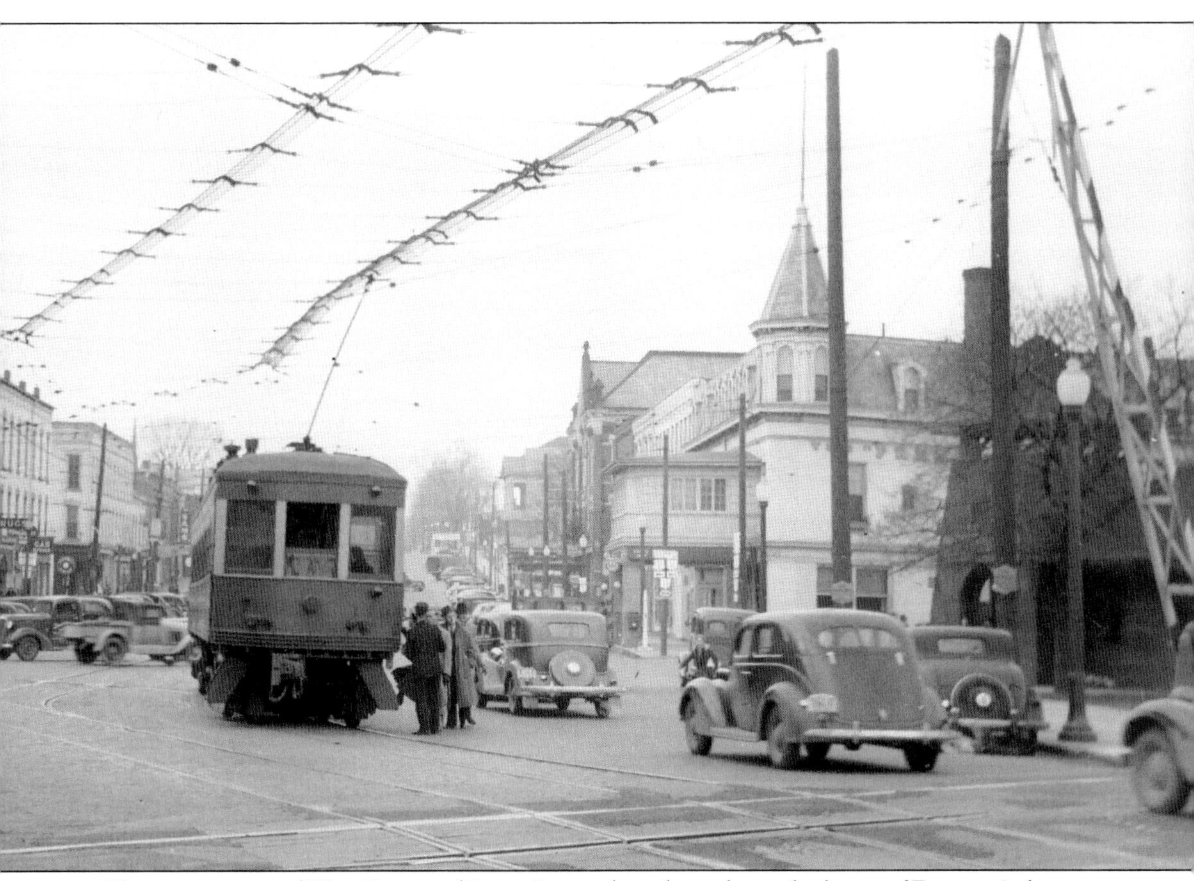

The intersection of West State and Front Streets has always been the heart of Fremont's downtown business district. This view looks west from the bridge on State Street across the tracks, and the Hotel Fremont and Fremont Opera House are on the right. Some passengers are braving heavy traffic to board Lake Shore Electric car 170, westbound for Toledo.

The river runs along the right side of this early map of Fremont dating from 1860. A number of the designated sites from over 150 years ago are still in existence today. The Maumee & Western Reserve Turnpike is now US Route 20, and the railroad line southwest of town on the map—less than 10 years old at the time—is now part of the North Coast Inland Trail.

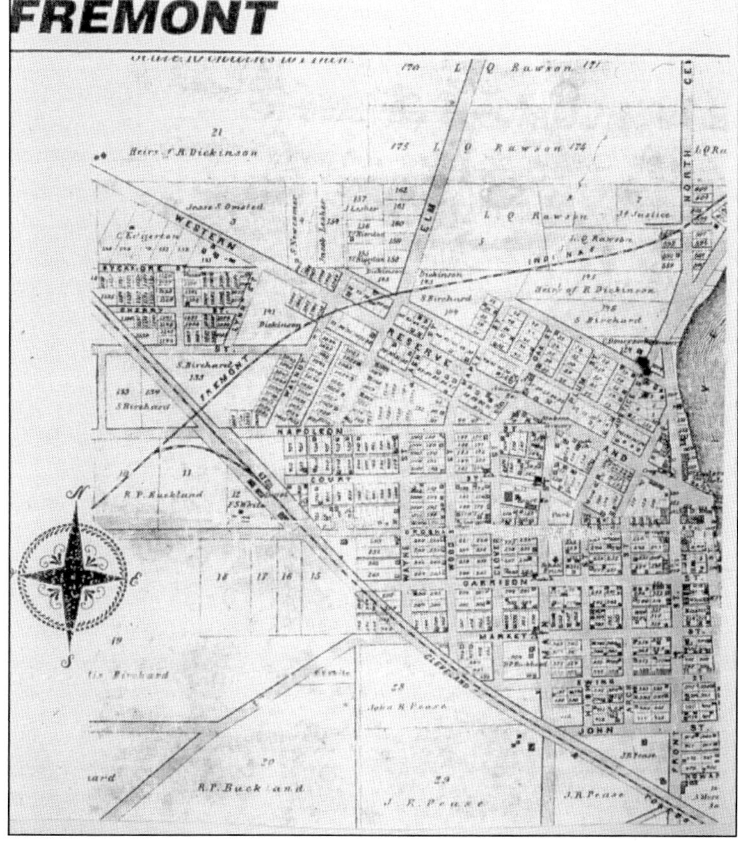

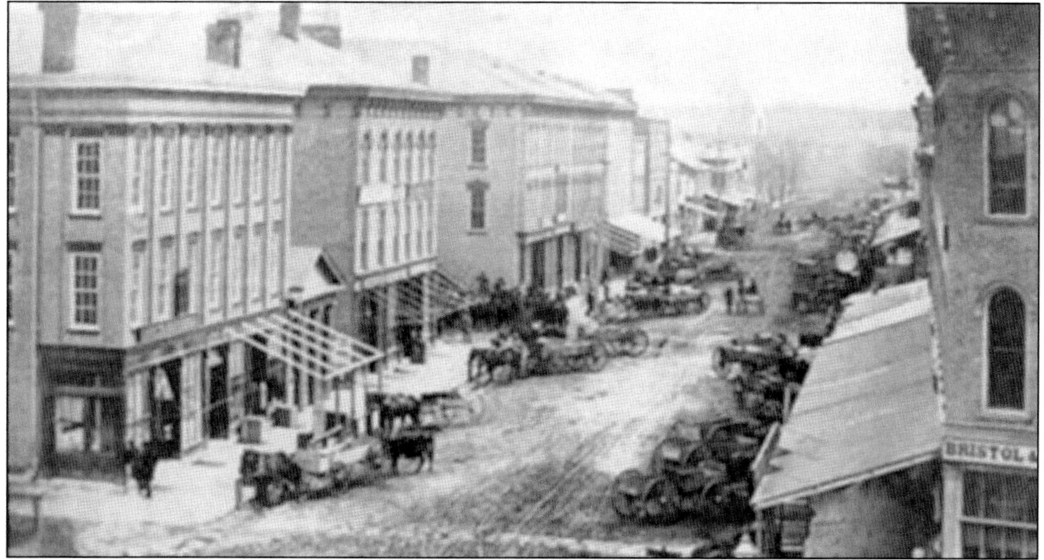

One of the oldest pictures of downtown Fremont, this photograph, taken about 1868, has a view that looks south on Front Street from the corner of West State Street. The buildings in the foreground are gone, but all those in the next block beyond Croghan Street on the east side of Front Street still remain.

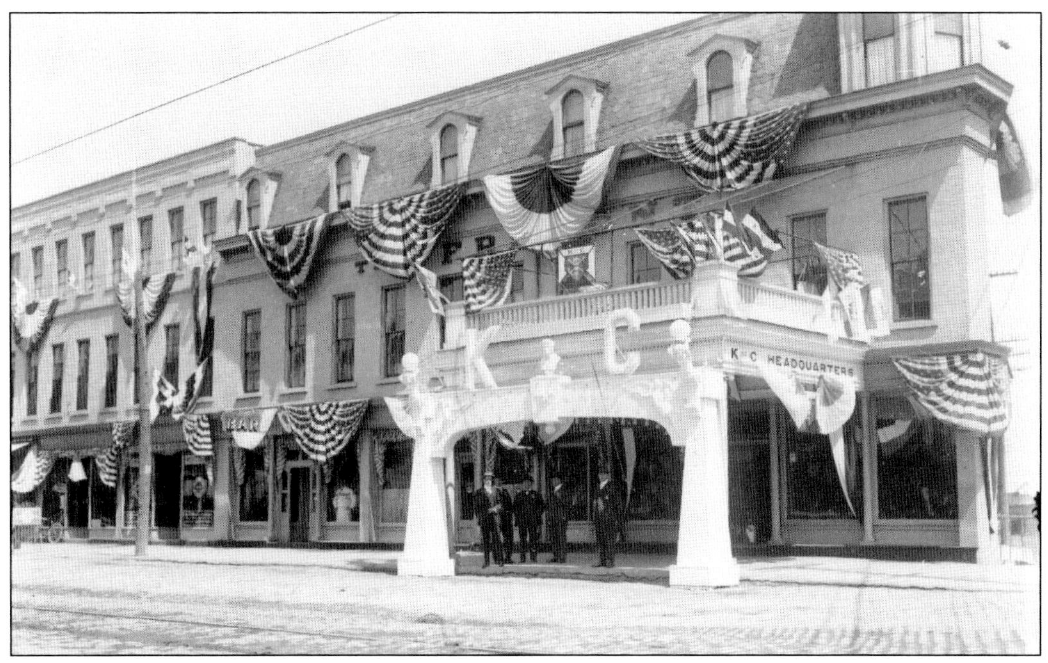

The Hotel Fremont was a landmark on the northwest corner of Front and West State Streets for over a century. It was often the first building visitors would see, as it stood in proximity to both the river and the train station. Built about 1875 on the site of an 1840s hotel called the Croghan House, the Hotel Fremont tragically burned in March 1881.

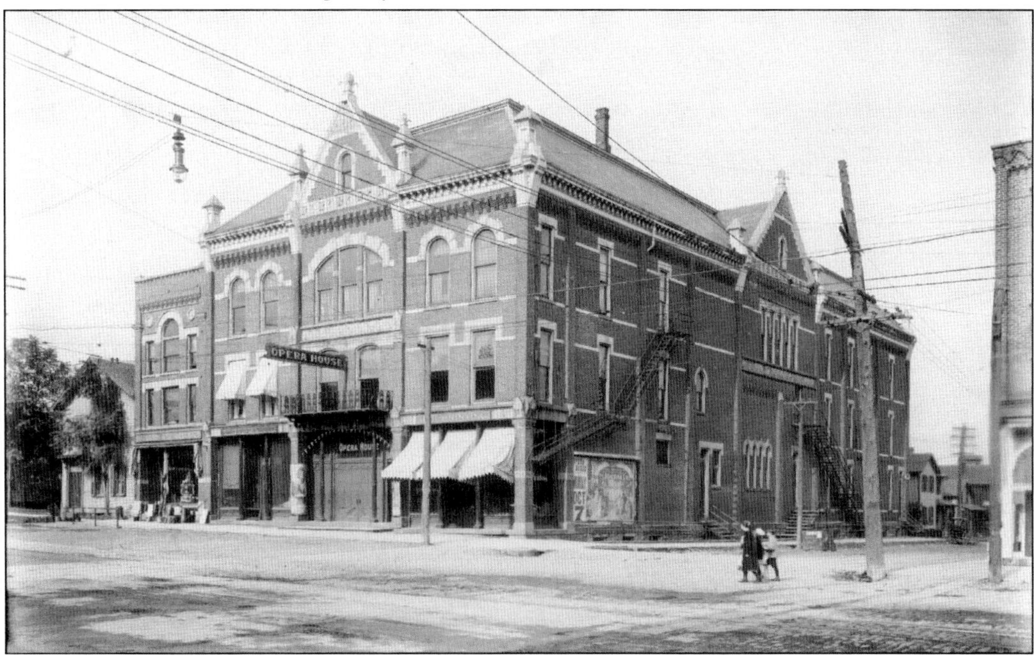

The massive Fremont Opera House is pictured on the northwest corner of West State and Arch Streets, one block west of the Hotel Fremont. It was built in 1891 and lasted until the age of television before being razed in 1958. The large auditorium was filled when top entertainers such as Buffalo Bill and Harry Houdini appeared here in the early 1900s.

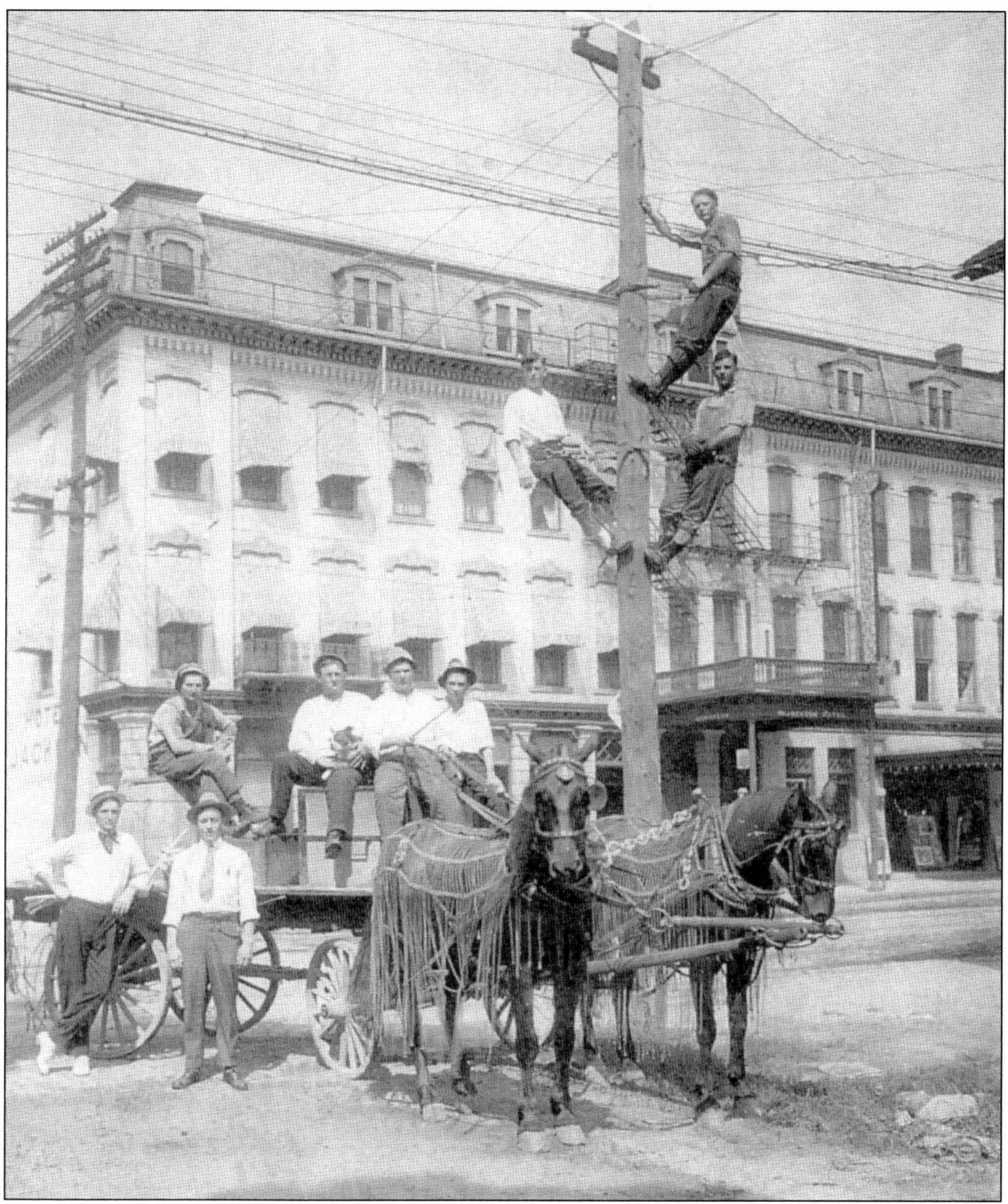

The Jackson Hotel was another impressive building that prospered in the days of large downtown hotels. It was built as the Ball House on the northwest corner of South Front Street and Birchard Avenue in 1874 and was purchased about the turn of the century by A.H. Jackson, who was at one time owner of the largest manufacturer of women's undergarments in the country. His factory on the east side of Front Street took up almost the whole city block between Birchard and Garrison Streets. In this photograph taken on August 19, 1916, it appears the men are working on the utility lines. If so, they have a lot of supervisors, and the horses are well-dressed.

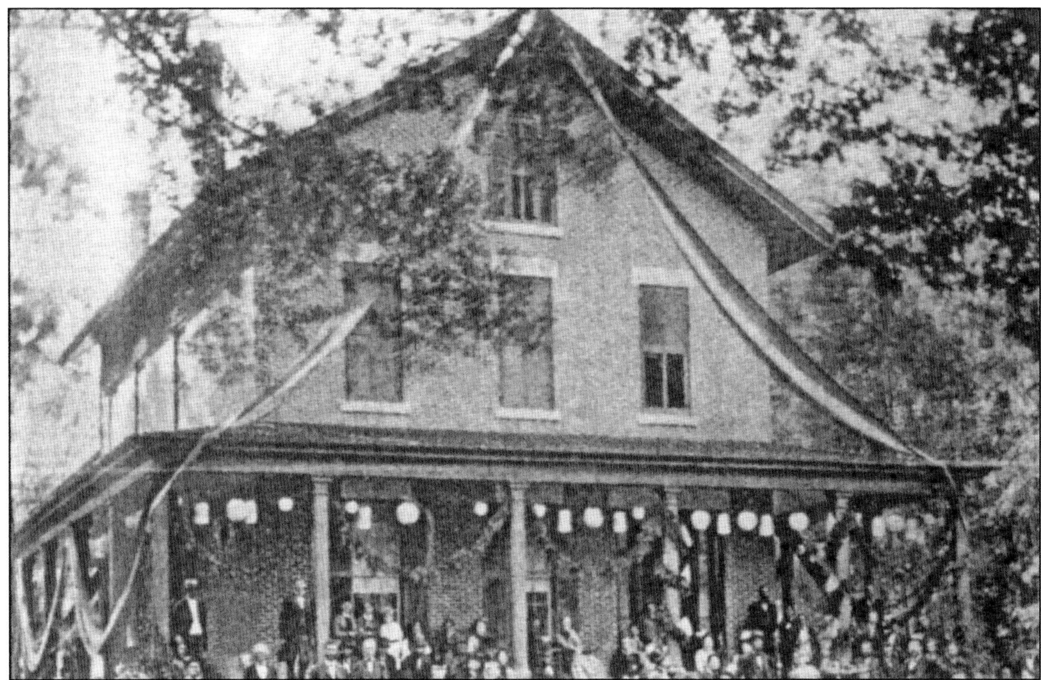

This is the earliest known photograph of the Hayes home in Spiegel Grove in Fremont. This original section was built in 1859 by Hayes's uncle Sardis Birchard, an important parental figure and mentor to Hayes who influenced him to return to Fremont in 1873. It appears that this picture was taken at a rally during the presidential campaign of 1876. Hayes would continue to live in the home until his death in 1893.

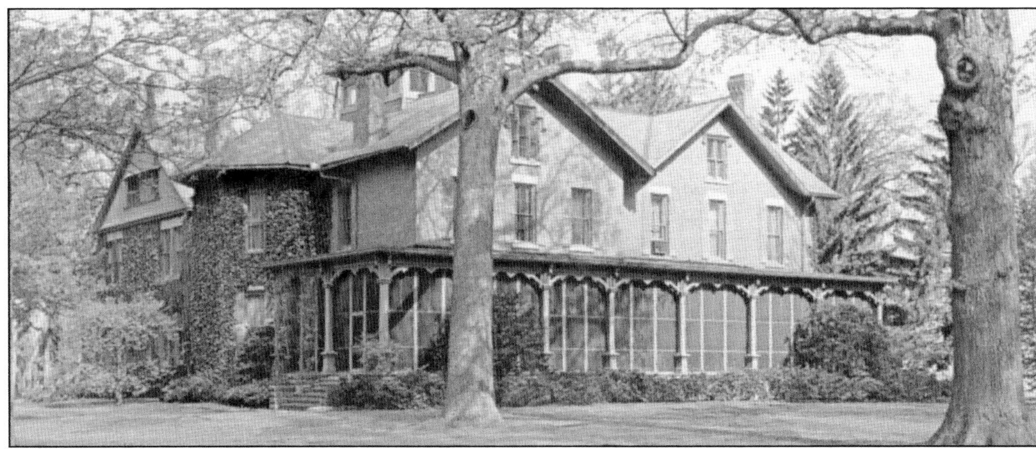

Another early photograph of the home shows the improvements made by the Hayes family before they returned from the White House in 1881. The addition to the right with the matching front gable was built in 1880, as were many other additions to the rest of the home. Deeded to the State of Ohio by the family in the 1960s, the home, along with the museum and library in Spiegel Grove, are now the Hayes Presidential Center, a treasure for the community and a nationally renowned research center.

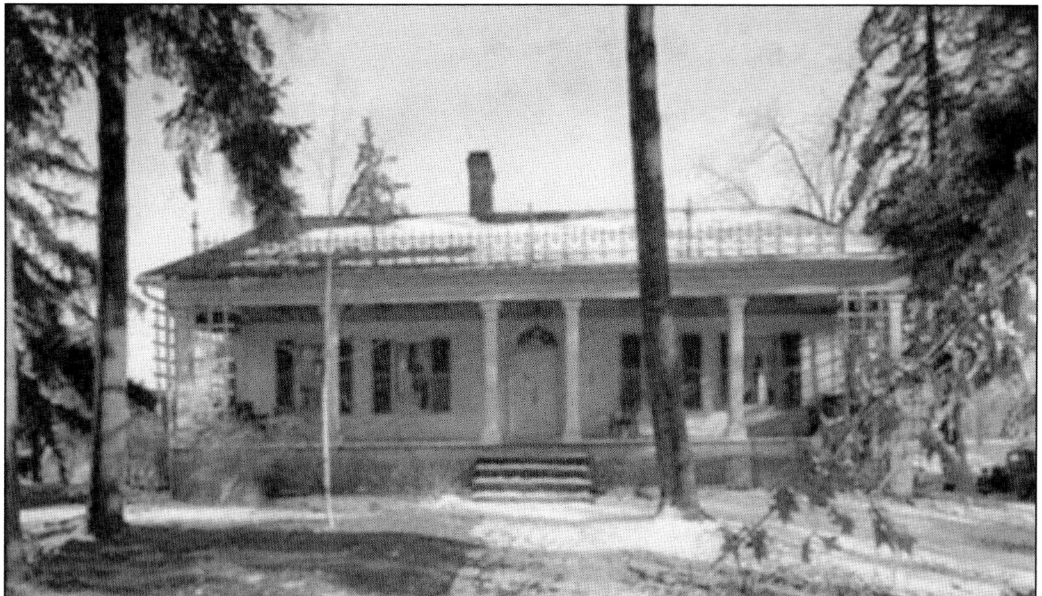

Perhaps the oldest dwelling in Fremont, the Vallette house on Buckland Avenue was built in 1828 and served as an early inn run by the Vallette family. While staying there, Sardis Birchard decided to purchase the charming wooded area he passed by every day. He named it Spiegel Grove (the German word *Spiegel* means "mirror"), because the trees would often be reflected in pools of water that collected in the area. Hayes also stayed at this house while he was recovering from the wounds he suffered in the Battle of South Mountain during the Civil War.

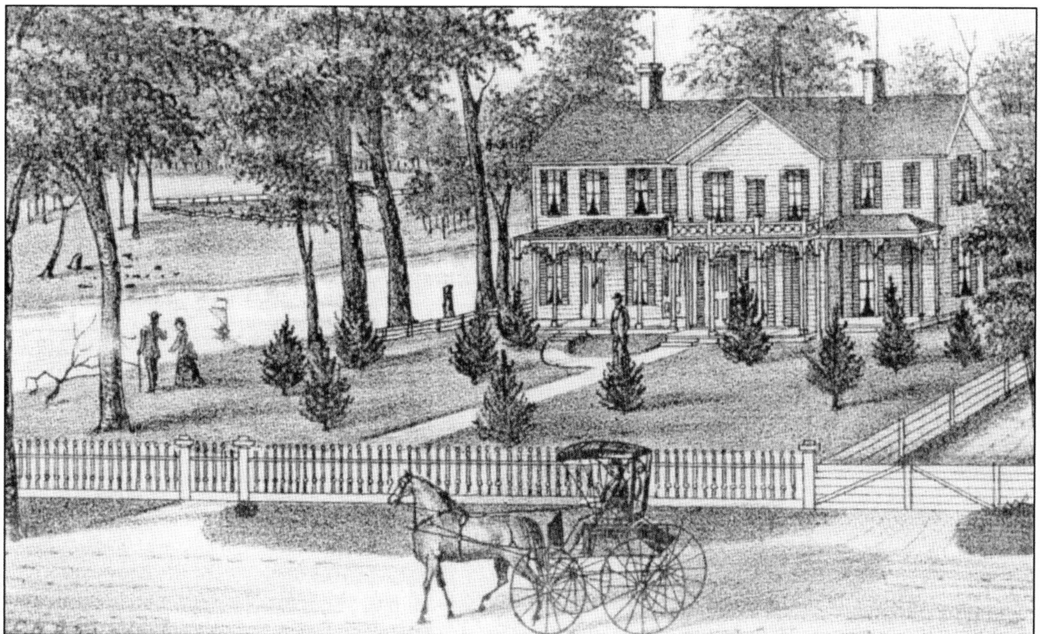

The George Reynolds house, pictured here in the 1874 county atlas, stands on Tiffin Road beside the Sandusky River at left. This was where the Ballville Bridge crossed the river, and several mills were located nearby. Later lived in by the Weller, Klingman, and Child families, the house has changed very little in the past 140 years.

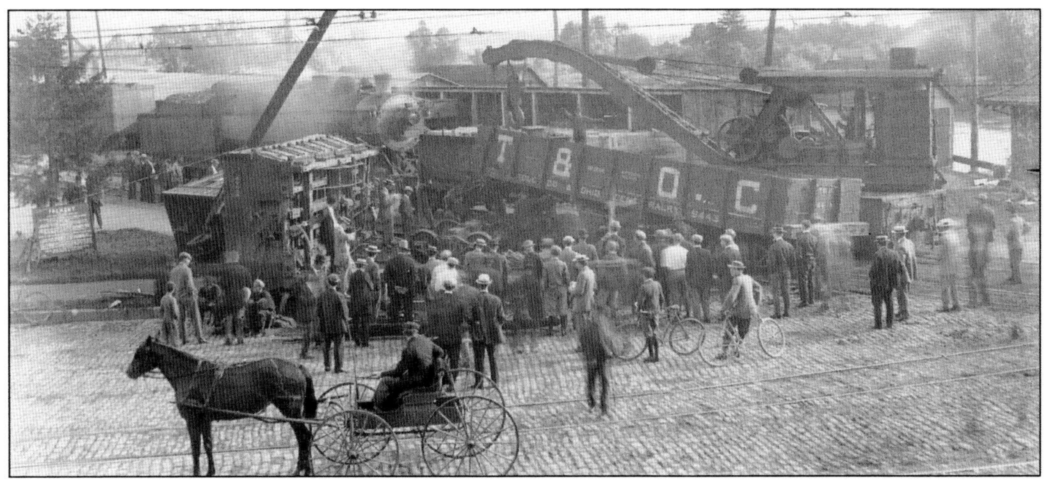

Spectators are standing perilously close to a train derailment, while a heavy crane is at work in this photograph taken about 1912. The view is looking northeast toward the Sandusky River in the background.

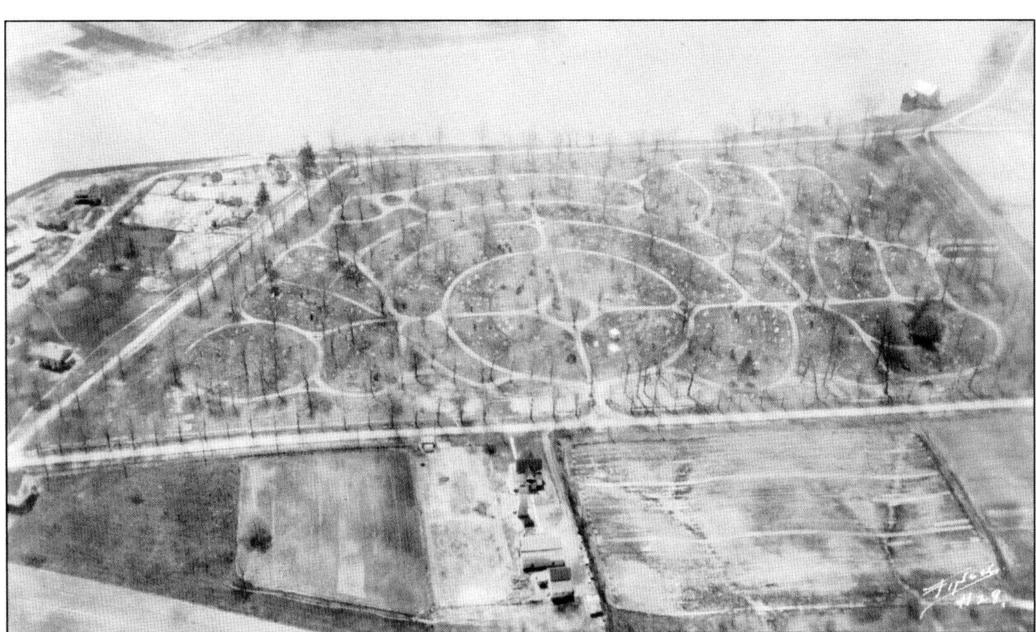

An early-1900s aerial view, with a view looking west, shows the spiderweb maze of Oakwood Cemetery, the largest in Fremont. The cemetery opened in 1858, and the large mausoleum at right was built in 1918. Members of the Hayes family were buried in the circle at the center of the picture. The river runs along the top of the photograph toward the Ballville Dam, and an old mill is visible in the upper right corner.

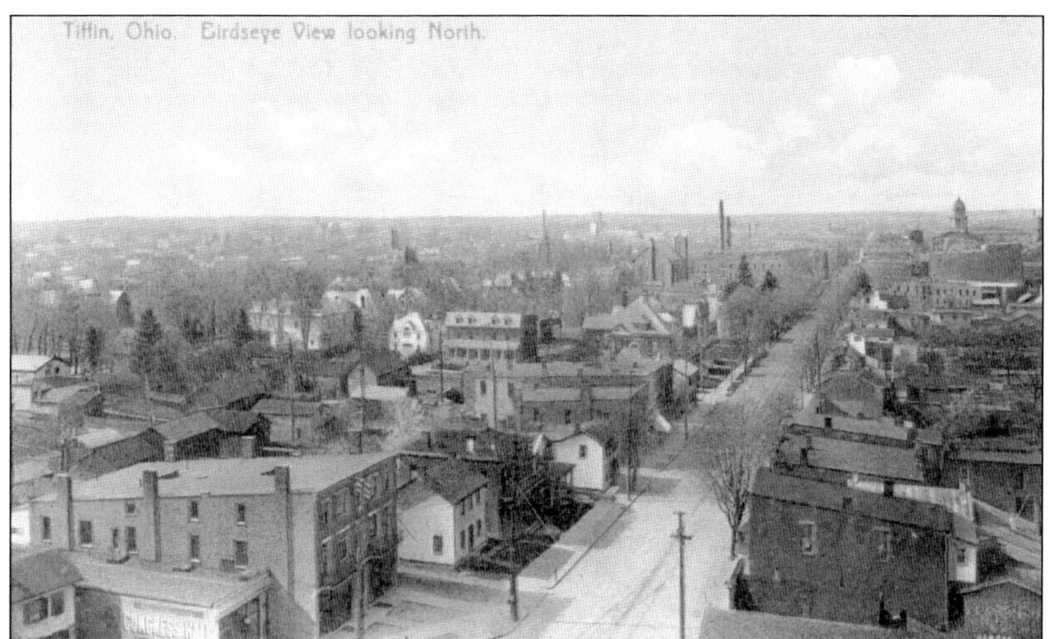

Pictured is a very early aerial view of downtown Tiffin, showing how the city was growing in the latter part of the 1800s. The view looks north, and the skyline mostly consists of church steeples and the dome of the old courthouse. (Courtesy of the Seneca County Museum.)

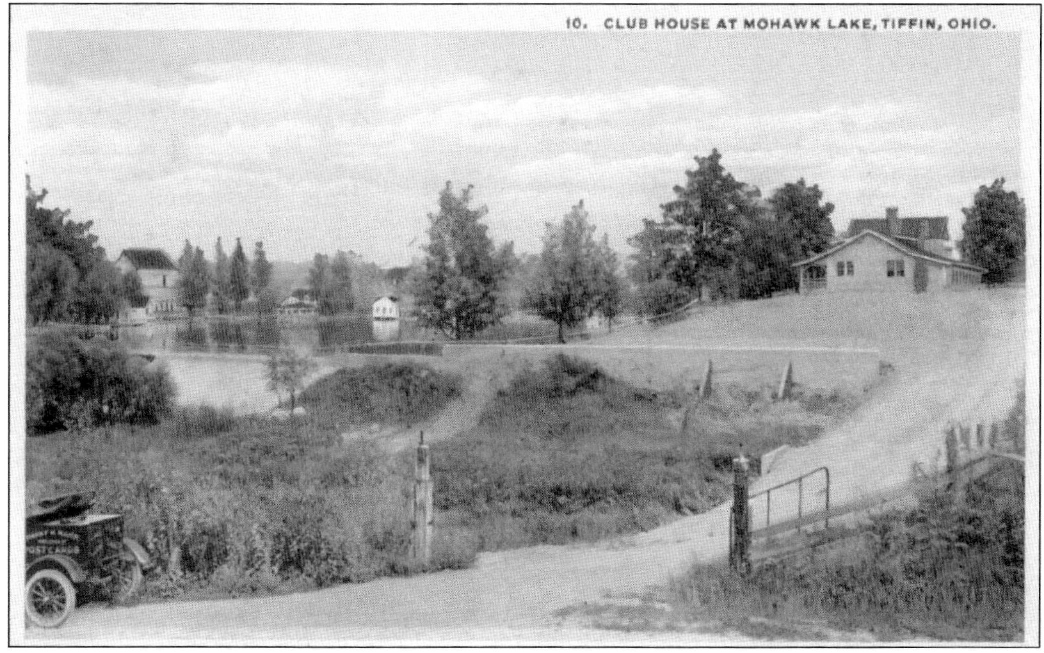

Scenic Mohawk Lake and its clubhouse are pictured in this turn-of-the-century postcard. It was a popular place near the river for Tiffin residents to visit in the days of short automobile excursions for family picnics or dates with a sweetheart. The vehicle at lower left is vending postcards. (Courtesy of the Seneca County Museum.)

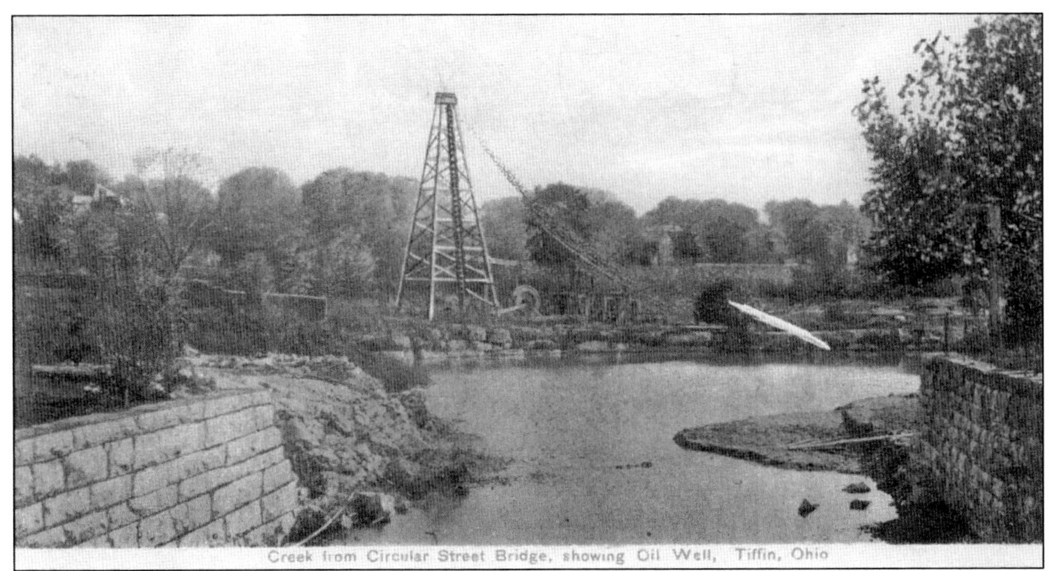

Rock Creek flows northwest through Tiffin to merge into the Sandusky River between Washington Street and the railroad bridge. This view of Rock Creek in 1910 looks east from the bridge on Circular Street at an oil derrick, which is still in use on what would later become part of the Heidelberg campus extensions. Heidelberg has been an important part of the city's intellectual life since its founding in 1850. (Courtesy of the Seneca County Museum.)

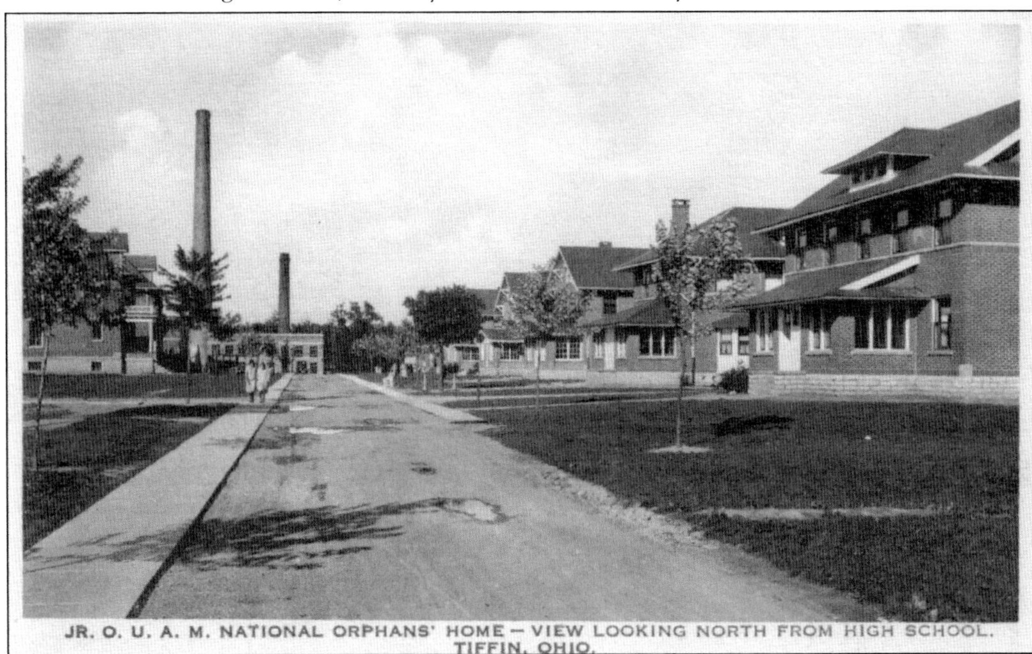

The Junior Order of United American Mechanics operated this orphanage, which was known in Tiffin simply as the Junior Home. Started in 1896 on a large tract of land in north Tiffin east of the river, it eventually grew to over 30 buildings. At its peak in 1935, the home had 1,105 children living on its self-contained campus. Early-20th-century dormitory houses are seen in this postcard, with a view looking north from the high school. The home closed in 1945, and the campus was sold to the state to be used as a mental hospital. (Courtesy of the Seneca County Museum.)

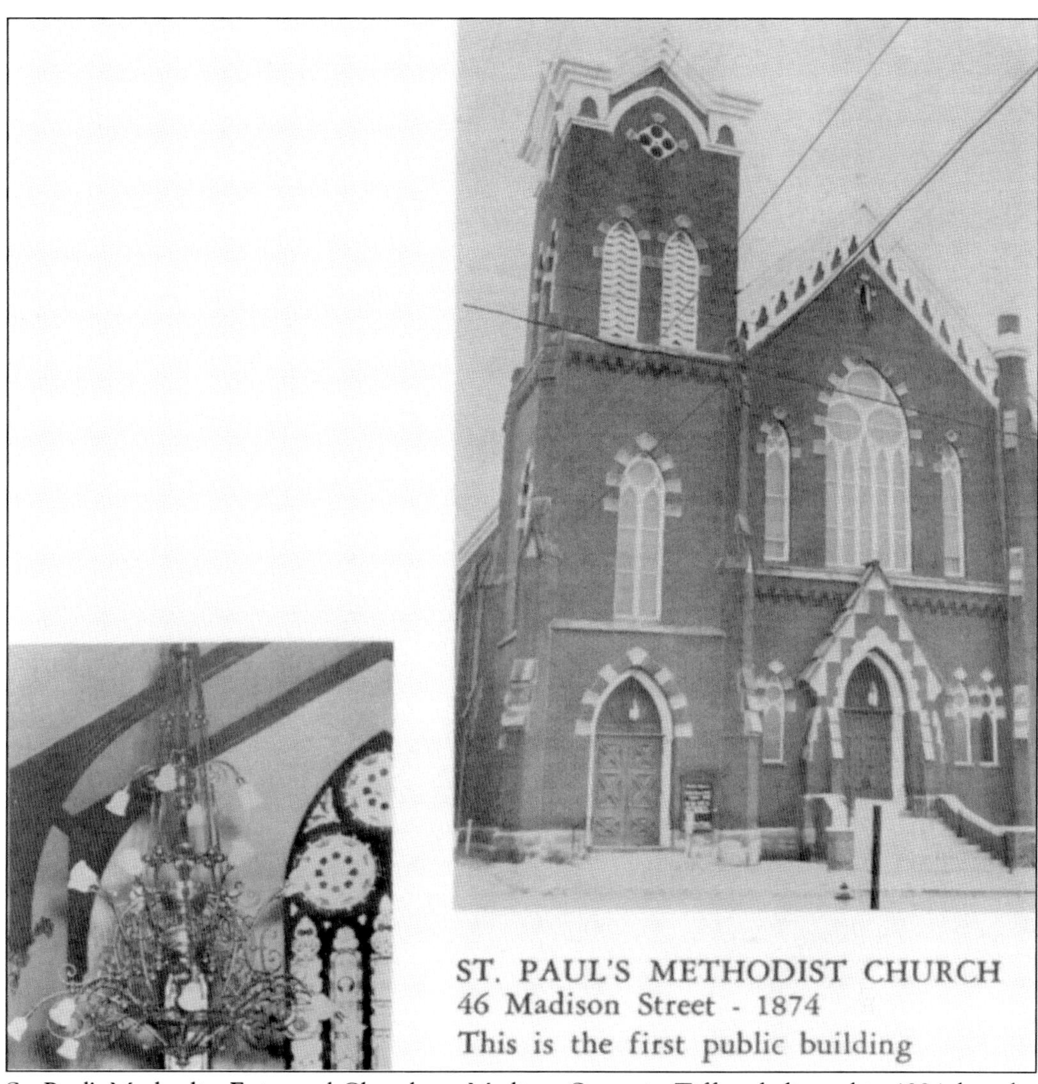

St. Paul's Methodist Episcopal Church on Madison Street in Tiffin, dedicated in 1884, has the distinction of being the first public building wired for electricity while it was constructed. A brass chandelier was presented to the church at its dedication, courtesy of Thomas Edison himself, and it still hangs in the church today.

Bibliography

Bristley, Pat. *Stories of Sandusky County: The 2001 History of Sandusky County, Ohio*. Fremont, OH: Lesher Printers, 2013.

Elchert, Keith and Laura Weston-Elchert. *Tiffin*. Charleston, SC: Arcadia Publishing, 2015.

Finch, Frank. *1913 Flood*. Fremont, OH: Finch Studios, 1913.

Grob, Ray. *Down the Sandusky*. Fremont, OH: Sandusky County Chamber of Commerce, 1971.

Historical Atlas of Sandusky County Ohio. Chicago: Everts, Stewart, & Company, 1874.

Keeler, Lucy Elliot. *A Guide to the Local History of Fremont, Ohio, Prior to 1860*. Columbus, OH: Fred J. Heer, 1905.

———. "The Sandusky River." *Ohio Archaeological and Historical Publications, Volume XIII*. Columbus, OH: Fred J. Heer, 1904: 191–247.

Lang, William. *History of Sandusky County, From the Close of the Revolutionary War to July, 1880*. Springfield: Transcript Printing, 1880.

Meek, Basil. *Twentieth Century History of Sandusky County, Ohio*. Chicago: Richmond-Arnold Publishing Company, 1909.

Michaels, Krista and Larry Michaels. *Fremont and Sandusky County: Then & Now*. Fremont, OH: Morrison Publishing, 2015.

———. *Fremont Panorama*. Fremont, OH: Morrison Publishing, 2012.

———. *Fremont: Then & Now*. Fremont, OH: Morrison Publishing, 2009.

Scranton, Nancy. *James and Elizabeth: A True Story of Brave Ohio Pioneers*. Compiled by Abigail Scranton Woodman, 2012.

Swickard, Lisa. *Calamity and Courage: Tiffin's Battle During Ohio's Deadly 1913 Flood*. Melmore, OH: Virgin Alley Press, 2010.

Tiffin-Seneca Sesquicentennial: 1817–1967. Tiffin County Commissioners, 1967.

INDEX

Discover Thousands of Local History Books Featuring Millions of Vintage Images

Arcadia Publishing, the leading local history publisher in the United States, is committed to making history accessible and meaningful through publishing books that celebrate and preserve the heritage of America's people and places.

Find more books like this at
www.arcadiapublishing.com

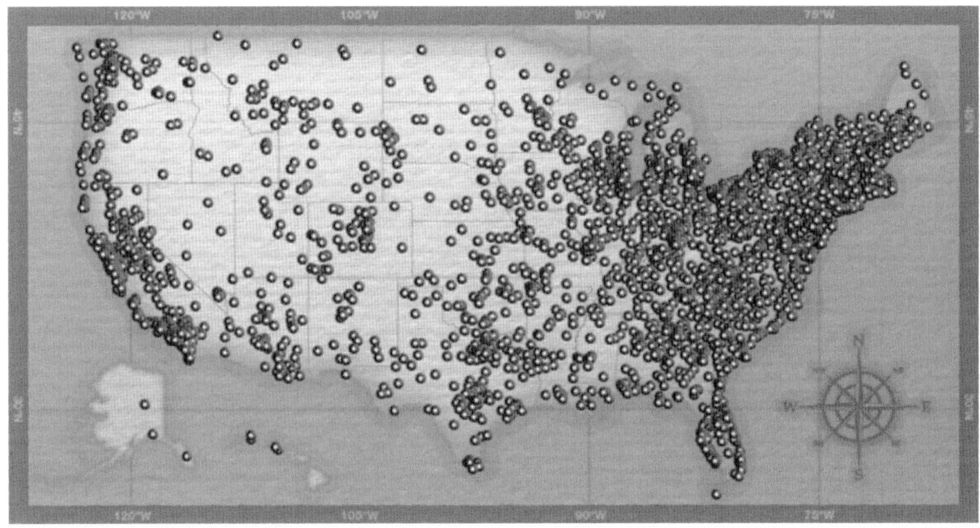

Search for your hometown history, your old stomping grounds, and even your favorite sports team.

Consistent with our mission to preserve history on a local level, this book was printed in South Carolina on American-made paper and manufactured entirely in the United States. Products carrying the accredited Forest Stewardship Council (FSC) label are printed on 100 percent FSC-certified paper.

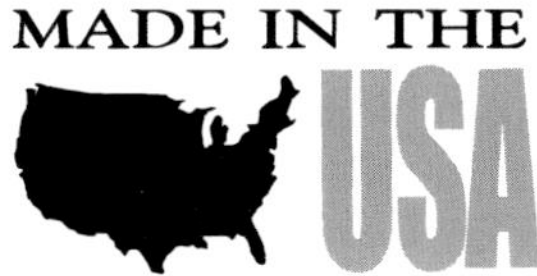